Sheffield Hallam University
Learning and IT Services
Adsetts Centre City Campus
Sheffield S1 1WS

Peer Gr   101 920 606 3   nent

D1332655

SHEFFIELD HALLAM UNIVERSITY
LEARNING CENTRE
WITHDRAWN FROM STOCK

ONE WEEK LOAN

2 8 MAR 2011

Understanding Children's Worlds
Series Editor: Judy Dunn

The study of children's development can have a profound influence on how children are brought up, cared for, and educated. Many psychologists argue that, even if our knowledge is incomplete, we have a responsibility to attempt to help those concerned with the care, education, and study of children by making what we know available to them. The central aim of this series is to encourage developmental psychologists to set out the findings and the implications of their research for others—teachers, doctors, social workers, students, and fellow researchers—whose work involves the care, education, and study of young children and their families. The information and the ideas that have grown from recent research form an important resource which should be available to them. This series provides an opportunity for psychologists to present their work in a way that is interesting, intelligible, and substantial, and to discuss what its consequences may be for those who care for, and teach, children: not to offer simple prescriptive advice to other professionals, but to make important and innovative research accessible to them.

Peer Groups and Children's Development

Christine Howe

WILEY-BLACKWELL

A John Wiley & Sons, Ltd., Publication

This edition first published 2010
© 2010 Christine Howe

Blackwell Publishing was acquired by John Wiley & Sons in February 2007. Blackwell's publishing program has been merged with Wiley's global Scientific, Technical, and Medical business to form Wiley-Blackwell.

Registered Office
John Wiley & Sons Ltd, The Atrium, Southern Gate, Chichester, West Sussex, PO19 8SQ, United Kingdom

Editorial Offices
350 Main Street, Malden, MA 02148-5020, USA
9600 Garsington Road, Oxford, OX4 2DQ, UK
The Atrium, Southern Gate, Chichester, West Sussex, PO19 8SQ, UK

For details of our global editorial offices, for customer services, and for information about how to apply for permission to reuse the copyright material in this book please see our website at www.wiley.com/wiley-blackwell.

The right of Christine Howe to be identified as the author of this work has been asserted in accordance with the Copyright, Designs and Patents Act 1988.

All rights reserved. No part of this publication may be reproduced, stored in a retrieval system, or transmitted, in any form or by any means, electronic, mechanical, photocopying, recording or otherwise, except as permitted by the UK Copyright, Designs and Patents Act 1988, without the prior permission of the publisher.

Wiley also publishes its books in a variety of electronic formats. Some content that appears in print may not be available in electronic books.

Designations used by companies to distinguish their products are often claimed as trademarks. All brand names and product names used in this book are trade names, service marks, trademarks or registered trademarks of their respective owners. The publisher is not associated with any product or vendor mentioned in this book. This publication is designed to provide accurate and authoritative information in regard to the subject matter covered. It is sold on the understanding that the publisher is not engaged in rendering professional services. If professional advice or other expert assistance is required, the services of a competent professional should be sought.

Library of Congress Cataloging-in-Publication Data

Howe, Christine.
Peer groups and children's development / Christine Howe.
p. cm. — (Understanding children's worlds)
Includes bibliographical references and index.
ISBN 978-1-4051-7945-4 (hardcover : alk. paper) — ISBN 978-1-4051-7944-7 (pbk. : alk. paper)   1. Child development.   2. Interpersonal relations in children.   3. Friendship in children.   4. Age groups.   I. Title.
HQ772.H65 2010
305.231083′4—dc22

2009035839

A catalogue record for this book is available from the British Library.

Set in 10/12.5pt Sabon by Graphicraft Limited, Hong Kong
Printed and bound in Malaysia by Vivar Printing Sdn Bhd

01   2010

SHEFFIELD HALLAM UNIVERSITY
wl
305.231
HO
ADSETTS LEARNING CENTRE

Contents

Contents

Series Editor's Preface

This is a most welcome addition to the series *Understanding Children's Worlds*, and more generally to the literature on children's experiences with their peers. The question of the impact of peers in the classroom and in breaktime at school on children's development is explored in detail. How do children experience their peers—do they facilitate mastery of the curriculum? Why do children differ in their relationships within the school environment? And what do we know about their peer experiences outside the school? What are the practical implications for teachers of the research on peers?

Christine Howe steers us through a large literature with care and precision, and identifies the gaps in the research as well as the lessons to be learned. Perhaps the broadest message is that an interdisciplinary perspective is needed, with both psychological and educational approaches and insights. She starts by highlighting the importance of cultural context—the impact of peers is not seen as a cultural universal—though commonalities in the themes and evidence are clear across countries and cultures. An important distinction is made between a *performance mode*, with a child as performer and peers as audience, and a *cooperative mode* in which children interact independently of the teacher as mediator. The former has little direct impact on children's mastery of the curriculum—though the social consequences are important and may therefore have an impact on what is learned. By contrast, the relatively rare cooperative mode impacts, she argues, on social judgment, and benefits mastery of the curriculum.

The chapters on status and on friendship, and their impact on children's wellbeing, are of particular interest and importance. She argues persuasively that it is inadvisable to look at status and friendship in isolation from each other. To understand the educational implications of friendship and status we should look at both; and it is evident that friendship is of particular importance. It plays a significant protective role in terms of children's susceptibility to being bullied and victimized, and provides a buffer against problems in personal adjustment. The point is strongly made that so much research to date has focused on the negative impact of peers, rather than on the role of peers in children's wellbeing; more study of the positive impact of friendship, and the positive implications of sociability, is urged. The practical implications for teachers described throughout the book are brought together in the last chapter: for instance, the arguments that peers are currently marginalized from classroom teaching and learning, that opinion exchange can promote reasoning ability and curriculum mastery, that mixed-ability groups should be the norm within the classroom, that children who have high-achieving friends are helped academically. Established cooperative learning programs should be employed as a starting point, modified to encourage discussion of contrasting opinions. These important lessons deserve our attention, as parents and as teachers.

Judy Dunn

Acknowledgments

My interest in peer groups and children's development crystallized during my time as a member of Strathclyde University's Centre for Research into Interactive Learning. The Centre's remit was to study the learning that results from interaction among novices, interaction between novices and experts (parents, teachers, and computers), and interaction among novices under expert guidance. The aim was to inform psychological theory and educational practice. Peer interaction among children was a key theme from the outset, with studies conducted into the learning and development that occurs when children work together on a range of topics. Literacy, mathematics, science, health, safety, reasoning, and social understanding all featured in the Centre's research. Inevitably, the work engaged with a wide-ranging literature, which included educational studies of how peer groups are used in classrooms, and psychological investigations of how peers impact upon development. However, as I mastered this literature, I gradually realized that some of the themes were hard to reconcile. For instance, educational analyses of class size and single-versus mixed-ability teaching implicitly sideline peers as influences on academic attainment. Psychological analyses, on the other hand, indicate that peers have a profound impact on children's development, including their academic attainment. Realizing that something must have been missed, I resolved to try to integrate the disparate strands, in the hope of more complete understanding of children's peer group experiences and their consequences for development. This book is the result.

Needless to say, the book is the outcome of many interactive experiences, often with peers. There are the collaborations over many years with other members of the Centre for Research into Interactive Learning, especially Donna McWilliam, Andy Tolmie, and David Warden. Pat Gallagher was the linchpin around whom our activities revolved. My move to the University of Cambridge facilitated direct exposure to the research of colleagues whom I have long admired, including Robin Alexander, Maurice Galton, Linda Hargreaves, and Neil Mercer. Some of the ideas presented in this book emerged during work that Neil Mercer and I carried out together as part of a review of primary education in England. Once the book started to take shape, Brigit Schroeter helped me to identify further references, Ed Baines commented on a draft chapter, and Barbie Clark introduced me to literature on the role of technology in children's peer groups. Lyndsay Upex and Miriam Robertson assisted with manuscript preparation. Once the first draft was complete, Judy Dunn as series editor and an anonymous reviewer provided feedback. I hope they will recognize their contribution to the final document. Many people have therefore contributed to the production of this book, and I want now to express my gratitude to all of them. However, I wish, above all, to thank my husband, Willie Robertson, for his love, patience, and support throughout the project. Without Willie, I should not have had a study with beautiful views over Scottish mountains in which to write, and I should not have had the privilege of completing the manuscript in the wonderful setting of Deogarh Palace in Rajasthan, India. I owe Willie more than I can say, and I want to acknowledge this here.

Chapter 1

Peer Groups in
a Cultural Context

Introduction

This book is concerned with children's experiences of peer groups, and the implications of those experiences for children's development. The *Oxford English Dictionary* offers two definitions of the word "peer," namely, "a person of the same standing or rank as the person in question" and "a person of the same age-group or social set as the person in question." According to Ladd (2005), psychologists typically emphasize the age dimension, referring "to people who are born around the same time as agemates or peers" (p. 2). Yet, like many anthropologists (Konner, 1975), Ladd also draws out the extrafamilial quality of peers: they are non-family members of similar age to the person in question, and (potentially at least) of similar standing or rank. Children's peers are conceptualized in a parallel fashion for the purposes of this book, in other words as other children who are of similar age to the child under scrutiny and potentially also of similar standing or rank, and who are not members of the same family. The interest is in children's experiences of the groups to which they belong together with one or more peers, and the groups containing two or more peers who they witness as outsiders. The developmental consequences of these experiences are analyzed with a view to informing both research and practice. Thus, the book is intended to address the research interests of psychologists and educationalists, as well as the practical concerns of teachers, parents, counselors, and policy makers. It is also intended to inform theoretical development.

While one of the book's goals is to be theory informing, the starting point is emphatically not a position of theoretical neutrality. On the contrary, facts about the status of peer groups in children's lives demand a perspective that is broadly sociocultural. This does not necessarily mean sociocultural in the specific sense developed by Vygotsky (e.g., 1962, 1978) and his numerous followers, and no doubt familiar to many readers. Rather, it means merely a perspective on peer groups that recognizes the broader cultural and historical contexts in which these groups are embedded. This perspective is consistent with Vygotsky but more general, and the present chapter starts by showing why it is necessary and what it implies. In particular, a sociocultural perspective on peer groups imposes constraints upon how developmental influences should be theorized, and the chapter's central section spells these constraints out. Having specified what amounts to a theoretical framework for taking matters forward, the chapter concludes with an overview of the material that follows. Key constructs like "groups," "children," and "development" are defined, and the structure and contents of subsequent chapters are summarized. The manner in which the book serves practical and research goals is outlined.

Cultural Dependency

I can perhaps best explain why a sociocultural perspective is needed through sketching two scenarios, both involving one day in the life of a 9-year-old girl. The first girl lives in the small village in Scotland (United Kingdom) where I myself resided for more than 20 years. This girl rises at about 7:30 a.m., has breakfast with her family, gets washed and dressed, and shortly before 9:00 a.m. is driven by her mother to the village primary school, which is located about one mile from her home. At school, she is placed in a class with 24 other children of similar age, but most of the morning's activity takes place with a subset of her classmates. After registration, she sits down with her "math set" (six children of similar mathematical ability), for instruction in mathematics. This involves cycles of teacher instruction directed at the whole set, followed by individual problem solving in workbooks while the teacher focuses on a different set. Mid-morning, the class breaks for playtime, and the girl goes outside to relax in the playground with her three closest friends (all girls). The second half of the morning is mostly occupied with language instruction (primarily reading and writing) in further ability-defined sets. The composition of the girl's language set differs slightly from the composition of her math set, although once more the session is structured around teacher instruction directed at the whole set followed by individual study. Shortly after midday, the class breaks once more, and the girl rejoins her close friends to eat lunch and play

outside. The afternoon's teaching is mainly devoted to an ongoing project on the Roman Empire, and in contrast to the morning involves teacher
instruction directed at the whole class plus follow-up exercises, which
the children address collaboratively in small, mixed-ability groups. School
finishes around 3:00 p.m., whereupon the girl is taken home by car, has
her tea, and in the early evening is driven to Brownies, where she finds
many girls from her school (from her own class and from one age band
above and one age band below). The girl's day ends with television and
mid-evening bedtime.

The second 9-year-old girl lives in the remote village in the Gambia
(West Africa) that I was privileged to visit during 2005. This girl's day
begins at dawn, whereupon she rises, gets dressed, and helps to dress
three younger members of the household (aged 2, 3, and 5 years) while
her mother feeds the baby. Her mother then prepares breakfast, which
the girl eats in a large family group that includes her father, her mother,
her father's other wives, and her siblings and half-siblings. After breakfast, the adults go to work in the fields, taking the baby with them,
and the 7- and 9-year-old boys set off on foot for the village school.
The girl is left with the 2-, 3-, and 5-year-old children, who accompany
her as she fetches water from the village well for washing up, and carries out other household chores. At the well, she chats with other girls
of similar age, who are also accompanied by younger siblings and half-
siblings. Once the chores have been completed, the girl has time for
playing at home with the younger children before one of her father's
wives returns to prepare lunch. Lunch is eaten with the full family group,
and as far as the girl is concerned, the morning routine is more or less
repeated from after lunch until supper. On the other hand, the 7- and
9-year-old boys do not return to school, but play soccer (and similar
games) with other village boys. The family group reconvenes for supper, which is followed by music and dancing with other families from
the village. With no electricity or gas, the village is poorly illuminated,
so bedtime comes early.

There are many similarities between the two scenarios. For instance,
both girls live in family units, receive care from their mothers, eat meals
at similar times, and engage in alternating cycles of work and play.
However, there are also many differences, including the one that is
crucial for this book: involvement in peer groups. Construed as non-
family members of similar age (and possibly similar standing and rank),
it is clear that peers play a significant role in the Scottish girl's life, for
she spends a great deal of time in groups that include her peers. Her
school class is one such group, as are her math set, her language set,

and the mixed-ability group in which she is studying the Roman Empire. Further peer groups are the friends with whom she spends school play-time and the lunch break, and the Brownies whom she meets in the evening. It is possible therefore that peer groups make an important contribution to her development. By contrast, the Gambian girl spends very little time in peer groups. She meets peers when fetching water from the village well, and during the evening's music and dancing. However, most of her day is spent with individuals of lower age, standing and rank (younger siblings and half-siblings) or higher age, standing and rank (parents, other adults in the family group, and other adults from the village). Thus, her development into an adult member of her society must take place largely independently of peer groups.

The contrast between the Scottish and Gambian scenarios over peer group experiences should not be regarded as a categorical statement about the two cultures, let alone about other cultures. Within Scotland, the extent of peer group experiences is influenced by geographical location, that is, urban, suburban, village, or truly rural. In the sparsely populated highland and island regions, school classes (and therefore also within-class subgroups) normally contain widely divergent age groups (Wilson, 2003). Location is undoubtedly also relevant in the Gambia, as of course is gender. The older boys in the scenario have more extensive peer group experiences than the female protagonist, by virtue both of attending school and of playing games in the village. Anthropological studies in Kenya (Whiting & Whiting, 1991), New Guinea (Herdt, 1987), and Nigeria (Ottenberg, 1988) indicate that gender differences over peer group experiences are typical in traditional societies. One reason is thought to be the role of peer groups in patriarchal cultures in "weaning" boys from the feminine culture of the household, especially when entry into the more formal of these peer groups is often associated with demanding initiation rites. Nevertheless, despite within-culture variation, the cross-cultural differences over peer group experiences that are highlighted in the two scenarios do seem to be valid *on average*. Crucial evidence has emerged from Whiting and Edwards' (1988) study of children aged 2 to 10 years from 12 communities located in India, Japan, Kenya, Liberia, Mexico, the Philippines, and the United States, but research has been conducted in other countries too (reviewed in Edwards, 1992). The general message is that while most children throughout Europe, and indeed North America and Australasia, have extensive experiences of peer groups, the limited experiences mapped here for a 9-year-old girl from the Gambia occur in other parts of Africa, and in many countries in Asia and South America.

Discussions of why peer group experiences are pervasive across some cultures and marginal across others have focused on schooling (Edwards, 1992; Rogoff, 2003). All cultures that provide schooling (and nowadays most do, to some degree) aspire to organize this around classes that are comprised of peer groups. This is not to say that the aspiration is always realized. As noted already in relation to Scotland, low population density is one factor that precludes this. Nevertheless, schooling is characteristically structured to approximate as closely as possible to the peer group target. Moreover, when schooling is organized around peer groups, other facilities follow. These include preschool institutions, such as nurseries, playgroups, and toddler groups, and formal out-of-school provision, such as sports associations (soccer, swimming), youth movements (Brownies, Scouts), and classes for the performing arts (dance, drama). Because informal relations like friendships are often forged in school and related contexts, these too will typically be peer based. The implication therefore is that in cultures where schooling is universal, most children will have extensive experiences of peer groups. In cultures where schooling is not universal, some children will have limited experiences. Insofar as gender often predicts access to schooling in such cultures, for reasons of patriarchy as discussed above, the influence of schooling is typically to perpetuate asymmetries over peer group experiences that already exist, while no doubt changing their form.

This book focuses on children who are members of societies where schooling is mandatory for all of the relevant age group, and therefore extensive peer group experiences are taken for granted. This is not to say that these experiences map precisely onto the Scottish scenario. On the contrary, there is, as we shall see, considerable variation within and between cultures in the form that the experiences take. However, the variation is in form not extent, for the extent of peer group experiences where schooling is mandatory can be assumed to be constant and substantial. Being constant as well as substantial, it is easy to forget that the experiences result from specific cultural practices, especially schooling, when (as here) focusing only on societies where schooling is mandatory. It is, in other words, easy to overlook Mueller and Tingley's (1989) point that peer associations are best understood as recent products of cultural evolution rather than as ancient outcomes of biological evolution. Nevertheless, overlooking the point would be a serious error, for, as signaled already, the sociocultural perspective that is necessitated carries important implications for theoretical analysis. These implications also apply to other "recent products of cultural evolution" such as television and the Internet, although not necessarily to the bonds forged between mothers and infants; after all, these bonds (no matter how culturally over-laid) do have foundations in evolutionary biology. Thus, it is important to spell out the implications of cultural dependency, and this is what the next section attempts to do. A theoretical framework is developed that acknowledges the cultural dependency of children's peer group experiences. The framework is extended and embellished as the book progresses.

Theoretical Framework

The fact that peer group experiences result from recent (and non-universal) cultural developments does not render them inconsequential in the cultures where they occur. On the contrary, just as many have argued in relation to television and the Internet, they could have profound implications for children's development. It is indeed possible that, as Ladd (2005) suggests, "peers make a significant and enduring contribution to children's socialization and development" (p. 11), so long as this claim is not taken as asserting a cross-cultural universal. Nevertheless, because peer group experiences are culturally dependent, any implications that they do have in cultures where they are pervasive are unlikely to be specific to peer groups. Equally, the mechanisms by which implications are realized are unlikely to apply only in peer group contexts. Specialized functions and specialized mechanisms usually depend on biological evolution, and the evolution of relevance is cultural.

The implications of cultural evolution need to be emphasized, for specialized contributions have frequently been proposed in the context of children's peer groups. They are implicit in mass media portrayals, where there is a tendency to treat peer groups in a uniquely negative light. In particular, peer groups are frequently depicted as having unrivaled capacities for leading children astray by undoing the "good work" that families and teachers achieve. Beyond this, specialized contributions have been proposed in the research literature, including from some extremely influential theorists. The present section begins by outlining two examples, with a view not to criticize but rather to developing an alternative approach that respects the cultural dimension. The approach is then contrasted with a further model that shares the present sociocultural perspective.

Piaget and Sullivan

The two theorists to be considered are the Swiss developmental psychologist (or, as he would have preferred, "genetic epistemologist") Jean

Piaget, and Piaget's American contemporary Harry Stack Sullivan. Discussing one of his earliest studies with school-age children, Piaget (1926) noted that children's speech to peers is considerably less "egocentric" than their speech to adults, egocentric speech being speech that is not adapted to what the listener has just said. Piaget suggested that the difference stems from contrasting power relations. Because adults are more powerful than children, children assimilate adult opinions unthinkingly, and therefore see no reason to engage with these opinions conversationally. By contrast, the more equal relations with peers motivate children to coordinate the opinions that peers express with their own views, compare the two sets of opinions, and when differences are detected comment accordingly. A few years later, Piaget (1932) suggested that coordination and comparison between existing views and alternatives are necessary conditions for cognitive development, and, in line with his earlier discussion of egocentrism, proposed that collaborative activity with peers is uniquely structured to support such coordination and comparison. He further claimed (in translation from French) that "if, then, we had to choose from among the totality of existing educational systems those which would best correspond with our psychological results, we would turn our methods in the direction of what has been called 'group work' and 'self-government' " (Piaget, 1932, p. 412).

As a psychoanalyst, Sullivan was primarily interested in the development of personality, in contrast to Piaget's emphasis upon cognition. However, like Piaget, he believed that peer groups have a crucial role to play for school-age children. In his classic book *The Interpersonal Theory of Psychiatry* (Sullivan, 1953), he spelled the role out, suggesting that it changes subtly across the "juvenile" and "preadolescence" eras. The juvenile era begins when children start school and continues for between three and five years. During this era, children learn to subordinate to non-family authority figures such as teachers, and also to accommodate to what they notice about their peers. Specifically, children compare their own characteristics with those displayed by peers, and conclude either that their own characteristics are superior (competitive accommodation) or that their peers' characteristics are worth emulating (compromise accommodation). For instance, writing about competitive accommodation, Sullivan comments that "when the juvenile acquires a pattern of relating himself to someone else which works and is approved, he simply knows that what he is doing is right" (Sullivan, 1953, p. 234). The preadolescence era starts around 8½ to 10 years of age when, according to Sullivan, children first acquire same-sex "chums." With chums, children engage in forms of interaction that require sensitivity to other people's feelings, forms of interaction that Sullivan styled as "collaborative." As with juvenile accommodation, collaboration with chums was regarded as crucial for the development of personality, with Sullivan claiming that "validation of personal worth requires a type of relationship, which I call collaboration, by which I mean clearly formulated adjustments of one's behaviour to the expressed needs of the other person in the pursuit of increasingly identical—that is, more and more nearly mutual—satisfactions" (Sullivan, 1953, p. 246).

Neither Piaget nor Sullivan believed that peer groups provide the only context for children's development. At least half of Sullivan's 1953 book is devoted to the critical role that the family plays in the pre-juvenile era, a role that is construed in more or less standard psychoanalytic terms. Piaget had little to say about social influences on preschool children, but he recognized substantial developmental change during the first years of life, and it would be inconsistent with his theoretical model as a whole (see also Piaget, 1985) to attribute this change purely to maturation. Nevertheless, as Youniss (1980) was among the first to point out, both Piaget and Sullivan identified aspects of development, occurring from middle childhood onwards, for which they believed peer groups to be essential. Indeed, both identified what were referred to earlier as specialized *functions* for peer groups, in their case promoting aspects of cognition and personality that emerge in middle childhood, and what were referred to as specialized *mechanisms*, for them triggering processes of social comparison that were regarded as central for stimulating growth. Enough has been said already to demonstrate that Piaget and Sullivan were profoundly mistaken in both respects. Because peer group experiences are consequences of recent cultural history, predominantly schooling, they cannot play roles that are specialized to peer groups per se. The functions, if any, which they support must be capable of being supported in other contexts, and the mechanisms by which support is given must be capable of being triggered in other contexts.

Taking a sociocultural perspective on children's peer groups, it is easy to dismiss Piaget and Sullivan's work as anachronistic. Nevertheless, despite its limitations, the work raises one issue of contemporary relevance. This is the reason why both theorists are revisited in subsequent chapters, with Piaget in particular playing a central role. The key issue stems from the fact that social comparison is highlighted in both Piaget's and Sullivan's work as the trigger for growth. For Piaget, it was comparison between own and others' opinions; for Sullivan, it was comparison between own and others' characteristics. However, as Piaget recognized, comparison is the kind of mechanism that seems to require symmetric power relations, and symmetry appears to be more likely in peer relations than in relations with adults. Thus, even though social comparison cannot be specialized to peer groups in any a priori sense, it may occur more often in peer group contexts in practice simply because the conditions on which it depends are more frequent in such contexts. As a result, it would be entirely consistent with a sociocultural perspective to hypothesize that the mechanisms by which peer groups influence development differ in some respects from the mechanisms that operate in other social contexts (e.g., in response to siblings, teachers, television, and the Internet), even though the mechanisms could in principle be activated in those contexts.

Indeed, de facto as opposed to a priori restrictions seem to be precisely what Michael Tomasello and his colleagues have been proposing to account for what they call "cultural learning" (e.g., Tomasello, 1999; Tomasello, Kruger, & Ratner, 1993). Tomasello and colleagues believe that imitation (where children reproduce another's actions) and instruction (where children are scaffolded into another's understanding) are the main mechanisms of social influence in asymmetric settings, such as adult–child interaction. Mechanisms that resemble Piagetian coordination and comparison are thought to predominate in symmetric settings, such as peer groups. However, there is no sense of impermeable barriers, such that imitation and instruction are impossible in peer groups, and coordination and comparison are inconceivable beyond these groups.

Group socialization theory

The preceding discussion implies a theoretical framework that rests upon three broad assumptions: (a) experiences of peer groups may have significant implications for children's development, but of course only in cultures where these experiences occur; (b) the developmental implications of peer group experiences are unlikely to be unique to peer groups, even in cultures where such experiences are common; and (c) the mechanisms by which peer groups influence development may differ from those that operate in other contexts, but only as a matter of practice and not of necessity. This is the framework that I shall adopt throughout the book, but before moving forward, I need to compare the approach with an alternative solution to the problems with which the chapter is grappling. This is the "group socialization theory" that has been developed by Judith Rich Harris (1995, 1998, 2000).

Harris surveys much of the cross-cultural research that was covered in the preceding section, and draws similar conclusions about the cultural dependency of peer group experiences. She realizes that, as a result, the roles of peer groups cannot be specialized at the levels of either functions or mechanisms. However, she regards peer groups as particular instances of extrafamilial groups in general, and believes that specialization is detectable across the broader category. Thus, group socialization theory rests on three assumptions that are rather different from the ones outlined above: (a) experiences of extrafamilial groups are universally significant for children's development, and in some cultures these groups may be predominantly peer groups; (b) the developmental implications of extrafamilial groups are unique to these groups, although not necessarily to peer groups in particular; and (c) the mechanisms by which extrafamilial groups influence development are unique as a matter of principle as well as practice.

Group socialization theory was developed because Harris was uncomfortable with attempts to explain individual differences in personality purely with reference to the interplay between genetic factors and the family environment. She was content with current thinking that attributes about 50% of personality to genetic influences, but was not persuaded that the family can account for the remainder. In her view, the associations reported in the literature between family practices and developmental outcomes are too weak and/or subject to a multiplicity of explanations, despite decades of detailed exploration (see also Maccoby & Martin, 1983). Familial factors that can be regarded as "uncontaminated" by genetic influences, such as children's birth order, have proved to be of limited relevance. Rejecting the family as a significant contributor to personality, Harris turned to the extrafamilial group, which she defined as an association with at least three members. In Harris's opinion, dyads do not constitute groups. She concluded that the norms, which groups evolve, operate as powerful influences on group behavior, via mechanisms that include within-group favoritism, or pressure to conform to within-group norms. Group influence is initially restricted to the group itself but subsequently, when circumstances permit, it can also have effects in other contexts. Harris points out that if family values are consistent with norms held within extrafamilial groups, which can be assumed sometimes to be the case, then the consequence of group socialization may be personality characteristics that are consistent with family practices. However, causality lies with the extrafamilial group, and not with the family.

Unsurprisingly, given its apparent marginalization of the family, surely one of modern society's most sacred of cows, group socialization theory has been repeatedly and roundly criticized (see, e.g., Vandell, 2000). The criticisms address a wide range of issues, including, but not restricted to, what is claimed about the family. For instance, Harris has been accused of holding an unconventionally broad and sometimes inconsistent conception of personality. She certainly includes language, for some of her most critical evidence (such as the fact that migrant children soon speak like their peers and not like their parents) comes from studies of language development. Harris (2000) acknowledges her breadth, but not her inconsistency. Harris has also been accused of selectivity in her use of research when minimizing family influences, and of jumping to conclusions before relevant work (longitudinal studies that control for genetic influences) has been conducted. Moreover, she is inconsistent here too, writing sometimes as if the family has no influence whatsoever, and at other times as if its impact, while real, is merely insufficient to account for the 50% of personality that is supposedly not determined by genes. In any event, Harris never explains how a firm line can be drawn between family and extrafamilial influences. After all, parents have significant, indirect effects upon children's peer group experiences through their choice of schools, neighborhoods, and who to invite to their homes.

All of the above criticisms may be valid, but they are not particularly relevant in the present context. As detailed later, this book covers all aspects of children's development, and it is immaterial how much is referred to as "personality." Moreover, since the book is concerned exclusively with the impact of peer groups, it can remain neutral about whether extrafamilial groups account for all or only some of the variance that is not explained by genetics. Indeed, considering that research estimating the genetic contribution to development has, to date, been conducted only in Western societies (and when, as we have seen, Western societies adopt specific, and non-universal, practices as regards one social structure at least, namely peer groups), it is unclear whether sufficient account has been taken of variation in the environment to warrant conclusions like "personality = 50% genes + 50% environment." With this in mind, neutrality about the proportion of the environmental component that comes from the family, the peer group, and so on may be the most prudent line to take. As for the fact that families exert indirect influences on peer group experiences, this would be more of a problem had families been the focus of the present book. With an emphasis upon peer groups, family factors can be ignored simply because they are indirect.

What is relevant here is the question of whether Harris's model suggests an alternative approach to the book's major aims than the one that is envisaged, and up to a point that does not seem to be the case. I am presuming that when children have extensive experiences of peer groups, these experiences may have implications for their development. Harris believes that experiences of extrafamilial groups are universally significant for children's development, and in some cultures these groups may predominantly be peer groups. Thus insofar as the focus is only on peer groups, as in this book, the expectations here are equivalent. I am presuming that the developmental implications of peer group experiences are unlikely to be unique to peer groups. Harris agrees insofar as she believes that what applies with peer groups will also apply with extra-familial groups in general. I am vague about how far the non-uniqueness spreads, while Harris sets clear boundaries. However, when the focus is limited to peer groups, this will be relevant only in the sense of signal-ing which alternative influences to watch out for and/or to control in research designs. On the other hand, I am open to a range of develop-mental mechanisms, constrained only by what is plausible when the individuals are similar in age, standing, or rank. Harris insists that the mechanisms are normative. I am happy to concede that, like social comparison as discussed above, normative influences are more likely under equivalence of age, standing, or rank. In situations of asymmetry, power, rather than norms, is often sufficient to dictate behavior! Nevertheless, for every social psychological study documenting normative influences, there seems to be another study on the same topic indicating so-called "informational influences," which include the exchanging and com-parison of opinions, the use of reasoned argument, and the comparison and resolution of differences (for a review see Van Avermaet, 2001). Interestingly, social comparison has featured prominently among the mechanisms used to explain such influences (Suls & Wheeler, 2000), although seldom with reference to Piaget or Sullivan. In general then, the social psychological evidence points against influences that are purely normative.

Once the normative requirement is relaxed, another tenet of group socialization theory becomes contestable. This is the differentiation of groups from dyads, for while it seems odd to think about dyads hold-ing norms, informational influences (as sketched above) seem as applicable to dyads as they do to larger groups. As it happens, Harris provides no research evidence to document the value of the group–dyad distinction, and admits (Harris, 1995) that it may sound like splitting hairs. Furthermore, making the distinction results in decisions that, on the face of it, seem arbitrary. For instance, chapter 5 in the present book discusses research which indicates that girls frequently organize them-selves into dyads in precisely the same contexts as those in which boys typically organize themselves into larger groups. Thus, if dyads are excluded from the concept of groups, analyses of peer group influences on girls' development would have to adopt a different frame of reference from the one adopted for boys. This may be warranted, but it seems undesirable to preclude other possibilities a priori. To avoid doing this, groups are conceptualized from now onwards as associations between *two or more* persons. Any differences between dyads and larger groups (or, for that matter, triads and foursomes, or small and large groups) will emerge as data permit. Given Harris's interest in social psychological evidence, it is noteworthy that Brown (1988) also defines groups as associations of two or more individuals in a book that focuses exclusively on such evidence.

Overall then, group socialization theory is a bold and interesting attempt to take a sociocultural perspective upon non-family influences on children's development. Nevertheless, because the present concern is purely with peer groups while group socialization theory's remit is broader, relatively few of its tenets turn out to be relevant. This includes the controversial claims about the relative importance of families compared with extrafamilial groups, along with the emphasis upon the broad concept of "extrafamilial group" as the unit of analysis. What is significant in the present context is group socialization theory's insistence that norms provide the mechanisms by which groups have their effects, and for connected reasons, that dyads should not be counted as groups. As noted, neither proposal is firmly grounded in evidence. Therefore, the strategy here is to be less restrictive at this stage, while being open to modification as research is forthcoming. Accordingly, the theoretical framework that the present book adopts presumes that: (a) children's experiences of peer groups (including dyads) have the potential to influence their development; (b) the aspects of development that peer groups can influence are also potentially influenced by other social experiences, and these alternative influences need to be considered when evaluating research; and (c) the mechanisms by which peer groups have their effects could be informational (including perhaps social comparison in the sense of Piaget and/or Sullivan) as well as normative.

Peer Groups and Children's Development

As noted, the purpose of the theoretical framework is to inform an analysis of children's experiences of peer groups, and the implications of those experiences for children's development. This analysis occupies the remainder of the book. As signaled already, the focus of the analysis is children's experiences in societies that require them to attend school. It is, in fact, also restricted to school-age children within those societies, that is, the age group from 5 or 6 years through to mid- to late teens. It is perhaps a little unnatural to refer to the upper end of the age range as "children," but a generic term is needed and "children" is preferred. When only the upper age group is of interest, alternative terms like "adolescents" are used. Normally, children are described in terms of age groups, but implementing this strategy has involved an element of guesswork. In many of the relevant research reports, samples are presented with reference only to school stage, for example Kindergarten, Grade 4, Year 9, Key Stage 3, High School. This is not very helpful to an international readership that may be unfamiliar with the conventions of specific school systems. Therefore, I have "translated" as accurately as possible into age levels, for example North American Grade 1 = 6-year-olds. For this reason, references to age groups should be treated as approximations.

The concept of "peer groups" should be clear from what has preceded, but essentially the term is used to designate associations between two or more children, who are not members of the same family but who are of similar age and (potentially) of similar standing or rank. The degree to which age, standing, and rank can vary while remaining "similar" is being kept deliberately vague. The emphasis upon "potential" similarities in standing and rank is intended to highlight the fact that children's peer groups do not involve predetermined differences in status, even though, as is discussed later, differences typically emerge. As regards "development," the book adopts a broad perspective, addressing social, personal, and academic development. Because the concern is with development rather than learning, little attention is paid to memorization of specific pieces of information, for instance a friend's telephone number, one's own blood group, or the capital of Peru. Rather, the emphasis is upon the social, personal, and cognitive structures that allow information to be integrated and, through this, to guide behavior.

Overview of contents

The analysis of children's experiences starts in chapter 2 with a discussion of the structural properties of classrooms. The Scottish scenario with which the present chapter began depicted a two-tier peer group structure, the whole class and its constituent subgroups. The latter included a math set, a language set, and a mixed-ability project group. Chapter 2 considers whether two-tier structures are universal properties of classrooms, or whether there is variation. It also discusses how tiers are organized, for instance what are their characteristic sizes and how children are assigned to them. Random assignment from the available set of peers is possible, but the Scottish scenario suggested selectivity in accordance with ability for certain subjects. Key questions discussed in chapter 2 relate to the extent of selectivity, and how much it is founded on ability.

With a clear sense of how classrooms are structured, chapter 3 considers the teaching and learning activities that the structures support. The emphasis is not, however, upon teaching and learning from the perspective of teachers. Rather, it is upon what the activities imply for how children experience their peers. There can be little doubt that children see teaching activities as something that their teacher wants them to engage with, whether or not they are inclined to comply. However, the teacher–pupil axis is not what this book is about. The focus is children's experiences of peer groups, and unless children have a strong sense of their classmates as members of their community, classrooms will be *constituted from* peer groups but will not necessarily be *experienced as* peer groups. Having drawn conclusions about the manner in which peers are in fact experienced in classrooms, the next issue to consider is the implications of these experiences. Do they, for instance, facilitate mastery of the curriculum? Moreover, are they always facilitative or only under certain conditions? These questions are discussed in chapter 4.

The focus of chapters 2–4 is on classrooms and the formal purposes of teaching and learning for which classrooms are constituted. This is not to say that the chapters are restricted to classrooms. Other peer groups that are created for formal purposes are referred to throughout. As signaled earlier, such groups include sports associations, youth movements, and extracurricular classes when school-age children are involved. However, it will not prove possible to say very much about these groups, simply because they are under-researched, and when research exists it seldom adopts a peer group perspective. Nevertheless, while chapters 2–4 occasionally move away from the classroom context, they concentrate exclusively on formal (i.e., institutionalized) functions. Classrooms are treated purely as contexts for teaching and learning, and sports associations are treated purely as contexts for coaching and performance. When such settings are analyzed as peer groups, this is manifestly a limitation. In her major exposition of group socialization theory, Harris (1998) remarks at one point that "To children in school, the most important people in the classroom are the other children" (p. 241). When she wrote this, Harris was not thinking about teaching and learning. She was concerned with the informal relations that children forge with each other while engaged in formal tuition. She was suggesting that these relations are significant.

Chapter 5 discusses informal relations in classrooms, and by implication in other peer groups that are constructed for formal purposes. It shows how these relations have traditionally been characterized in terms of friendship and status. Located in formal settings like classrooms, friendships amount to informal subgroups that may or may not be related to the formal subgroups (math sets and so on) that can also occur. Status depends on the relative popularity of children in the eyes of their peers, when considered across the setting as a whole. Status is, in other words, an informal dimension of the overarching formal structure. The book is concerned with school-age members of societies that require children to attend schools. Therefore, insofar as friendship and status are characteristics of classrooms (among other settings), they can be assumed to be universal aspects of experience as far as the target age group is concerned. However, this does not necessarily mean that all children have identical experiences. On the contrary, some children have many friends and experience friendship directly, while others have few or no friends and experience friendship as observers of others. Some children are popular, while others witness the popularity of others. Chapter 6 considers why children differ, and whether the differences are stable across time and place. Does friendlessness in school predict friendlessness in other contexts, and are friendless 5-year-olds typically friendless five or ten years later?

In considering stability across time and place, chapter 6 broadens the discussion to some extent from the formal, predominantly classroom, contexts considered in the early part of the book. Thus, by chapter 7, a picture of children's peer group experiences will have been painted that is as comprehensive as current research permits. Chapter 7 begins an analysis of the implications of this picture for children's development, focusing on social and personal growth. A substantial literature is surveyed that links negative experiences of friendship and status with, on the one hand, aggression, criminality, and substance abuse, and, on the other, anxiety, depression, and low self-esteem. However, once the circumstances are probed by which experiences of status and friendship have these troubling effects, an intriguing possibility emerges. Rather than being separate from the formal structures within which status and friendship are embedded, the developmental consequences may be partially dependent on those structures. In other words, they could result in part from the fact that status (by definition) and friendship (in practice) are informal dimensions of classrooms and other formal settings, and these settings have the peer group structure sketched in chapters 2–4.

Chapter 8 addresses the cognitive aspects of development, particularly those relating to academic achievement. In this respect, it revisits issues discussed in chapters 3 and 4 but with a new twist. It shows that the informal dimensions of friendship and status influence children's classroom attainment. Thus, whether or not education relies on direct learning from peers in the sense introduced in chapter 4, children's experiences of peer groups do have relevance for their performance in schools. Harris (1998) may have overstated the case when she suggested that, as far as children are concerned, other children are the most important people in classrooms. However, she was certainly correct to indicate that by virtue of informal experiences, other children are relevant. The book concludes in chapter 9 with a discussion of the implications of the material covered in earlier chapters for research and practice. One key point from chapter 8 is that teachers should recognize and work with the peer groups that comprise their classrooms because, whether they like this or not, these groups influence their effectiveness. Chapter 9 offers suggestions about what this means in practical terms.

An interdisciplinary perspective

Chapters 2–4 present material that addresses classic educational concerns. Research is summarized that informs debates around optimal class size, mixed-versus single-ability teaching, and the role of talk in instructional practice. Scholars located in university faculties of education are responsible for most of this research. The material presented in chapters 5 and 6 relates to venerable issues in the psychological analysis of social and personal development. For instance, studies of friendship and status date back more than a century. Here, investigators based in academic departments of psychology have conducted virtually all of the reported research. The separation between chapters 2–4 on the one hand and chapters 5 and 6 on the other means that contemporary educationalists and psychologists will have little difficulty locating the material that reflects their respective traditions. For instance, all of the empirical research that is included on the notorious class size debate appears in chapter 2.

The separation between educational and psychological material should assist readers in reviewing specific topics, but it will be disappointing if it leads educationalists to stop reading midway through the book or encourages psychologists to jump to chapter 5. If this happens, neither group will obtain a complete picture of the issues that concern them, for these issues are much more interwoven than commonly assumed. As signaled already, the message from chapter 8 is that psychological material on peer group experiences is needed to address the central educational issue of academic performance. Of equal importance is the fact that the psychologically informed message from chapter 8 implies a perspective on class size, ability-based teaching, and instructional talk that could not emerge from educational research alone. This perspective is developed in chapter 9. On the other hand, one message from chapter 7 is that educational research is relevant to deciphering the inherently psychological problem of social and personal development. Developing this theme, chapter 9 argues that, without an educational dimension, attempts to assist children experiencing social and emotional difficulties are unlikely to achieve more than partial success. In short, resolving dilemmas of educational practice requires psychological research into peer group experiences, and interpreting psychological research requires understanding of how peer groups are used in schools. So the book's broadest message is that an interdisciplinary perspective is needed to study the nature and consequences of children's peer group experiences in the depth that the topic deserves. It is hoped that the chapters to follow make a contribution to the large body of work which, adopting that perspective, remains to be done.

Chapter 2

Peer Groups and Classroom Structure

Introduction

As noted in chapter 1, all schools aspire to a peer group structure, for the universal preference is for classes where children are of similar age. The same applies with formal out-of-school provision, like youth movements, sports associations, and classes relating to the performing arts. As was pointed out in chapter 1, there is probably a close connection between the peer group structure of schooling and the equivalent structure in out-of-school contexts, with the former, historically, driving the latter. For sure, practical constraints, such as shortage of children in specific age bands, mean that the aspiration is not always attainable, but it remains the target to which most organizations involving children approximate to some degree. Nevertheless, despite its contemporary status as the universal target, the peer group structure of formal activities involving children has not been a constant practice throughout human history. In ancient times (e.g., classical Greece), teaching was usually delivered on a one-to-one basis, and one-to-one instruction still survives in special circumstances. The practice of employing governesses and private tutors has never quite died out, and one-to-one coaching remains the norm at elite levels within out-of-school activities, such as sports, athletics, and the performing arts. Remedial teaching in schools is sometimes delivered on a one-to-one basis. Historically, the "normal" peer group arrangement has been superimposed upon one-to-one foundations, as education (and related activities) has become less exclusive, and funded through tax revenues rather than private wealth. Public funding has so far only stretched to one (teacher/coach/group leader)-to-many (children) provision.

However, the fact that *peers* are the favored principle of grouping in classrooms and other formal contexts, rather than the countless other possibilities for one-to-many arrangements, suggests something more than merely an *alternative* to one-to-one provision. By minimizing individual differences along the age dimension, a peer group structure is a means of homogenizing children in one respect, and thus taking a small step toward the de facto re-creation of a one-to-one relation. The implication is, therefore, that peer group structures have emerged historically as a *compromise* between what resource realities necessitate, and an ideal that remains one to one. The contexts in which one-to-one provision survives, and particularly their association with elitism and privilege, support this interpretation. Moreover, it is not difficult to find commentaries upon contemporary practice that re-echo the ideal. For instance, Wood (1998) writes: "We have known for a long time that individual teaching by an expert human tutor leads to faster learning and better performance on academic tests than classroom teaching in groups" (p. 105). In one sense, such commentaries are irrelevant in the context of this book, for the focus is on the consequences of peer group structures (including "classroom teaching in groups"), given that these structures already exist. The merits of peer groups when compared with alternative arrangements are neither here nor there. Nevertheless, from another perspective, views like Wood's could prove highly relevant, and that is if they influence how peer groups are actually experienced. This chapter and the chapter that follows address children's experiences of the peer groups they encounter in formal contexts like classrooms. Repeatedly the chapters highlight instances of policy and practice that can only be interpreted in terms of tacit subscription to a one-to-one ideal. Sometimes subscription is relatively explicit.

The present chapter focuses on the structural properties of the peer groups that bring children together for formal purposes. The next chapter considers the activities that take place within those structures. As signaled in chapter 1, the emphasis in both chapters is upon schooling, for that is the context that has attracted most research. On the face of it this seems unfortunate, when the issue that the two chapters address—characterizing the formal dimension of children's peer groups—should apply equally with formal out-of-class activities. However, at present, research relating to such activities is concerned with their overall effects on children's development, which appear to be beneficial (Cooper, Valentine, Nye, & Lindsay, 1999; Fredricks & Eccles, 2006; Marsh, 1992; Posner & Vandell, 1999). It has not yet segmented the influences of peer groups from those of other factors, for example adult leadership, or removal from alternative, informal activities. Being obliged, then, to focus on schooling, one point that proves crucial for the analysis to follow was flagged at the start of chapter 1, and this is that the peer group structure of classrooms can be layered. It will be recalled that the Scottish scenario, with which chapter 1 began, portrayed a young girl being taught in a whole-class context on some occasions, and in smaller subgroups on other occasions. Specifically, mathematics, language, and the Roman Empire were all studied in such subgroups. Thus, the analysis to follow considers first the basic organizational unit—the classroom in the case of schools—and then any constituent subgroups. In both cases, the key issue is the parameters of group composition in addition to the underlying constant that groups comprise peers. The critical features of composition overlap across the two layers and, indeed, prove to be interconnected. Nevertheless, there is also one striking difference: while the basic organizational unit is universal in the sense discussed already, there is considerable cross-cultural and intra-cultural variability in the use of subgroups. The structures in which children receive their schooling are therefore not homogeneous.

The Peer Group Structure of Classes

The present section focuses on the composition of classes, for as noted classes are the basic organizational unit around which much else revolves. Two features of composition have attracted particular attention in the literature: (a) class size, and (b) selectivity along dimensions in addition to age. The features are interdependent, for if class size is set at levels such that all children in given age cohorts can be accommodated in single classes, no further selectivity is achievable. It is only when several classes are possible at specific age levels that choice becomes feasible. Nevertheless, despite their interrelation, the features can be (and have been) discussed separately, and this is the practice in the present section. As regards class size, Blatchford (2003) notes a tendency to confuse the concept with "pupil–teacher ratio," an index that is derived by dividing the total number of children in some school by the total number of teachers. Without doubt, the two indices are strongly correlated, but nevertheless class size, which relates to the total number of children within specific classrooms, is the most relevant to peer groups as actually experienced. With respect to selectivity, the dimension that is most commonly considered in addition to age is ability, but gender, ethnicity, social class, and a host of behavioral characteristics are sometimes also taken into account. In recognition of its salience, the section focuses on ability, but other dimensions are mentioned briefly.

Class size

During the 1940s, my mother-in-law was a teacher in what, in the United Kingdom, is called a "primary" school, that is, a school for 5- to 11-year-olds. She regularly had 60 children in her class. The class that I most vividly remember from my own primary school days was the one that I was placed in during 1960. It contained 48 children. My children attended primary school in the late 1980s and early 1990s, and the size of their classes never exceeded 25 children. A recent report from the Organisation for Economic Cooperation and Development (OECD, 2008) suggests that the current class size average for public-funded primary schools in the United Kingdom is 25.8 children. This compares with a primary school average class size of 21.5 children across OECD countries as a whole, with relatively low averages reported for Luxembourg (15.6), Iceland (18.3), and Italy (18.4), and relatively high averages reported for Korea (31.6), Japan (28.2), and Turkey (27.5). With public-funded schools at secondary level, the average class size across OECD countries as a whole is 23.8 children, with Switzerland (19.1), Luxembourg (19.5), and Iceland (19.8) recording relatively low averages, and Korea (36.0), Japan (33.2), and Mexico (29.8) recording relatively high averages.

Moving beyond OECD countries, a recent case study of three secondary schools in South Africa (Xolo, 2008) reports a class size of 25 in a rich urban school. However, there was an average of 40 children per class in a school located in one of the townships, and the school that was targeted in a poor rural location had classes that contained as many as 75 children. In research to be discussed in more detail later, Alexander (2001) reports that class sizes at the primary school level in India vary between 36 and 70 children. A study in Kenya described in Pontefract and Hardman (2005) and involving 27 classes of 5- to 13-year-olds indicates class sizes of between 45 and 75 children. In general then, the above mixture of anecdote and systematic research serves to highlight two central points. First, there is considerable variation over typical class sizes, both between cultures at any moment in time, and within cultures historically. Second, typical class size is negatively correlated with wealth: as resources increase, class sizes decrease. The implication is that small class sizes are valued, and therefore the aspiration is to minimize within resource constraints. This is undoubtedly why Blatchford, Bassett, and Brown (2008) report class size reduction initiatives in China, England and Wales, Hong Kong, Japan, Korea, Macau, the Netherlands, New

Zealand, Taiwan, and the United States. In the United States, 33 states have passed legislation endorsing class size reduction programs.

Given apparently universal endorsement of the advantages of small classes, it is surprising to discover that the research literature provides an ambiguous message about their effectiveness. This can be illustrated by comparing two key studies (for a comprehensive literature review see Blatchford, 2003). The first is the STAR project (e.g., Finn & Achilles, 1999), which was conducted in 72 schools across Tennessee in the United States. The crucial aspect of the project for present purposes is that it involved randomly assigning a large cohort of children to small classes (13–17 pupils per class) or regular classes (22–25 pupils per class) upon entry to school. All participating schools had both types of class. The children remained in their classes for three years whereupon the small classes were disbanded, and all children were reallocated to regular classes. The children who were initially placed in small classes made more rapid progress than the other children in literacy and mathematics. Moreover, the small class advantages were found not just during the three years that the children were actually in small classes but also on follow-up assessment during subsequent years. These results have proved robust against more sophisticated analyses of the STAR data that have been conducted since the project's completion (Goldstein & Blatchford, 1998). Nevertheless, despite the robustness, concerns have been expressed about the lack of baseline attainment measures before the project started. This would have allowed guarantees that the "small class" and "regular class" children were comparable at the outset, instead merely of the presumption of comparability that random allocation provides. It would also have permitted systematic analysis of the effects of the relatively high dropout rates, when for instance the children moved schools. In addition, the use of what is technically known as an "experimental design" means that the children in the small classes (and their teachers) must have known of their "special" status. This may have resulted in atypical behavior, for instance particular efforts to succeed, which may have exaggerated the effects.

Blatchford's (2003) work in 199 schools spread across England (involving 669 classes encompassing more than 7,000 children) was, in part, an attempt to address the difficulties with the STAR project. It involved baseline measures upon entry to school, and it exploited the variation in class size that occurs naturally rather than creating variation artificially. This resulted in four bands becoming the focus of analysis: 10–20 children per class, 21–25 children per class, 26–30 children per class, and 31 or more children per class. In terms of academic performance, Blatchford's data indicate marked effects during the first year of schooling: the smaller the size band, the higher the children's attainments on tests of literacy and mathematics administered at the end of the year. However, the effects dissipated over subsequent years, such that no attainment differences could be detected as a function of class size two years later. For sure, Blatchford's research, like the STAR project, is an impressive and important piece of work. Nevertheless, its naturalistic approach means that it was restricted to the range of class sizes that currently exists in English schools. As intimated already, this range is relatively small when judged against changes over time and differences between cultures. To make a truly convincing case about the effects of class size, it would be necessary to introduce greater variation by examining "possible" class sizes as well as actual ones. This would require experimental intervention, which would need to be carefully planned to pre-empt the special status dangers that have already been indicated in relation to the STAR project. Even though the valuing of small classes signaled above means that it would probably be regarded as unethical to assign children to classes that were larger than the current range, there could be no such objections to assigning them to classes that were smaller. This of course is the approach that the STAR project adopted.

In addition to examining children's performance, both of the projects discussed above obtained data on teachers' attitudes to class size. Unsurprisingly, an overwhelming majority of teachers favored class sizes at the lower end of the range that they were familiar with. What is more interesting in the present context is the tendency to justify the preference in terms of greater potential for individualized treatment. Thus, it emerged from the STAR project that teachers in small classes felt that

> they were better able to individualize instruction [and achieve] increased monitoring of student behavior and learning, opportunities for more immediate and more individualized re-teaching, more enrichment, more frequent interactions with each child, a better match between each child's ability and the instructional opportunities provided, a more detailed knowledge of each child's needs as a learner, and more time to meet individual learners' needs. (Pate-Bain, Achilles, Boyd-Zaharias, & McKenna, 1992, p. 254)

Likewise, Blatchford (2003) begins his report with a case study that characterizes his findings. He cites a teacher, whose comments are echoed by many other teachers quoted subsequently, who "felt very strongly that hearing children of this age read individually in school was important—the small class size allowed almost daily sessions in which there was a stress on individualized support" (p. 3). The significance of such attitudes in the present context is not only that they provide the first evidence for tacit subscription to what was earlier called the "one-to-one ideal"; they also suggest that for many teachers, the peer group structure of classrooms is incidental. The main issue is the interactions that individual children engage in with their teachers, and not any relationships between the children themselves. To put it differently, the imagery is of a wheel in which the teacher is the hub, and the pupils are spokes arranged around the hub.

Of course, the fact that teachers believe that small classes support individualized teaching does not necessarily mean that they behave in an individualizing fashion in reality when faced with small classes. The social science literature is replete with mismatches between beliefs about behavior and what actually happens. Thus, over the years, there have been various attempts to document teaching activity directly, and relate observations to the number of children in the class. This was a further component of Blatchford's (2003) study, and these data have now been supplemented with observations recorded in English schools during 2005 and 2006 (Blatchford et al., 2008). Observations were made of 5- to 6-year-olds and 7- to 8-year-olds in 27 primary schools, and of 11- to 12-year-olds and 14- to 15-year-olds in 22 secondary schools. Eight children were observed in each school, with children selected to ensure gender balance and a spread of ability (high, medium, and low as nominated by teachers). Class size was assessed via the number of children present in the classroom at the time each observation was recorded. The larger the class size at primary school level, the less likely children were to engage in on-task behavior or to interact with their teachers. For low- and medium-ability children only, large classes were also associated with more off-task behavior, and more time spent by teachers on dealing with misdemeanors. At secondary level, the relation between class size and on- and off-task behavior was limited to the low-ability children. However, once more, the likelihood of direct pupil–teacher interaction was inversely related to class size, regardless of pupil ability.

Blatchford et al.'s evidence on direct interaction between pupils and teachers suggests that reducing class size promotes individualizing treatment *to some degree*. Nevertheless, it is important not to overinterpret. Blatchford et al. looked for evidence that interaction was (a) initiated, (b) responded to, (c) sustained for at least 10 seconds. Fulfilling these conditions goes only a small way toward providing what current research highlights as effective practice during one-to-one teaching. The research in question is grounded in the work of Vygotsky (e.g., 1962, 1978), particularly Vygotsky's concept of a "zone of proximal development." This is defined as "the distance between the actual developmental level as determined by independent problem solving and the level of potential development as determined through problem solving under adult guidance or in collaboration with more capable peers" (Vygotsky, 1978, p. 86). The role of teaching is to assist children in crossing their personal zones, so that what they can achieve under guidance becomes their "actual developmental level" on subsequent occasions. To put the work on class size into perspective, it may be useful to consider what is known about effective assistance.

Research relating to effective assistance has focused on mother–child interaction rather than classrooms. For instance, Wood and Middleton (1975) and Wertsch (1979) recorded mothers assisting preschool children with, respectively, the construction of pyramids from blocks and the completion of jigsaw puzzles. Wood and Middleton found that child progress depended on mothers providing "contingent control," that is, prompting with increasing specificity until task success is achieved, and then with decreasing specificity until success is possible unaided. Thus, to be effective, the initial prompt should be relatively general, for instance "Now you make something," with specific instructions like "Get four big blocks," and then physical demonstration used, as necessary, later. Gradually the sequence should be reversed. Similarly, Wertsch identified four levels in the transition from "other-regulation" to "self-regulation." At the first level, the mother's goal should simply be to engage with the task that exists for the child, rather than aspire to solution. At the second and third levels, she should gradually increase the scope of her guidance, and then decrease this. At the fourth level, the child will be capable of taking full responsibility for task completion, perhaps inviting assistance when they recognize a challenge rather than depending on the challenge being identified by the mother. Dispiritingly, Wood (1986) reviews evidence showing not only that mothers vary considerably in their ability to optimize guidance, but also that teachers find this virtually impossible, even when (implausibly in authentic contexts) working with children on a one-to-one basis. This is not to suggest that class size reduction is irrelevant. Quite the opposite; the recommendations for practice outlined in chapter 9 presuppose manageable numbers. Rather, the aim is to introduce circumspection into what is currently a highly politicized arena, and perhaps also to understand what Wood (1998) was thinking about when he wrote so scathingly of "classroom teaching in groups" in the text quoted earlier.

Selective assignment

Regardless of the effectiveness data, it can be assumed from the values and historical trends sketched above that at any point in time children are assigned to the smallest classes that resources permit. The OECD statistics indicate that this currently averages between 15 and 30 children per class across affluent countries. Blatchford's (2003) research suggests considerable variation within countries too, with a range of at least 15–30 children per class in England alone. Whatever the current situation, it is unlikely to be stable, for as noted, the pressures are always for further reduction. It is interesting that policy debates about class size seldom, if ever, specify the desirable minimum! Moreover, as class sizes reduce, so the possibility increases for being selective about how children are assigned within the constraints imposed by age. There is, as noted earlier, always a class size that corresponds to the full age cohort and if this is the size that a particular school adopts, then selectivity along other dimensions becomes impossible. The pupil intake to schools catering for the younger age groups (primary schools, elementary schools, and so on) is often set to allow one class per age cohort, while complying with whatever legislation is currently in force about class size. However, small intake is less often the case at older age levels (in secondary schools, high schools, etc.), where the possibility of several classes per cohort is commonplace. Thus, the issue of selectivity is particularly pertinent at these age levels, and this is where research has been focused.

In the early part of the 20th century, it was common to find selectivity at the school level, again particularly in secondary/high schools. Entrance examinations segregated children by ability, and single-sex schools were the norm. Selectivity on grounds of race, ethnicity, and/or religion is also well documented. Nowadays, most public-funded schools in most countries are required to operate coeducational, multiethnic, multifaith, comprehensive entrance policies with catchment area demographics expected to be the main determinant of intake composition. Any deliberate selectivity is supposed to be restricted to within-school practices. Indeed, coeducation is so strongly entrenched in the United States that Haag (1998) despaired of being able to compare its efficacy with single-sex arrangements. All that seemed possible was hopelessly confounded comparison between private single-sex schools (restricted socioeconomic distribution) and public coeducational schools (full socioeconomic distribution). Haag identified less compromised comparisons conducted in other countries, but most were extremely dated, since it is not just the United States where coeducational arrangements prevail. In any event, the results are inconclusive.

Within coeducational schools, selectivity with respect to gender is sometimes attempted, although this remains rare. Research into its efficacy, which was "fledgling" at the time that Haag conducted her review (Haag, 1998, p. 22), has produced mixed results. Reporting on examination performance in a coeducational school that had used single-sex classes since the 1970s, Younger and Warrington (2002) document impressive results for both sexes. In England, where the study was conducted, all pupils take the General Certificate of Secondary Education (or GCSE) at about 16 years of age. National data show steady improvement in GCSE results on a year-by-year basis, but the improvement in Younger and Warrington's school was almost twice as steep as the national average. This was true for both boys and girls. Working in Germany, Kessels and Hannover (2008) found that single-sex teaching boosted the confidence of 14-year-old girls in their ability to achieve in physics, while having no adverse effects on the (relatively high) confidence of boys. The study is impressive for: (a) its large sample ($N = 401$); (b) its sustained intervention (lasting one year); (c) its control for school and pupil effects by formulating all-boy, all-girl, and mixed classes within each of the four participating schools; and (d) its control for teacher effects, through ensuring that each of the 10 teachers who were involved in the project taught a mixed-sex class, and at least one single-sex class.

Yet against these positive results, Jackson (2002) found that while 80% of the girls in a sample of 12- to 13-year-olds ($N = 125$) preferred single-sex teaching when this was introduced into an English secondary school, 64% of the boys preferred the traditional mixed arrangements. Reporting on more than 4,000 children who had been followed from birth, Sullivan (2006) demonstrates that once prior attainment is taken into account, there are no discernible effects of single- versus mixed-sex teaching on pupil confidence. Harvey (1985) examined the science test results of 2,900 pupils attending 17 secondary schools in England. Two of the schools were coeducational but used single-sex science classes, six were coeducational with mixed science classes, six were all-girls schools, and three were all-boys schools. Verbal reasoning (as a proxy for IQ) was controlled in data analyses. Harvey found no differences in science test results between the single-sex and mixed classes in the coeducational schools, for either the boys or the girls. For the boys there were also no differences between the coeducational and single-sex schools, but the girls performed better in the coeducational schools.

There are undoubtedly many reasons why the studies summarized in the previous paragraph are more ambivalent about single-sex arrangements than the studies presented in the one before it. Schools that introduce single-sex provision are always going to be "special" when the prevailing ethos at the national level is coeducational. Therefore, generalizable results are not necessarily to be expected. Effects of special status will be compounded when the number of schools participating in the research project is relatively small. In addition, interview and questionnaire data reported in Shah and Conchar (2009) indicate that parents are proportionately more in favor of single-sex provision than their children. This suggests that the community pressures that lead to such provision may come from different sources than those directly affected.

One implication from the above is that the more typical the principle of within-school selectivity, the greater the likelihood of generalizable results. If so, it ought to be possible to draw conclusions about selectivity on grounds of ability that are relatively compelling, for ability is the main basis for selectivity within contemporary schools. At the classroom level, ability-based selection has traditionally taken one of two forms (Harlen & Malcolm, 1997; Sukhnandan & Lee, 1998). The first involves stable classes defined by ability, an approach that is usually termed "streaming" with the United Kingdom and "tracking" in the United States. It presupposes of course that ability is a general characteristic, with level of ability in one subject predicting level of ability in other subjects. The second approach is intended to sidestep this assumption, by employing mixed-ability classes as the basic unit, but regrouping by ability for specific subjects, for instance bringing all of the mathematics high achievers from each class together to create a new class for instruction in mathematics. This approach is usually called "setting" within the United Kingdom, but as we shall see later, setting has other uses too, which make the term confusing. Hence, following North American practices, the approach is characterized as "regrouping" or "regrouped classes" in the discussion to follow.

Unfortunately the hopes of straightforward conclusions about ability selectivity are quickly dashed. Research has been beset by methodological problems, albeit of a slightly different variety from the ones that apply with gender. Evidence for the value of ability selectivity depends on controlled comparison with mixed-ability equivalents. Comparisons with mixed-ability arrangements are the norm, but it is debatable whether these comparisons have ever been fully controlled. For instance, no study has equated across all potentially relevant characteristics of pupils (e.g., ethnicity, gender, socioeconomic status, awareness that groups are/are not based on ability) and teachers (e.g., expectations of specific pupils, pre-ferred methods of teaching, attitudes to grouping by ability). Moreover, few studies have made repeated assessments over sustained periods of time, in a fashion that takes present and past experiences of grouping into account. Research designs have improved over the years, but one side effect of this improvement is that evidence relating to stable classes (i.e., streaming cum tracking) is weaker than evidence relating to regrouping. As with the work discussed earlier on class size, the tradi-tion is for research to focus on the forms of ability groupings that currently exist, not the forms that existed in the past and/or might exist in the future. In the United Kingdom and the United States, where the bulk of the work has been conducted, stable ability-based classes are rapidly disappearing. For instance, they are currently used in less than 5% of English schools (Kutnick, Sebba, Blatchford, Galton, & Thorp, 2005b; Sukhnandan & Lee, 1998). As a result, such classes were the focus of early, relatively weak, research, and for this reason evidence about their consequences should not be regarded as conclusive. For the record, findings suggest no advantages over mixed-ability arrangements as regards pupil attainment, and possible disadvantages as regards social and personal development (Harlen & Malcolm, 1997; Slavin, 1987, 1990; Sukhnandan & Lee, 1998).

As regards regrouping, which remains common in schools and increases with pupil age (Sukhnandan & Lee, 1998), it is possible to detect two distinct lines of research. The first makes comparisons with mixed-ability arrangements, and the second examines the consequences of being assigned to high-, medium-, or low-ability groups specifically. Surveying literature that relates primarily to the former, Kutnick et al. (2005b) write that "the research evidence on the impact of pupil group-ing practices leads us to conclude that no one form of grouping benefits all pupils" (p. 12). Some research indicates that the pre-existing achieve-ment spectrum is simply preserved, no matter whether teaching groups are homogeneous or mixed with regard to ability. This is, for instance, the message from work conducted in Belgium, Germany, and the Netherlands that Kutnick et al. review. Whether this is regarded as good, bad, or neutral most likely depends on one's personal values, and on whether maintaining the current spectrum means preserving relative or absolute differences. Studies are not always clear on this point. Other research suggests that some pupils gain more than others from specific arrangements, and these differences can be predicted from their ability, but there are no overall differences. For example, in a study conducted in Israel, Linchevski and Kutscher (1998) found that children with high mathematical ability performed very slightly better in mathematics when working with other children with high mathematical ability than when working in mixed-ability classes. However, children whose mathematical ability was in the low or medium range performed considerably better in mixed-ability contexts than with other children whose mathematical ability was equivalent.

One problem with assessing the effects of ability regrouping is that designation of ability levels is not a precise science, and it is recognition of this problem that underpins the second line of research of the two pinpointed above. Here, the focus is on the implications of which class children are regrouped into, regardless of actual ability. A particularly comprehensive example is the work of Ireson, Hallam, and Hurley (2005), for this involved 45 secondary schools spread across England. Ireson et al. observed only loose association between the classes that pupils were regrouped into for various subjects and their grades for those subjects on earlier national tests (so-called KS2 taken around 11 years of age and KS3 taken around 14 years, with "KS" an abbreviation for "Key Stage"). For instance, one school had placed pupils who achieved Level 5 in KS3 English in all 12 of its regrouped classes. Moreover, class placement mattered. Ireson et al. found that average performance in GCSE mathematics, English, and science was significantly higher from pupils who had been placed in relatively high-ability classes than from pupils *with comparable KS3 grades* who had been placed in lower ability classes. Working on a smaller scale (that is, with six schools rather than Ireson et al.'s 45, and with one subject rather than Ireson et al.'s three), Wiliam and Bartholomew (2004) replicate the findings. Pupils placed in the top groups obtained significantly higher grades in mathematics than would be expected from their KS3 scores, and pupils placed in the lower groups obtained significantly lower grades. Interviews conducted as part of the study pinpoint teacher expectations as one key factor. As one pupil memorably reminisced: "Sir used to normally say 'You're the bottom group, you're not going to learn anything' " (see Boaler, Wiliam, & Brown, 2000, p. 639).

The work of Ireson et al. (2005) and Wiliam and Bartholomew (2004) is relatively recent, and therefore can be read as confirming the continuing vitality of ability-based grouping. Children may be assigned to mixed-ability classes in the first instance, but regrouping means that selectivity along ability lines remains prevalent at the level of classrooms. It increases with age, but few children finish their school careers without experiencing some differentiation at the classroom level according to ability. Yet as we have seen, there is no research evidence to support the practice, and administratively it must impose burdens. There can, after all, be nothing simpler than the random assignment that mixed-ability teaching implies. So why does ability-based grouping continue? It is impossible to be certain, but it could be yet another manifestation of the one-to-one ideal. After all, selectivity with regards to ability (or gender, religion, or whatever) continues the homogenizing process that, as argued at the start of the chapter, the peer group structure itself reflects. As a result, it contributes to the creation of a singular "individual" (albeit an imaginary one) out of diversity.

Hard evidence for the role of homogenization may be difficult to obtain, but even if the interpretation is only partially true, it both confirms and strengthens the earlier portrayal of peer groups in the context of school-ing. As regards teachers, the peer group structure of classrooms is not merely incidental rather than central to primary concerns; it may even be tacitly regarded as obstructive. As regards pupils on the other hand, the structure is anything but incidental. Children think about the gen-der composition of their classrooms, as evidenced in Jackson's (2002) and Shah and Conchar's (2009) demonstration that they have attitudes toward this. As the above quotation from Boaler et al. (2000) makes clear, they are also aware of ability composition, sometimes painfully so. The implication is therefore that ability and gender are not merely principles for organizing classroom peer groups; they are also part of peer groups as actually experienced by children.

The Structure of Classroom Subgroups

In discussing the peer group structure of classrooms, the previous section addressed what can be regarded as a universal of schooling. The class is the basic organizational unit within all schools, and, by aspira-tion at least, membership of classes always depends on age. However, as noted earlier, some schools can, like the school in chapter 1's Scottish scenario, also deploy a subgroup structure within the overall classroom. When subgroups are used, precisely the same issues apply as were dis-cussed above, that is, issues of size and selectivity. Therefore, these issues are considered once more in the present section, this time with respect to classroom subgroups. The overall aim also remains as before, to portray the structural features that children are exposed to when they join peer groups for the formal purpose of schooling. Nevertheless, while many themes recur, the section starts by discussing one key difference between classrooms and their constituent subgroups. As flagged already, the universality of classes is not replicated at the subgroup level. Subgroups are only deployed in a subset of schools, and the section begins by discussing the factors that predict this variability.

Cultural and local influences on classroom structure

Mention has already been made of Alexander's (2001) cross-cultural study of primary schools. As well as covering five countries (England, France, India, Russia, and the United States), the study takes a multilevel approach to each country, moving from national policy through school organization to the microcosm of classroom activity. Research methods include analysis of documentation, surveys and interviews with key personnel, and observations in classrooms. Many of Alexander's conclusions about classroom activity are covered in chapter 3, but one is highly relevant here. This is that teaching in the schools in India and Russia that featured in the research was conducted exclusively at the whole-class level. No use of subgroups was detected. Furthermore, while the schools in England, France, and the United States all made use of subgroups to some degree, usage proved to be considerably more extensive in England and the United States than it was in France. Osborn (2001; with Broadfoot, McNess, Raven, Planel, & Triggs, 2003) compared practices in Denmark, England, and France, using questionnaires, interviews, documentary analysis, and observations of teachers and pupils. Her results replicate the differences between England and France over subgroup usage that Alexander reports, while suggesting that small-group activity is even more frequent in Denmark than it is in England.

Both Alexander and Osborn see the differences over subgroup usage as reflecting and reinforcing differences at the levels of national policy and school organization. Moreover, they regard the interaction between levels as mediated by cultural values and traditions. For instance, France and Russia have long traditions of centralized curricula, which teachers have delegated responsibility to deliver. This undoubtedly supports a monolithic perspective on teacher–class relations. Education in India, an ex-British colony, is heavily influenced by the English model, which has traditionally (although no longer) been decentralized. However, when, as noted earlier, class sizes in India can reach 70 pupils, school organizational factors press toward a single layer. Think, after all, how much time it would take simply to divide 70 children into subgroups, let alone to engage them in meaningful activity. Schooling in England and the United States has been strongly influenced by the conception of "democratic education" propounded by John Dewey (e.g., 1916), and therefore emphasis has long been placed upon pupils' rights to have their individuality recognized. At the very least, this implies movement away from a single "whole-class" layer, with the deployment of subgroups being an obvious consequence.

Focusing like Alexander and Osborn on underlying cultural values and traditions, Tweed and Lehman (2002) draw a distinction between "Socratic" and "Confucian" philosophies of education. Socratic philosophy emphasizes questioning beliefs, implanting doubt, evaluating others' knowledge, esteeming self-generated knowledge, and looking for reasons (see also Billig, 1996). According to Tweed and Lehman, it is a philosophy that underpins much educational thinking in the English-speaking world, of which America, Canada, and Australia are highlighted specifically (but presumably Ireland, New Zealand, and the United Kingdom would also be included). Confucian philosophy stresses effortful learning, individual conduct, essential knowledge, a pragmatic, career-focused orientation to learning, and above all respect for academic authorities. Tweed and Lehman associate this philosophy with the "culturally Chinese," including but not restricted to the citizens of China. Of particular relevance here is the evidence that Tweed and Lehman present that students whose educational systems are underpinned by a Confucian philosophy have limited experience of teaching units below the whole-class level. For instance, an Australian study is cited which finds Asian university students reporting four times as much difficulty with tutorial discussions as local students. The point is made that this reflects the absence of small-group activity from earlier experiences of teaching.

There seems little question that cultural traditions and values are relevant to the peer group structure of classrooms, and there are undoubtedly other aspects of such traditions and values to be considered. For instance, developmental psychologists have placed considerable emphasis upon the distinction between "individualism" and "collectivism" (Tamis-LeMonda et al., 2008), and it would be surprising if this distinction did not have implications for education. Equally though, it is inconceivable that variations in the use of classroom subgroups are fully explicable at the level of culture. In the first place, traditions and values are multidimensional, and it is unlikely that they ever point in a fully consistent direction. Secondly, practices change without discernible changes in basic values. For instance, Galton (1999) draws attention to the growing interest in Hong Kong and Singapore (despite being "culturally Chinese") in using small-group activity in classrooms. Thirdly, as Alexander (2001) emphasizes, no country is fully prescriptive with respect to pedagogy, and therefore there is always scope for individual preference as regards methods of delivery. In chapter 3, we shall look in detail at two large-scale observational studies conducted in English primary schools (Galton, Hargreaves, Comber, Wall, & Pell, 1999; Galton, Simon, & Croll, 1980). One of these studies was completed in the late 1970s when classroom subgroups were in vogue, and the other was completed in the mid-1990s when political pressures were pointing toward whole-class provision. Both studies identified "class enquirers" among their samples of teachers, that is, teachers who concentrated activity at the classroom level. However, both also identified "group instructors," who deployed subgroups to a significant degree. Both types of teacher could be found in a single school.

Moreover, it should not be imagined that when cultural conditions support the use of two-tier, class/subgroup systems, variations in usage are purely a matter of teacher preference. Research reported by Baines, Blatchford, and Kutnick (2003), covering 378 primary and secondary schools located in many parts of England, shows considerable variation in the use of subgroups as a function of academic subject. For instance, while 28% of the primary classes observed by Baines et al. used subgroups for science, only 5% did this for mathematics. The equivalent figures at the secondary level were 52% for science, and 14% for mathematics. Information and Communication Technology (ICT) was not specifically targeted in Baines et al.'s research, but earlier work suggests that small groups are common in that context too. For instance, surveys by Jackson, Fletcher, and Messer (1986), covering 110 English primary schools, and McAteer and Demissie (1991), covering 111 Scottish secondary schools, established that between 80% and 97% of ICT teaching involves pupils working in small groups. Science and ICT both rely on equipment, which is relatively expensive for schools to provide. It seems likely therefore that the heavy use of groups in these contexts is resource driven: most schools simply cannot provide the requisite facilities on a one-to-one basis.

Overall then, a range of factors determines whether the peer group structure of classrooms involves a single, classroom-level layer, or a two-tier system where the classroom level is embellished with smaller subgroups. At the very least, children's chances of experiencing one form rather than the other depend on the country they are born in, the preferences of their teachers (influenced no doubt by the views of school management), and the resources that are available. These factors need to be borne in mind when considering the effectiveness of the two forms of organization, something which can perhaps best be done with reference to a review article by Lou et al. (1996). Using all previously published research of relevance, Lou et al. used a statistical technique called meta-analysis, which considers mean difference across studies and strength of effect, to ascertain the impact of classes with and without subgroups on academic achievement (51 studies), pupil attitudes (21 studies), and self-concept (10 studies). The results indicate consistently more positive effects when subgroups were used than with the single-tier arrangement. However, from what has already emerged, it can be assumed that, across the studies, subgroups were used when cultural conditions and local preferences favored them, and with some school subjects rather than others. Lou et al.'s findings are important, but they cannot be presumed to imply positive effects in all circumstances.

Size and selectivity

As noted above, Baines et al. (2003) report large-scale research examining the relation between subgroup usage and school subject. This research is also one of the most comprehensive investigations ever attempted of the composition of subgroups when these are used. Therefore it also provides an excellent starting point for the discussion to follow. The research is actually an amalgam of three separate studies, one of which underpins the analysis of class size by Blatchford (2003) that was considered earlier. As will become clear, some results of relevance to subgroup composition appear in Blatchford's book, or alternatively in Blatchford, Baines, Kutnick, and Martin (2001), rather than in the Baines et al. report. The three studies had a common methodology, which involved preparing maps of each participating classroom. At a preassigned time on a preassigned day, teachers were asked to use the maps to indicate the whereabouts of each pupil, the groups they were part of, and the activity they were engaged in. Pupil gender was to be noted, as was the location of all adults who were present at the time. Later in the day (whenever was convenient), teachers were invited to complete questionnaires, which elaborated on the maps through information about class size, pupil ability, and so on. In total, 920 teachers completed maps, and these maps provided information about 4,924 classroom subgroups. The groups covered three primary school age bands (5 years, 7 years, and 10 years), and two secondary school age bands (12 years and 15 years).

Baines et al. found that the average number of subgroups increased with age from a mean of 4.4 groups per class with the 5-year-olds to a mean of 6.5 groups per class with the 15-year-olds. At the same time, subgroup size decreased with age from a mean of 5.6 children per group with the 5-year-olds to a mean of 3.4 children per group with the 15-year-olds. Blatchford (2003) and Blatchford et al. (2001) report analyses, based on the primary school data only, which indicate a relation between class size and subgroup size. Specifically, groups with between four and six members were the most frequent arrangement regardless of class size, accounting for between 45% and 50% of the primary school groups. Dyads and triads were less common, with neither accounting for more than 9% of the subgroups. Nevertheless, their frequency decreased to about 5% dyads and 5% triads as class size increased. As regards larger groups, around 25% of the subgroups observed in classes with more than 26 pupils had 7–10 members, while this was true of only about 8% of the subgroups observed in smaller classes. The picture was more or less reversed with subgroups containing 11 or more members. These groups accounted for 26% of the total when class size ranged between 10 and 25 members, presumably because the "11 or more" category often covered the whole class. However, the category only encompassed about 17% of the total when class size was larger. In contrast to the mixed-ability nature of the classes (as documented earlier), Baines et al.'s report suggests that about 60% of the primary school subgroups at all three age levels were stratified by ability. Stratification was at similar levels with the younger secondary pupils, while at 15 years of age, 81% of the groups were based on ability. Although groups were typically mixed sex, boys were disproportionately likely to be in lower ability groups and girls to be in higher ability groups (see Kutnick et al., 2005b, for detail of the relation between gender and ability).

The implications of ability-based grouping at the classroom level were discussed earlier in this chapter, and many of the excellent reviews on the topic also discuss ability-based grouping at the subgroup level (e.g., Harlen & Malcolm, 1997; Kutnick et al., 2005b; Slavin, 1987, 1990; Sukhnandan & Lee, 1998). Some draw attention to the absence of straightforward terminology for this form of grouping, in contrast to "streaming" or "tracking" for stable, ability-based classes, and "setting" or "regrouping" for temporary classes based on ability in specific subjects. Chapter 1's Scottish scenario included examples of ability-based subgroups, the so-called sets in which the protagonist studied mathematics and language. The term "set" was selected deliberately because this is how the (real) school in which the scenario was located refers to ability-based subgroups. Baines et al. (2003) occasionally use the term in an equivalent manner. However, the term "set" is bound to cause confusion if applied with subgroups, given its alternative (and probably more conventional) role in designating regrouped classes. "Ability-based subgroup" is probably as good a term as any in the absence of pithy alternatives. Whatever term is used, most literature reviews draw attention to the same methodological problems that emerged in relation to ability-based grouping at the classroom level, such as failure to control all potentially confounding variables, or to obtain repeated measures of pupil attainment (including before and after assignment to groups). Here, it is sometimes even unclear what "ability" means, for instance whether some general capacity is referred to, or whether it is ability in specific subjects (as in the Scottish scenario). Unfortunately, the research of Baines et al. (2003) is open to criticism on this score, despite its general significance.

Vagueness over the concept of ability is a limitation that also applies to what, in other respects, are arguably the strongest reviews in the field: the review reported by Lou et al. (1996) in the article discussed earlier, and a further review presented in Webb (1989). Most of the other surveys cite these two pieces of work. As well as comparing classes with and without subgroups (as summarized above), Lou et al. used their meta-analytic techniques to compare the relative effectiveness of ability-based subgroups with mixed-ability subgroups. Moreover, they did this in a fashion that allows potentially confounding characteristics of pupils and teachers to be controlled for statistically. Focusing on mathematics and computer science, Webb conducts comparable analyses via systematic comparison of correlations. Lou et al. base their analyses on 20 published studies, which (inevitably) overlap with the 19 published studies considered by Webb. Both Lou et al. and Webb conclude that, overall, there is little evidence for differences between ability-based subgroups and mixed-ability subgroups as regards pupil attainment. Nevertheless, low-ability children appear to gain most from working in mixed-ability subgroups, while medium-ability children seem to profit most from ability-based arrangements. High-ability children perform well within both types of grouping. As regards low- and high-ability children, these findings mirror what Linchevski and Kutscher (1998) detected at the classroom level in research discussed earlier. On the other hand, Linchevski and Kutscher found that mixed-ability arrangements were more profitable than ability-based grouping for medium-ability children as well as low-ability children, so here there may be differences between the classroom and subgroup levels.

Competing pressures

So, once more, the question has to be asked of why schools go to the additional trouble of ability-based subgroups, when there appears to be no net advantage over the administratively more straightforward mixed-ability arrangement. On the face of it, the answer that was proposed earlier for ability-based selectivity at the classroom level seems just as plausible at the subgroup level. The formulation of ability-based subgroups is perhaps an additional strategy for rendering children as similar as possible along an educationally relevant dimension, so that they become, in effect, a composite "individual." In other words, it continues yet further the homogenizing process that, as argued earlier, the peer group structure itself reflects. Indeed, interview material presented in Blatchford et al. (2001) suggests that the valuing of homogeneity is not far from the surface of some teachers' consciousness. One teacher, for instance, stated: "If I teach larger groups and therefore get around more often, the quality is more likely to be reduced as there are more children working together—all of differing abilities" (p. 295).

Nevertheless, whatever its apparent plausibility, such homogenizing (and the one-to-one ideal that it implies) does not rest comfortably with the cultural values which, as discussed at the start of this section, contribute to the use of subgroups in the first place. These values stress the recognition of variability through "democratic education," and the celebration of doubt, questioning, and divergent opinions following "Socratic philosophy." They are therefore difficult to square with structural features that are directed at ironing differences out. One way of reconciling the inconsistencies is to suggest that although cultural values provide the foundations for organizational practices, these foundations have been overridden by homogenizing tendencies. This may be so. Nevertheless it needs to be remembered that, as suggested at the start of the chapter, schooling began historically as a one-to-one process. Preservation of that ideal and the associated homogenization has origins that are at least as ancient as Socratic philosophy. Indeed Socrates himself was the arch proponent of doubt, questioning, and divergence—and intense one-to-one teaching. A more plausible line of argument in the present context is perhaps to suggest that the two strands coexist, as competing and contradictory pressures upon contemporary practice.

Preliminary evidence that is consistent with this interpretation comes from further research by the team whose work has been used extensively throughout the chapter, Ed Baines, Peter Blatchford, and Peter Kutnick. Based on interviews held in England with 36 secondary school teachers, Kutnick, Blatchford, Clark, MacIntyre, and Baines (2005a) find that on the one hand teachers express views like "When you are trying to develop an idea you need the whole class to develop it together" (p. 12), while on the other hand they can also believe that "Looking at it from different angles, getting other people's opinions and what other people think makes them a bit more aware" (p. 10). The United Kingdom has already been pinpointed as lying within the Socratic "sphere of influence," and these divergent strands could reflect tension between the respecting of difference that this perspective implies, and a concurrent drive for homogeneity. This said, it is important not to overinterpret the findings. Kutnick et al.'s sample was small, and there is no evidence that the quoted comments are representative of views held across the sample, let alone elsewhere. In any event, the current interpretation is mine, and there are no independent grounds for believing that Kutnick et al. would accept it.

Summary and Conclusions

The aim of the present chapter was to survey literature relating to the peer group structure of children's classrooms. It was anticipated that some features would be interpretable with reference to a one-to-one teaching ideal, which was once common practice. It was hypothesized that the organization of schooling around peer groups reflects a historic compromise between ideals and resource realities, and therefore remnants of one-to-one aspirations might be detectable. As formal out-of-school activities are strongly influenced by the structure of schooling, a parallel hypothesis was formulated about these activities. However, a dearth of relevant research meant that this latter hypothesis could not be examined. It would be interesting to know if scholars involved with such activities recognize relevant material in the preceding paragraphs, and/or identify promising avenues for future investigation. As regards schooling, the chapter's conclusions are relatively straightforward at the descriptive level. The classrooms that children are assigned to will be as small as resources permit, which in relatively affluent countries currently averages around 21 pupils per primary class and 24 pupils per secondary class. More often than not, the basic classroom unit will be mixed ability and coeducational, and as multiethnic, multifaith, and socio-economically diverse as local demographics allow. However, children are often regrouped into ability-based classes for specific subjects, and occasionally into gender-based classes too. The practice of regrouping by ability increases with age. Depending on cultural traditions, teacher preferences, and available resources (and probably other factors in addition), some children will also find themselves working in classroom subgroups, the size of which decreases with age. Some of these subgroups will more likely than not be homogeneous with respect to ability from the earliest years of schooling, although as with classrooms, use of ability-based subgroups increases with age.

Without acknowledging the one-to-one ideal, the above practices would be hard to understand, for their research warrant is far from conclusive. Even the "holy grail" of class size reduction is not firmly grounded in empirical support. As for ability (and gender) homogeneity, there is no evidential basis whatsoever for believing that they have facilitative effects upon children's development. Yet class size reduction and within-class selectivity are both perfectly comprehensible from the one-to-one perspective. Indeed, it also becomes possible to understand why ability is conceptualized in the way that it is, because in reality current conceptions are problematic. Mention has been made of the dilemmas that educators (and researchers) face over whether to refer to generalized ability or ability in specific subjects. Measurement of either is not above question. However, no matter which perspective is adopted, ability is typically treated as a categorical variable (e.g., low, medium, or high), when it is actually located on a continuum. The treatment of children, whose ability is thought to lie within some specific range but can vary within that range, as identically "low," "medium," or "high" is further evidence for tacit homogenization.

Evidence presented throughout the chapter about teachers' attitudes and beliefs suggests that the one-to-one ideal is not simply an undercurrent within historical processes; it can also be an explicit shaper of individual aspirations and practices. Thus, it can be expected to influence the classroom activity that teachers orchestrate, as well as the organizational structures that they provide. The former possibility is examined in chapter 3, where, as noted earlier, the emphasis is upon children's experiences of classroom peer groups in terms of teaching activities. For now, the only point that remains to be made is that the within-class homogenization that follows from the one-to-one ideal does not merely have no net advantages; for some children at least, it appears to have definite drawbacks. Children categorized (or in some cases miscategorized) as "low ability" are disadvantaged through having to work in homogeneously low-ability groups. This disadvantage is revisited as the book develops, where it will become apparent that the research discussed so far only scratches the surface of what is really going on. It only applies, for instance, to children who remain in the educational system, and who can therefore complete whatever tests are administered. Children who have dropped out altogether do not feature in the statistics. However, when some children are disadvantaged, it strikes me as unsatisfactory to talk exclusively about net effects, important though these are. It is also necessary to contemplate changes elsewhere in the system so that gains are not always offset through losses. From time to time, the chapter has highlighted the way in which the reviewed research presupposes much of the educational status quo. Perhaps matters might be different if this presupposition was challenged. By chapter 9 sufficient material will have been presented not only to warrant such a challenge but also to suggest a viable alternative.

Chapter 3

Performance and Cooperation in Classrooms

Introduction

Chapter 2 began the discussion of how children experience the formal dimension of peer groups, focusing on schooling because virtually all research has been conducted in educational contexts. The chapter emphasized that from one perspective peer groups are fundamental to the educational process, insofar as the universal aspiration is for classes where children are of similar age. However, from another perspective peer groups are peripheral, for from the viewpoint of many teachers it is the pupil–teacher axis that is paramount, and not the relations among pupils. However, this latter perspective results in a dilemma, for the fact that teachers are dealing with peer groups rather than single individuals means that they have no hope of providing what chapter 2 highlighted as optimal instructional guidance. Chapter 2 identified a series of organizational principles that could (speculatively, of course) be interpreted as attempts to deal with the dilemma. These principles serve to negate diversity and therefore to create de facto individuals within the peer group reality.

Chapter 2's focus was the structural properties of classrooms, especially their size and composition. Nothing was said about whether the supposedly individualizing values influence what happens when lessons are actually conducted. Equally, nothing was said about how such values interact with what chapter 2 identified as a competing set of values, which in principle at least could also be relevant to classroom activity. These values, which chapter 2 associated with Socratic philosophy, highlight doubt, questioning, and difference of perspective—in other words, the very qualities that the individualizing approach seeks to suppress. At the structural level, the inherent incompatibility between Socratic values and individualizing tendencies will not necessarily become apparent. This explains why, as chapter 2 documented, practices consistent with both perspectives are being used in schools. Nevertheless, once the focus switches from structure to teaching activity, it is hard to see how practices could simultaneously be informed by both sets of values. Tension must be predicted, for instance, between the "single-mindedness" implied by individualized treatment and the expression of contrasting viewpoints that lies at the heart of the Socratic approach. So how is the tension resolved and what does this mean for how children experience their peers? By the end of the present chapter, the situation should have become clearer.

The chapter starts, like its predecessor, with an analysis of whole-class teaching. Research stretching back 30 years indicates that most whole-class activity is orchestrated via talk, and to the extent that children participate in classroom talk, they are typically required to *perform* for their peers. As a result, children usually experience their peers as performers or as an audience for their own performance. Individual differences are well documented in who characteristically performs and who characteristically sits in the audience. The chapter argues that the performance mode of activity can be associated with individualizing values, and shows that it is predominant not just at the whole-class level but also within subgroups. Nevertheless, a second strand is discernible at the whole-class level, and even more strongly with subgroups. This strand involves children *cooperating* with each other in the service of learning. It may not be too fanciful to align the cooperative mode with Socratic values, although as the chapter demonstrates classroom implementation stresses the provision of assistance as much as the exchange of views. With the provision of assistance, there is scope for role division between children, for example one child providing assistance and another child receiving assistance. Thus, as with the performance mode, the cooperative mode allows children to experience their peers in several ways. Once more, there are characteristic individual differences over what this implies.

Whole-Class Interaction and the Performance Mode

During the 1960s, there was increasing acceptance that, from the perspective of maximizing teaching outcomes, research into classroom processes is at least as important as cataloguing attainment. This led to a number of studies, which typically involved observing whole-class behavior, classifying observations as they were made using predefined categories, and recording category usage on coding sheets. The categories were invariably rather broad, for example "praise" or "response," for only a small number of distinctions are possible when coding in situ. Moreover, analyses were based exclusively on category frequencies, and therefore were normally restricted to global quantitative statements. Nevertheless, the results of these studies have not only provided the foundations for a research tradition that continues to the present; they have also proved robust across refinements of both research methodology and classroom design. For instance, the introduction of technologies such as interactive whiteboards ("smart boards" in American terminology) or data projection seems to have changed very little. Therefore, the present section begins with the early research, and outlines a selection of studies that attest to its continuing relevance. As signaled already, the key point to emerge is that whole-class activity typically requires pupils to play circumscribed roles in classroom scripts. As a result, peer group experiences amount either to performing one of these roles or observing the roles performed by classmates. The second half of the section summarizes a sizeable body of research that documents differences between children in the roles that they play and the roles that they observe.

The ubiquitous IRF

One set of conclusions to be drawn from early research is encapsulated in Flanders' (1970) "two thirds" rule. This rule states that: (a) for about two thirds of the time someone is talking; (b) about two thirds of this talk is the teacher's; and (c) about two thirds of the teacher's talk consists of "lecturing" or "asking questions." The implications from the first two points are that talk is a pervasive component of whole-class activity, and such talk is dominated by teachers. The implication from the final point is that while a great deal of classroom talk is limited, via lecturing, to what Barnes (1973) referred to as the "transmissive" mode, some talk is interactive. Questions, after all, require answers. However, insofar as it is teachers who ask questions, whole-class interaction is teacher led. Using a further set of observations, Sinclair and Coulthard (1975) confirm that questions are typically asked by teachers rather than by pupils. However, they subsume questions within a broader category of "initiations," and report that when initiations occur, they usually trigger a three-turn "initiation–response–feedback" (or IRF) sequence. Pupils characteristically provide responses, and teachers offer feedback as well as initiating. Sequence 3.1 below, reported originally in Coulthard (1977, p. 103), can be interpreted as a paradigm example of the IRF sequence. It also illustrates, via the teacher's concluding question, how feedback is swiftly followed by further initiation.

Sequence 3.1

TEACHER: Those letters have special names. Do you know what it is? What name do we give to these letters?
PUPIL: Vowels.
TEACHER: They're vowels aren't they? Do you think you could say that sentence without having any vowels in it?

Subsequent research has sometimes referred to initiation–response–*evaluation* (or IRE) sequences rather than IRF. However, as Cazden (2001) points out, feedback is a broader concept than evaluation, since it includes confirming that knowledge is shared as well as appraising its quality. I shall therefore use the term "IRF" from now on. Whatever term is used, there can be little doubt about the pervasiveness of the underlying sequence. Commenting on Sinclair and Coulthard's work in relation to classroom talk recorded at least 10 years later, Edwards and Mercer (1987) assert that the IRF sequence is "once seen, impossible to ignore in any observed classroom talk" (p. 9). Nowadays, the IRF sequence (with teachers initiating and providing feedback, and pupils responding) is regarded as such a well-established feature of classroom interaction that few researchers examine it specifically. Nevertheless, high frequency of occurrence remains apparent. For instance, this is the subtext within other studies conducted in the United Kingdom, the location of Sinclair and Coulthard's original research. A recent example is Burns and Myhill's (2004) TALK project, based on 54 episodes involving teachers and classes of 6- or 10-year-old children.

Initiation–response–feedback sequences are so embedded in classroom practice in the United States that Cazden (2001) feels comfortable about referring to them as "traditional" structures. She cites the large-scale investigation of Nystrand and colleagues (see, e.g., Nystrand, Wu, Gamorgan, Zeiser, & Long, 2003) as one of several sources of evidence. In research that was mentioned in chapter 2, Alexander (2001) documents IRF sequences during whole-class interactions observed in all five of the target countries (England, France, India, Russia, and the United States). Of course, as noted in chapter 2, there were cross-cultural differences in the proportion of time devoted to whole-class activity, but when such activity occurred, IRF sequences were discernible. An article by Pontefract and Hardman (2005), which was also referred to in chapter 2, reviews studies of classroom interaction conducted throughout Africa, and reports in detail on observations made in Kenya of 27 teachers working with 5- to 13-year-olds. Initiation–response–feedback sequences proved the norm across mathematics, science, and English. Finally, noting the mass introduction of interactive whiteboards into British schools (by 2005, available in 94% of primary schools across England and Wales), Mercer (2007) describes the use that four teachers made of the technology while working with 7- to 11-year-olds. He includes associated patterns of social interaction. Despite the potential for revisiting and restructuring that interactive whiteboards afford, the essentially linear IRF style was predominant in the talk that actually occurred.

While confirming the ubiquity of initiation, response, and feedback/evaluation, several reports (e.g., Alexander, 2001; Burns & Myhill, 2004; Pontefract & Hardman, 2005) also indicate frequent usage of "truncated" IR sequences. In other words, sequences occur where there is no explicit feedback. In reality, use of such sequences may reflect little more than the conversational convention that, in the absence of overt rejection, claims should be regarded as accepted. Thus, the tacit assumption is made that responses will be heard as receiving *implicit* feedback (and therefore the sequences remain de facto IRF), even though the feedback is not expressed. This interpretation leads to the hypothesis that IRF sequences will be more frequent than IR sequences when children's responses are incorrect, while IR sequences will usually be associated with correct answers. The hypothesis remains to be tested, and until it is, the main source of support lies with teacher *repetition* of pupil responses. In the sequence that Burns and Myhill use to illustrate IR interaction (an extract from which is presented here as Sequence 3.2; see Burns & Myhill, 2004, p. 43), the teacher almost invariably responded by repeating what the children had just said.

Sequence 3.2

TEACHER: Can anyone think of anything that travels on the road?
CHILD: Motorbike.
TEACHER: Motorbike. How many wheels has a motorbike got?
CHILD: Two.
TEACHER: Two.

Edwards and Mercer (1987) report occasional instances where teachers repeat incorrect responses, no doubt with a particular tone of voice, to highlight inaccuracy. By contrast, teacher repetition in Pontefract and Hardman's Kenyan research was normally restricted to *accurate* contributions from pupils. Repetition is known to be the major assent term within young children's discourse (Baines & Howe, in press; Keenan, 1974; Keenan & Klein, 1975; Martinez, 1987; McTear, 1985; Pellegrini, 1982), and this surely is also how adults normally use it. As such, its occurrence in classroom interaction can be treated as evidence that, functionally, IR and IRF sequences are not significantly different.

Whatever the comparability (or otherwise) of IRF and IR sequences, both offer considerable scope for variation in how sequences unfold. Recognition of this scope has provided the backcloth for most recent analyses of classroom interaction, with particular emphasis placed upon the "I" component (see, e.g., Alexander, 2001, 2006; Burns & Myhill, 2004; Galton et al., 1999; Mercer & Littleton, 2007; Nystrand et al., 2003; Pontefract & Hardman, 2005). There has been extensive discussion of the extent to which teachers use closed initiations, such as "Which king led the English troops at the Battle of Agincourt?", as opposed to open initiations, like "Let's imagine the atmosphere in the English and French camps on the eve of the battle." Open initiations facilitate diversity, for instance the identification of a range of emotions among the troops (and perhaps the contextualization of speeches made by Shakespeare's Henry V within those emotions). In relation to Henry V, a classroom sequence can be envisaged, where several children identify the specific emotions that occur to them, and their suggestions are synthesized as a prelude to analyzing the play.

The hypothetical sequence sketched for Henry V appears to have many of the characteristics that Alexander (2006) associates with "dialogic teaching." It certainly exemplifies Cazden's (2001) concept of "non-traditional" teaching, and there can be little doubt that it occurs in classrooms. Cazden provides examples, and it plays a central role in the teacher-guided "communities of enquiry" that epitomize Lipman's *Philosophy for Children* program (e.g., Lipman & Sharp, 1978). Nussbaum and Novick (1981) describe science lessons where 12- to 13-year-olds were invited to "brainstorm" about what happens to the air that remains in a closed jar when some air is pumped out, for example sinks to the bottom, rises to the top, lies in patches throughout, acquires a looser molecular structure. Pupils' ideas were debated and evaluated, as much by themselves as by their teacher. Yet, such sequences cannot be frequent, for if they were frequent, the literature would routinely discuss I–R–R–R (etc.)–F sequences in addition to IRF/IR. This is not the case.

The occurrence of brainstorming, whether about soldiers' emotions, philosophical debates, or evacuated air, depends on a range of factors in addition to open initiations. Alexander (2006) lists many of them. Nevertheless, they would seem inconceivable in the absence of open initiations, and this is the point that the various commentators make (e.g., Galton et al., 1999; Mercer & Littleton, 2007), for there is extensive evidence that closed initiations predominate in whole-class interaction. Closed initiations demand single responses, for example "1415," which may or may not be correct. The only way in which more than one child could generate such responses is if they speak out in chorus. Choral responses are actually a well-documented feature of classrooms (e.g., Alexander, 2001; Pontefract & Hardman, 2005), and children have little difficulty deciphering when these are required. They presumably rely on cues like teacher intonation, teacher nomination, or even custom and practice ("Good morning, Upper 5Y," "Good Morning, Miss—"). Nevertheless, while choral responding within closed IRF sequences is commonplace, the modal format involves a single child providing a single, constrained response to the teacher's initiation. Given everything that has been said already, this convergence upon closed initiations and constrained responses will not be surprising. Unlike the brainstorming discussed above, it focuses on homogeneity rather than diversity. It can therefore be seen as part-and-parcel of the same processes that, as outlined in chapter 2, press for unrelenting class size reduction and single-ability teaching. It is moreover what led me earlier to suggest that peer group experiences in whole-class settings involve a performance mode. One child performs by virtue of responding to the teacher, and those classmates who are listening become the audience.

In sum then, whole-class activity is dominated by talk, and this talk characteristically follows an IRF sequence. Initiations are typically (although not invariably) closed, and closed initiations generate closed responses. These responses are frequently (although again not invariably) provided by individual children. The implication as regards peer group experiences is role differentiation, with one child operating as the performer and the other children operating as the audience. However, as soon as this conclusion is drawn, a further issue is raised. Over the course of a lesson, a school day, a term, and so forth, occupancy of the performer and audience roles may rotate, in which case children's experiences will average out equivalently. On the other hand, it is also possible that some children play the performer role disproportionately often, and others are most frequently in the audience. What happens in practice? The paragraphs to follow summarize some of the research that bears on the issue. Its conclusions are that role differentiation does not typically average out. On the contrary, the balance between responding or observing responses and receiving or witnessing feedback varies considerably across children. Moreover, once full account is taken of the form that feedback takes, especially whether it is positive or negative, it becomes clear that here too there are stable differences.

Individual differences in performance roles

In discussions of the factors that predict roles in whole-class performance, one characteristic has been paramount, attracting the lion's share of research over the longest period of time. This factor is pupil gender, and in the mid-1990s I was commissioned to review the research into its significance that was then available (Howe, 1997). The following begins with my conclusions and then considers if (and how) they have been qualified through more recent work on gender or through research addressing other factors. By way of background, it should be noted that the research I reviewed was mainly conducted in mixed-sex classrooms—not necessarily to be regarded as a serious limitation when, as noted in chapter 2, coeducation is currently the modal arrangement. The research covered the full school age range, and was virtually always based on direct observations of classroom activity. However, there was a shift around the mid-1980s in the observational techniques that were used. Before then, the usual method was in situ categorization of behavior, as described above in relation to early work on the IRF sequence. Subsequently, most research involved tape-recording, either video or audio. Moreover, when in situ categorization was continued, it was associated with rigorous observer training and checks on reliability.

My 1997 review resulted in three broad conclusions about whole-class interaction, the first of which was that on average boys contribute more than girls. Available research indicated that, averaged across class members, boys make a disproportionately high number of responses to teachers' initiations. Specifically, this was the major finding from three British studies (Bousted, 1989, with 15-year-olds; French & French, 1984, with 10- to 11-year-olds; and Swann & Graddol, 1988, with 9- to 11-year-olds), and one Australian study (Dart & Clarke, 1988, with 14-year-olds). Dart and Clarke found that boys' contributions dominated regardless of whether the discussion addressed curriculum content, classroom management, or pupil behavior. However, the predominance of boys did not result from behavior that was consistent across all class members. Rather, the studies showed that it stemmed from the extreme talkativeness of a subgroup. Thus, it was no surprise to find research that focused exclusively on "silent students" (Jones & Gerig, 1994) reporting boys among the silent group as well as girls. On the other hand, the superior contribution of non-silent boys did not appear to be limited to the sheer volume of talk. Extended explanations were relatively likely to come from boys, with girls' contributions often limited to simple statements of fact (Good, Sikes, & Brophy, 1973; Swann & Graddol, 1988). In a large-scale American study involving 60 teachers and more than 1,300 pupils, Jones and Wheatley (1989) reported that boys were more likely than girls to conduct demonstrations in science classes.

The second broad conclusion drawn in Howe (1997) was that the high frequency of contributions from boys resulted from a mixture of self- and teacher selection. Self-selection covers instances where children call out without being explicitly invited, perhaps because they jump the gun or perhaps because the invitation is for a general "choral" response (along the lines detailed earlier). Bousted (1989), Sadker and Sadker (1985), and Swann and Graddol (1988) all reported boys self-selecting to a greater degree than girls, with the difference in Sadker and Sadker's study being as extreme as eight self-selections from boys to every one from girls. As regards teacher selection, Swann and Graddol found that when teachers nominated specific pupils to answer questions, these pupils were disproportionately likely to be boys. This was partly because the sooner that pupils' hands went up, the more likely they were to be selected, and in Swann and Graddol's study, boys reacted relatively quickly. However, the study also indicated that boys were more likely to be the focus of teachers' attention, even before questions were asked. They were, for instance, gazed at approximately twice as often as girls. Research available in 1997 suggests several possible reasons for this. First, boys were shown by Good et al. (1973) and Morgan and Dunn (1988) to be more restless than girls in classrooms, and their movement may have attracted attention. Second, they were found by Morgan and Dunn and by Good, Cooper, and Blakely (1980) to misbehave more than girls, and teachers may be monitoring where misbehavior is anticipated.

The third conclusion relating to whole-class interaction in my 1997 review was that boys receive more feedback from teachers on their contributions, both positive and negative, although a greater percentage of their feedback is negative. The gender differences as regards volume were documented, for American children at least, in Good et al. (1973) and Jones and Wheatley (1989). In some respects, the differences are scarcely surprising: given that boys contribute more, they necessarily create more opportunities for feedback. Less obvious, particularly in view of the gender differences over misbehavior mentioned above, is the greater likelihood of boys' contributions receiving positive feedback when compared with girls'. Nevertheless, this was reported in Good et al. (1973),

Jones and Wheatley, and Simpson and Erickson (1983). The only exception is the work of Stake and Katz (1982), which detected no gender differences over positive feedback. By contrast, all four studies documented higher levels of negative feedback to boys than girls, so perhaps it was here that misbehavior was relevant. Moreover, because the gender differences over negative feedback were more extreme than the gender differences over positive feedback, the ratio of negative to positive remarks was greater for boys than for girls (Good et al., 1973).

This, then, was what the literature suggested in 1997. Has the position as regards gender changed in recent times, and is gender the only factor to be relevant to whole-class interaction? Research into gender differences has evolved in two directions since the mid-1990s, while continuing to explore the issues that earlier work flagged as significant. First, the quantitative indicators examined in earlier research (e.g., number of contributions, proportion of positive and negative feedback) have been reappraised with enhanced rigor. One example is the work of Duffy, Warren, and Walsh (2001), which was conducted in Canadian high schools. It involved a large sample ($N = 597$ pupils), included observations across 36 lessons, covered mathematics and literature/language classes, and took account of teacher gender in addition to pupil gender. In many respects, its results confirm the earlier picture. Teachers addressed more interactions toward boys than toward girls, boys being the recipients of between 52% and 71% of teachers' remarks depending on curriculum discipline and teacher gender. Boys' contributions were more likely than girls' to be accepted, but also more likely to be criticized. The gender differences over criticism applied with both schoolwork and classroom conduct. However, Duffy et al. added the feedback category of "remediation" to the traditional set, and found that remediation was more frequently directed toward girls. Moreover, the tendency for boys to initiate interactions (i.e., to "self-select" in the terms used above) was less marked than in work conducted before 1997. Nevertheless, the one statistically significant difference to emerge was for boys to initiate 64% of the interactions with female literature/language teachers in comparison with girls' 36%.

Two further examples of recent, quantitative research into gender differences are reported in Altermatt, Jovanovic, and Perry (1998) and Hardman (2008). Altermatt et al. observed 70 science lessons involving 11- to 14-year-old pupils ($N = 165$ pupils) and their teacher ($N = 6$ teachers, 3 male). Observations were restricted to whole-class teaching. Altermatt et al. found that boys were more likely than girls to volunteer to answer their teachers' questions, such that 14 of the 17 most responsive pupils were boys. In fact, three boys accounted for 53% of the male volunteering, suggesting once more that male dominance is limited to a subgroup. Teachers were more likely to select boys to answer than girls, but this could be fully accounted for with reference to the gender differences over volunteering. In no classroom did teachers call upon boys more often than would be expected from their heightened volunteering. As regards Hardman (2008), the research is interesting because it was conducted in Nigeria and Kenya rather than, as with most of the above, Europe and North America. Yet here too, boys were found to respond to over twice as many teacher initiations as girls.

Alongside developments within quantitative research, there has also been a growing tendency to attempt detailed qualitative analyses. For instance, Rampton (2006) reports qualitative analyses of recordings made during the late 1990s in London secondary schools. Although the numbers of children involved was inevitably smaller than in the work discussed above, the recordings still amount to more than 80 hours of classroom interaction. Moreover, their "recognizability" has been confirmed through interviews with teachers—both teachers who featured in the recordings and teachers from different schools who listened to the recordings subsequently (see Rampton & Harris, in press). Rampton indicates gender differences in classroom interaction that are broadly in line with my 1997 review, but, if anything, are more polarized. Subgroups of boys were found not only to dominate the "R" component of IRF sequences, but also to infiltrate the "I" and the "F" components. For instance, teachers' initiations were completed (unsolicited) on their behalf by a subgroup of boys, and (equally) noisy classmates were silenced. Contributions from other pupils (and occasionally teachers) were evaluated. At the same time, other boys were relatively silent, just as Dart and Clarke (1988) and Jones and Gerig (1994) reported in research summarized earlier. As for girls, none matched the vociferousness of the dominant boys, but while some were quiet but engaged, others were transparently disaffected. Interestingly, many of the teachers who listened to the recordings applauded the dominant boys, noting that despite their apparent riotousness, they were invariably "on-task" and attentive to the subject matter.

With any topic, there is always scope for additional research. Nevertheless, the broad message from work on gender differences seems, from the above, to have remained constant for some considerable period of time. Boys are more likely than girls to fill the "R" slot in IRF sequences, and this results in more "F" of both a positive and negative kind. Equally though, there is a consistent subtext that gender cannot be the only factor, for classroom dominance is associated with some boys, but not all. Thus, over the years, there have been attempts to explore further factors, usually in conjunction with gender, in the hope of more pene-trating analysis. Pupil ethnicity is a popular choice, although even now the number of available studies is minuscule when compared with gender. For example, Tenenbaum and Ruck (2007) identified a mere 11 studies, when attempting a meta-analytic review of teachers' positive (or neutral) and negative speech as a function of pupil ethnicity. For the record, they found robust evidence of teachers addressing more positive/neutral remarks to European Americans than to pupils from minority ethnic backgrounds, but no differences over negative remarks. However, inspection of available studies on a case-by-case basis reveals such complex relationships between pupil ethnicity and IRF behaviors that such general conclusions may be premature.

For instance, working in the United States, Simpson and Erickson (1983) explored the verbal and non-verbal feedback (specifically praise and crit-icism) given to Black and White children aged about 6 years. Trained observers recorded eight Black teachers and eight White teachers in 16 separate classrooms. Black children were found to receive more verbal praise than White children, but there were no differences over non-verbal praise. Boys received more verbal and non-verbal criticism than girls, but the differences were particularly marked when the boys were Black and the teachers were White. So both teacher ethnicity and the verbal versus non-verbal dimension were relevant in addition to pupil ethnicity. Tennant (2004) collected observational data in 10 English secondary schools (and therefore with pupils who were at least 11 years of age, although precise age is unspecified). He found that boys engaged in more interactions with teachers than girls regardless of pupil ethnicity. (Teacher ethnicity is not mentioned, but presumed to be White.) African Caribbean and White children engaged in more interactions with teachers than Asian children regardless of gender. However, the difference between the African Caribbean and Asian children arose because the former were subject to higher levels of disciplinary action, indicative of criticism. The difference between the White and Asian children was because the former were more likely to be the recipients of remarks concerned with educational content. So here it is not a question of overarching charac-teristics like majority versus minority ethnicity, but rather of subtle differences depending on the actual group being studied.

Reviewing the discussion of gender and (more briefly) ethnicity high-lights results that are both important and inconclusive. The results are important because they demonstrate systematic individual differences in the roles that children play during classroom interaction. Boys are most likely to occupy the respondent slot in IRF sequences, and girls are most likely to operate as onlookers. Boys are most likely to receive critical comments from teachers, especially if they are Black and their teachers are White. Girls and Asian children are most likely to be in a position of watching this happen. The results are inconclusive because, for all their significance, gender and ethnicity are manifestly insufficient to predict classroom roles. Taking volume of contributions (and therefore responsiveness) as an illustration, the loose association with gender has been documented in the distinction between talkative and silent boys. As regards ethnicity, it does not take more than the two studies summarized in the previous paragraph to show how its influence depends on a range of additional factors. Far from supporting straightforward conclusions (let alone plugging the explanatory gap that remains once gender has been considered), research relating to ethnicity will have to proceed descriptively on a case-by-case basis for some considerable period before its precise significance is known.

Nevertheless, even though factors like gender and ethnicity are only partial predictors of whole-class behavior, they are meaningful predictors. As Sequence 3.3 below illustrates for gender, they make sense to the participants in just the way that they make sense to researchers. In the sequence, which is extracted from Rampton (2006, p. 65), a teacher attempts to subvert the gender norms that have been discussed above, and this does not pass unnoticed.

Sequence 3.3

TEACHER: Can I have a couple of girls' hands up?
JOHN: The girls are embarrassed.
TEACHER: Let's try.
[*Inaudible contribution from a girl*]
TEACHER: We've had the feud' already. Ninette, you [*Inaudible*] about these characters. Ninette.
UNIDENTIFIED PUPIL: Feudal system.
GUY: Ninette don't know.

When regrouping by ability was discussed in chapter 2, material was presented which made it clear that designated ability relative to peers is a construct that children use to interpret their classroom experiences. We have now seen that the same applies with gender. The implication is clear. The features that have been highlighted, no matter whether they relate to principles of selection like ability or to modes of interaction like the IRF sequence, are not simply heuristics for representing class-room peer groups in research reports; they are also part of children's lived experiences within those groups.

Subgroup Interaction and the Cooperative Mode

With some understanding of how whole-class interaction translates into experiences of peers, we can move now to classroom subgroups. As stressed repeatedly, the use of such subgroups is not universal, in contrast to classrooms. Moreover, the values that support usage do not rest comfortably with the homogenizing tendencies, which, as we have seen, apply as much to the organization of subgroups as they do to classrooms. Thus, it is difficult to anticipate what subgroup activity involves, always assuming that such activity occurs in the first place. After all, nothing has been said yet to guarantee that there is such a thing as subgroup activity. Because classrooms are the basic unit for purposes of school-ing, activity can be presumed at that level. However, the "optional" character of subgroups means that this assumption can no longer be made. The use of subgroups documented in chapter 2 may, in some cases at least, signify little more than seating arrangements, and not contexts for educational activity. Accordingly, the present section begins with research that examines the issue, and shows that the "seating arrange-ment" perspective is not misplaced. Nevertheless, classroom subgroups are not invariably restricted to this function, and as the section develops, a sense of activity emerges. At the same time, a picture is drawn of peer group experiences that complements but extends the picture drawn from the previous discussion of the whole-class setting.

Sitting in groups versus working with groups

The best place to start an analysis of whether classroom subgroups are functioning units or merely places to sit is with two large-scale observa-tional studies conducted in English primary schools by Maurice Galton and his colleagues. The studies were alluded to in chapter 2. The first study, which was designated the ORACLE study (Galton et al., 1980), involved observations in 58 schools over a three-year period starting in 1976. Around 47,000 observations were made of teachers, and 84,000 observations of children, with 489 children observed in total. Data for the second study (Galton et al., 1999) were collected in the mid-1990s, mostly in the schools that featured in the ORACLE study. In total, 28 schools (and 29 classrooms) participated, with 6,663 observations made of teachers and 8,562 observations of children. The ORACLE study indicated that around 90% of the time, children were seated in pairs or other small groups. The follow-up study added an extra (non-group) coding category, but still found that about 80% of the time, children were seated in pairs or small groups. However, the children in the ORACLE sample only worked with the children they were seated with 7% of the time, and the corresponding figure for the follow-up sample was 15%. Whole-class activity occurred about twice as often as subgroup activity on both occasions, but the predominant activity in both the 1970s and the 1990s was individual study.

Also mentioned in chapter 2 was the research of Blatchford et al. (2001) on class size, subgroup size, and their interrelation. It will be recalled that Blatchford et al.'s methodology involved teachers drawing maps of their classroom structures, and responding subsequently to questions about these structures. In addition to documenting the classroom structures themselves, Blatchford et al. also obtained information about associated activity. Confirming Galton et al.'s (1980, 1999) low values, they found that children only "worked together to produce a group product" about 12% of the time. This said, the percentages increased to 24% when the children were seated in dyads specifically as opposed to any small group, and 31% of the time when they were seated in triads. Going beyond Galton and colleagues, Blatchford et al. found that for a considerable proportion of the time that children were seated in groups but not working together, they were under direct instruction from the teacher. In conjunction with a considerable proportion of individual study when seated in groups (63% of the time on average), this mirrors chapter 1's Scottish scenario. There, the protagonist's mathematics and language sets received teacher instruction, and then engaged in individual problem solving while the teacher worked with different sets. The implication is that even when subgroup activity does occur (and this is infrequent) it is more like a miniature whole-class session than anything distinctive. This in fact is precisely what MacQuarrie, Howe, and Boyle (2008) found when they observed teachers interacting with classroom subgroups during science and English lessons (incidentally, in schools located in Scotland). Patterns of dialogue were indistinguishable from whole-class teaching, amounting of course to further bouts of teacher-dominated IRF.

Observations made by Galton and colleagues suggest that even when subgroup activity is directed at peers, its quality is questionable. Both the ORACLE project and the follow-up study indicate that pupils rarely talk to each other, and when they do talk, their conversation is quite likely to be about non-school topics, for instance to involve gossip about out-of-school events. In fact, talk during subgroup activity was nearly three times as likely to be off-task as on-task in the ORACLE study. The results from the follow-up study were somewhat more positive, but even there off-task talk was at least as frequent as on-task. Similar findings have been reported in Alexander (2001), Bennett, Desforges, Cockburn, and Wilkinson (1984), Boydell (1975), and Galton and Patrick (1990), with Alexander's research of particular interest because, as noted earlier, it covers subgroup activity in the United States as well as in the United Kingdom. A specific example of the problem emerged in the so-called SLANT project (for Spoken Language and New Technology; see Wegerif & Scrimshaw, 1997). The project focused on children working with computers, an important context when, as noted in chapter 2, a relatively high proportion of classroom activity around computers involves small groups. Detailed analysis of group interaction suggested that the activity was not typically task focused, productive, or equitable. In some groups one child so completely dominated the discussion that the other group members either withdrew from the activity, becoming increasingly quiet and subdued, or else participated marginally, for example as passive scribes of the dominant child's ideas. In other groups, the children seemed to ignore each other altogether, taking turns at the computer, each pursuing their own ideas when "their turn" came round.

Nevertheless, while the picture that Galton and others have painted is almost certainly consistent with the generality of cases, it may be inappropriate to regard it as a universal truth. In the first place, the picture rests upon average tendencies, specifically upon mean scores. Little evidence is provided about variability, via for example standard deviations or frequency ranges. In addition, the literature contains occasional reports of more intensive group activity in classrooms. For instance, in addition to observing teachers as noted above, MacQuarrie et al. (2008) also recorded the dialogue and action of the 12- to 15-year-old pupils, obtaining over two hundred 40-second data samples in total. In both science and English, on-task behavior was more than three times as frequent as off-task behavior during small-group activity. Moreover, virtually every sample of small-group interaction contained instances of pupils asking their partners for assistance, receiving information, and resolving task difficulties. A further project, like MacQuarrie et al.'s work conducted in Scotland (Anderson, Tolmie, McAteer, & Demissie, 1993; McAteer, Anderson, Orr, Demissie, & Woherem, 1991), involved analyses of talk recorded around eight contrasting software packages in literacy and mathematics. Participants were children aged 12 to 13 years who had moderate learning disabilities. These children were recorded in pairs ($N = 10$ pairs) or in one-to-one interaction with teachers ($N = 10$ children, each with a different teacher). Virtually all talk was on-task, something that other researchers have also found in computer environments (e.g., Fish & Feldman, 1987; Webb, 1987). Moreover, although interaction in the child–child pairs was largely limited to acquiescing and repeating, there were occasional signs of more active engagement. For instance, with five software packages (some literacy and some mathematics), child–child pairs exchanged information more frequently than child–teacher pairs, and with two packages such information was as likely to be challenged as passively accepted.

It may be significant that style of interaction varied with software package in the second of the two studies summarized above, and that the variation was independent of subject matter. After all, it suggests that the *manner* in which material is presented plays a critical role in determining the extent and nature of child engagement in subgroup activity. The implication is that one reason why engagement is low in the majority of cases is that the contextualizing of material is seldom as effective as it might be, perhaps because sound principles of contextualization are not well known—in which case, the occasional impressive exceptions may reflect little more than good luck. Nevertheless, the structuring of materials for active engagement in classroom subgroups has been extensively discussed in one body of literature, and a degree of consensus over effective practice has emerged. This is the literature relating to the "cooperative learning" movement, and therefore the next part of this section will outline briefly what cooperative learning involves, and whether its design principles have genuinely been found to be effective. To the extent that the principles are both effective and implemented in classroom settings, it can be anticipated that, in some classes in some corners of the world, the situation as regards classroom subgroups will be rather different from the one sketched so far. Active engagement should occur, and its occurrence will be a matter of principle, not lucky chance.

Cooperative learning

The concept of cooperative learning can be traced to the "theory of social interdependence" developed by Morton Deutsch (e.g., 1949). The theory rests upon the assumption that members of social groups are rendered interdependent by virtue of common goals. Interdependence can be positive when group members perceive that their goals can only be attained through cooperating with other group members (as with a soccer team), but it can also be negative when group members perceive that they are in competition with each other for goal attainment (as with athletes grouped by virtue of running the same race). Deutsch believed that positive interdependence is a prerequisite for "promotive interaction," where individuals encourage each other's efforts to reach shared goals, and through encouragement achieve good results.

Although the earliest applications of Deutsch's theory did not include education, by the mid-1960s David and Roger Johnson were developing teaching programs that incorporated the basic ideas. It was in relation to these programs that the term "cooperative learning" was introduced. The programs involved children working in classroom subgroups, and were designed to display five characteristics that were regarded as critical to successful results (Johnson, 2003; Johnson & Johnson, 1992, 1999; Johnson, Johnson, & Holubec, 1994). Following Deutsch, the characteristics included positive interdependence and promotive interaction. Deutsch's emphasis upon encouragement toward joint goals was continued in the concept of promotive interaction, and was seen to include explanation, elaboration, listening to other perspectives, providing help, getting feedback, and engaging in intellectual conflict. In other words, a form of interaction was aspired to that was considerably richer than what was described at the start of this section. The three characteristics that were added to Deutsch's features were: (a) individual accountability, where the performance of individual group members is assessed, and assessments are fed back to both the individuals and the group as a whole; (b) training in interpersonal and small-group skills, for example trust-building and communication exercises; and (c) group processing, that is, periodic reflection on how well the group is performing, perhaps incorporating teacher feedback. Taken together, the characteristics imply that the extent and nature of engagement in classroom subgroups depends on preparation (e.g., skills training), task design (e.g., positive interdependence, individual accountability, consistency with promotive interaction), and post-task activity (e.g., group processing).

Although the Johnsons' framework is largely taken for granted within the cooperative learning tradition, further conditions have sometimes been proposed. Most importantly, Slavin (e.g., 1992, 1995) has argued that in addition to the five characteristics, successful outcomes also depend on team rewards. Slavin has used a variety of subgroup arrangements in his research on the issue, for instance: (a) Student Teams-Achievement Division (STAD), where four-member teams of mixed ability, sex, and (when possible) ethnicity work on a joint project; (b) Teams-Games-Tournament (TGT), where joint activity within the team is supplemented with weekly, competitive tournaments against other teams; and (c) Jigsaw II (see also Aronson, 1978), where team members are randomly assigned to become experts in some aspect of the project, with expertise subsequently pooled. In all cases, individual team members take quizzes prior to group activity and after its completion, and rewards (e.g., certificates) are allocated if the improvement averaged across team members reaches some criterion (and/or in the case of TGT exceeds that of other teams). While Johnson (2003) accepts the added value of what he calls "reward interdependence," others (e.g., Hertz-Lazarowitz, 1992) are skeptical. Remembering Deutsch's negative interdependence, there are particular concerns when, as with TGT, team rewards are associated with competition. Such considerations have led Elizabeth Cohen (e.g., 1994) to argue that the key refinement that is needed to the Johnsons' framework is not the introduction of rewards, but the adoption of tasks that, by virtue of being challenging, open ended, and inherently group based, are intrinsically motivating. Cohen cites Sharan and Sharan's (e.g., 1992) "group investigations," where classroom subgroups work on joint projects in formats that resemble STAD without the rewards.

Cooperative learning is, in other words, an interweaving set of procedures, with common themes. One such theme is conducting tasks in subgroups, for although cooperative learning in some guises includes individual activity (e.g., Jigsaw II) it invariably requires children to work together in small groups at least some of the time. A second theme is that successful implementation requires compliance with specified characteristics during preparation, task design, and follow-up. A third theme is that talk should not merely be on-task but also of the elaborate variety that promotive interaction implies. Thus, to the extent that the themes are followed, subgroup activity can be envisaged that is much richer than what was presented earlier as the picture of normal practice. Over the years, many schools have signed up to the cooperative learning approach, particularly in the United States but also elsewhere (most notably Israel; Hertz-Lazarowitz, 1992), and under guidance from the originators attempted to implement the central themes. The consequences for pupil learning have been extensively studied, and found to be positive. For instance, Johnson and Johnson (2000) identified 158 articles covering eight cooperative learning methods, which included STAD, TGT, and group investigation. Using meta-analysis (see chapter 2) to compare impact on learning, they conclude that teachers could be confident about employing any of the methods. Meta-analyses of the effects of cooperative learning in the specific domain of mathematics education have obtained positive results at both the elementary school level (Slavin & Lake, 2008) and the high school level (Slavin, Lake, & Groff, 2007).

Encouraging though evaluations of cooperative learning have proved to be, they are typically restricted to outcomes. They seldom examine how the programs were implemented, and therefore whether they remained faithful to the core themes, let alone whether this had any bearing on the successful results. Without clarity here, it is difficult to address what, in the present context, is the critical issue, namely whether by virtue of engaging in cooperative learning some children have richer experiences of classroom subgroups than is normally the case. Thus, it is fortunate that within the general dearth of relevant research a small number of studies have addressed program implementation, and most of these studies provide data relating to subgroup interaction. For example, Hertz-Lazarowitz (1992) reviews 10 studies conducted in Israel and the United States and covering the full school age range (plus, in two cases, adults), which include evidence about classroom interaction. In general, the studies show that the adoption of cooperative learning approaches boosted on-task interaction within classroom subgroups, and within that interaction, enhanced assistance and explanation. Intriguingly, success in several of the studies seemed to be *negatively* related to the degree of teacher intervention into small-group activity. Slightly later, Shachar and Sharan (1994) report a six-month group investigation program in history and geography, which was also conducted in Israel, and included 197 children aged about 14 years. Classroom observations showed that prior to the program only 4% of the total communication involved children interacting with other children about the topics they were studying. During the program, the figure increased to about three quarters of the total exchanges.

Cooperative learning has traditionally had little impact on education within the United Kingdom, which may of course be a further reason why many of the negative findings about subgroup activity were obtained in that country. Of the studies summarized at the start of this section, all but Alexander (2001) were restricted to data obtained within the United Kingdom. Nevertheless, there have been two recent attempts to embed cooperative learning principles in British teaching practices, and to assess the consequences for classroom activity. The first is the SPRinG project (for Social Pedagogic Research into Groupwork), which was conducted in England with 5- to 14-year-olds (see Blatchford, Kutnick, Baines, & Galton, 2003). SPRinG made heavy use of subgroups, and through a combination of teacher training and task design tried to promote all of the Johnsons' (e.g., Johnson, 2003) key characteristics, with the exception of individual accountability. Results are promising. Reporting on the aspects of SPRinG that were implemented with 5- to 7-year-olds, Kutnick, Ota, and Berdondini (2008) show that children who participated in the program displayed steadily increasing amounts of joint, on-task interaction when working in classroom subgroups. This was not true of control children who experienced standard teaching. Equivalent results are presented for 8- to 10-year-olds in Blatchford, Baines, Rubie-Davies, Bassett, and Chowne (2006) and for 11- to 14-year-olds in Galton, Hargreaves, and Pell (2009). Blatchford et al. indicate that 87% of subgroup activity was on-task with the program participants, as opposed to 69% with a control group. Program participants were nearly three times as likely as the control group to produce "high level talk." Such talk was defined as "making suggestions, giving opinions, and giving reasons-justifications" (Blatchford et al., 2006, p. 764). Galton et al. report that SPRinG procedures boosted on-task behavior in mathematics and science (although not English), and promoted discourse that amounted to Blatchford et al.'s "high level talk" in all three subjects.

The second project is a partial replication of SPRinG that was conducted in Scotland, and referred to as SCOTSPRinG (see Christie, Tolmie, Thurston, Howe, & Topping, 2009). Its participants were 9 to 12 years of age. SCOTSPRinG data also indicate increases attributable to the program in the extent to which the children provide information, offer explanations, and grant assistance when working in subgroups. Moreover, as with the Israeli and American studies that Hertz-Lazarowitz (1992) reviews, SCOTSPRinG results indicate that direct teacher intervention into subgroup activity is a deterrent to rich interaction (see Howe et al., 2007). Earlier, it was suggested that when teachers intervene in classroom subgroups, they often implement IRF sequences, therefore activating the performance mode. The implication may be incompatibility between the forms of interaction associated with performance mode and the forms that occur when children are cooperating. Although not limited to formal cooperative learning as we have seen, the latter forms can perhaps be referred to as the "cooperative mode."

Summing up then, research in the cooperative learning tradition confirms the message that has already emerged from other sources, that classroom subgroups are not necessarily quite as "flat" as work summarized at the start of the section suggests. It may be true that when subgroups are used, they often (perhaps normally) operate as seating arrangements or as arenas for teacher-dominated IRF interaction rather than as contexts for interaction among pupils. Nevertheless, this is not invariably the case. When schools embark upon cooperative learning programs, children will work actively with their peers at the tasks they have been given. Such programs are not widespread, but equally they are far from insignificant, especially in the United States and Israel. Therefore, they need to be factored into the overall picture. Moreover, when children are in cooperative mode, whether or not in the context of formal cooperative learning, their interaction seems to display the features that David and Roger Johnson associated with "promotive interaction" (Johnson & Johnson, 1992, 1999; Johnson et al., 1994). In other words, there is evidence of explanation, elaboration, listening to other perspectives, providing help, getting feedback, and engaging in intellectual conflict.

Role differentiation in classroom subgroups

The evidence for promotive interaction when children are in cooperative mode is significant from a number of perspectives. Insofar as promotive interaction as observed in children involves listening to other perspectives and engaging in intellectual conflict, it displays features that, as we saw in chapter 1, Piaget (e.g., 1932) associates with cognitive growth. This point is developed in chapter 4. However, insofar as promotive interaction as observed involves task-related assistance, for example information, help, explanation, and so on, it also places children in asymmetric roles. One child needs help, and another child supplies this. Thus, precisely the issues raised earlier for the performance mode in whole-class interaction apply with the cooperative mode in subgroup interaction. On the one hand, it is possible that the asymmetry is short lived, surviving no longer than the specific interaction. One moment after this interaction, the child who requested help may be providing help on a different topic. Equally though, it is also possible that the asymmetry lasts longer. Some children may habitually provide help, and others may habitually require this. In other words, stable role differentiation may be found within classroom subgroups, at least when the cooperative mode is involved, just as it was found across classes as a whole.

In fact a substantial body of research now exists relating to role differentiation at the subgroup level, and as with the whole-class context, gender has been a key dimension. One recurring finding is that girls are more likely to request assistance than boys. Webb (1984) found this with 13- to 14-year-olds organized into small groups (normally foursomes) for teaching in mathematics. Moreover, when girls asked for help, it was more likely than boys to be for general strategic explanation, for example "What kind of sum is it?" Boys' requests typically focused on specific procedural information, for example "Which column do you add first?" Similar observations have been made in computer environments, for instance by Lee (1993) working with children of similar age to Webb's sample, and Siann and McLeod (1986), working with 5- to 7-year-olds. Interestingly, Webb's results arose because of marked gender differences in groups where girls were in the majority. There were no differences in balanced groups or in groups where boys predominated. Another of Webb's findings is arguably relevant to explaining this, namely that both girls and boys tended to request assistance from boys. After all, when girls are in the majority within the foursomes that Webb typically used, only one boy will be present, and therefore this boy will have no other boy to address. If boys regard other boys as the only acceptable source of assistance, it is little wonder that they seek help less frequently than girls, when they are in a minority of one.

As regards the provision of assistance, there is evidence in the research of both Lee (1993) and Webb (1984) of girls doing this proportionately more than boys. Similar results are reported in Jones et al. (2000) and Conwell, Griffin, and Algozzine (1993) from research conducted in science classrooms. Scanlon (2000) and Underwood, Underwood, and Turner (1993) confirm the picture based on observations made during computer-based activities. The implication is mismatch between acting as the target of help-seeking, most likely from the previous paragraph to be associated with boys, and acting as a ready source of help, now found to be associated with girls—in which case, boys must be ignoring proportionately more requests than girls, and children in general must be receiving less help during subgroup activity than they feel they need. This said, there are signs that these effects are diminished when the sex ratio is balanced. Petersen, Johnson, and Johnson (1991) detected a tendency toward equalization of help giving among 12-year-olds working in foursomes, when the groups contained two boys and two girls. McCaslin et al. (1994) found that although groups (again predominantly foursomes) with a balanced sex ratio were relatively slow to engage in helping, they sustained their helping activities longer than groups with an unbalanced sex ratio, such that by the end of a two-week period they were providing assistance to a greater degree. Nevertheless, mixed *pairs* are necessarily balanced as regards sex ratio, and in the study with 5- to 7-year-olds mentioned above, Siann and McLeod (1986) found girls resenting the assistance that boys provided when working in mixed pairs around computers. This was particularly the case when the assistance was offered practically rather than verbally. In other words, the girls disliked it intensely when their male partners manipulated the mouse or the keyboard on their behalf. Chapter 1 discussed Harris's (e.g., 1998) insistence that pairs be differentiated from larger groups; the research discussed here is perhaps one area where Harris's views can be warranted.

While gender has played a major role in studies of role differentiation in classroom subgroups, it is not the only factor to be examined. As with whole-class interaction, ethnicity has been considered, once more without straightforwardly interpretable results. Shachar and Sharan (1994) summarize a number of studies indicating that children from minority ethnic backgrounds typically play relatively passive roles in small-group interaction. However, Conwell et al. (1993) found few significant differences in their study of science classrooms, merely a tendency for White boys (rather than Black boys or girls of any ethnicity) to adopt what were designated the roles of "ideas person" and "equipment handler." As with the whole-class research, it seems likely that account needs to be taken of the specific minority ethnic group that is being studied, and the cultural milieu that surrounds this group. At present, the factor that, together with gender, has provided the most compelling data is not ethnicity, but ability. Perhaps unsurprisingly, research with 13- to 14-year-olds reported in Webb (1982) indicates that in mixed-ability triads or foursomes, high-ability children give more explanations than low-ability children. Reviewing this study and 18 further pieces of work in the article discussed in chapter 2, Webb (1989) not only finds consistent evidence for a positive association between ability and the provision of assistance in mixed-ability groups; she also finds that children whose ability is in the middle range are liable to be excluded from explanatory dialogue. She notes a tendency for high- and low-ability children to forge teacher–learner relationships which bypass their medium-ability peers, who actually obtain a better deal as regards assistance in single-ability groups.

The research covered in Webb (1989) focuses on children in the normal ability range, but equivalent results have been obtained in research that compares children with registered learning disabilities with their mainstream classmates. Children with learning disabilities typically make relatively limited contributions to subgroup interaction, partly due to their own passivity (Gresham, 1982; Kemp & Carter, 2002; Nabuzoka & Smith, 1993) but also thanks to their partners' avoidance (Roberts & Smith, 1999; Zic & Igri, 2001). Furthermore, when children with learning disabilities are engaged in interaction, they are seldom in control. It is usually their non-disabled classmates who initiate conversation and provide whatever assistance is needed for task completion (Guralnick,

1990; Guralnick & Paul-Brown, 1984; Thomson, 1993). An illustration of this is provided in Pender (2003), based on observations of 7- to 10-year-old children playing in triads, and (of greater relevance to the present focus on classrooms) engaging in problem solving. There were 23 triads in total, and each contained one child with learning disabilities. Pender found that the group member with learning difficulties was twice as likely to ask for assistance as the other children, and half as likely to provide assistance. Consistent with Webb's alignment of high ability with the adoption of an instructional role, the provision of assistance was largely the prerogative of the non-disabled children. Furthermore, when these children needed assistance, they were three times as likely to direct their requests to their non-disabled partner as to the child with disabilities.

As with the discussion of gender and ethnicity in relation to whole-class interaction, the material presented in the previous few paragraphs is significant because it demonstrates systematic individual differences in the roles that children play. Moreover, the identification of these systematic differences is at least as important as the specification of the factors that predict them. Thus, while it is helpful to know that, on average, high-ability girls are most likely to be the source of assistance in interacting subgroups, it does not matter that ability and gender (and perhaps ethnicity) are imperfect correlates rather than defining features. The key point is that children differ in their habitual modes of subgroup behavior, because this implies systematic variation in peer group experience.

Summary and Conclusions

The chapter has identified two modes of classroom activity, both heavily reliant on talk but also encompassing physical behavior. Reference has, for instance, been made to use of computers and science apparatus. The first mode was designated the "performance mode" and its occurrence was associated with traditional IRF sequences. It was found to be predominant within whole-class activity including (it can be assumed) when children are seated in subgroups but working as a class. It also occurs when subgroups are separately instructed by teachers. The performance mode was linked earlier in the chapter with values that seek to minimize peer group diversity. In fact, it also confirms chapter 2's imagery of classrooms as wheels with teachers as hubs and pupils as spokes.

The second mode of activity was referred to as the "cooperative mode," and because it includes alternative perspectives and intellectual conflict, it can perhaps be related to Socratic values. It was discussed in the context of subgroup activity, where it was found to be a feature of so-called "cooperative learning." However, cooperative learning programs are utilized in only a small number of countries, and in only a small number of contexts within those countries. In the absence of formal programs, the cooperative mode looks to be the exception rather than the rule as regards classroom subgroups, and likely to be a matter of chance as much as design. Earlier in the chapter, reference was made to "dialogic," "non-traditional" teaching at the whole-class level, and the style of interaction associated with such teaching displays features that can be related to the cooperative mode. However, dialogic/non-traditional teaching appears to be even less frequent than its subgroup equivalent, perhaps because (as documented above) it appears to be undermined rather than strengthened through direct involvement from teachers.

Chapter 2 ended by stressing the way in which research into class size and mixed- versus single-ability teaching presupposes the educational status quo. The identification of the performance mode as the prevailing form of classroom activity has added a further dimension to our understanding of what the status quo involves. Indeed, the findings about class size (no clear advantages associated with small classes) and ability-based grouping (no clear advantages over mixed-ability arrangements) now have to be qualified as results relating to the performance mode. The question therefore has to be raised of whether equivalent results would be obtained if the cooperative mode was more widely used. It seems unlikely. On the face of it, large classes pose more challenges with the cooperative mode than with the performance mode. So stronger class size effects could be anticipated if the cooperative mode ever became prevalent. At the same time, the cooperative mode depends on diversity, and mixing ability levels more or less guarantees diversity. Therefore, with the cooperative mode, ability-based groupings might not merely lack net advantages over heterogeneous arrangements; they might actually prove inferior. Writing about the class size debate in particular, Pedder (2006) stresses how conclusions about structural issues should not be divorced from consideration of process. The point that I am making here is that the performance versus cooperative distinction is a key element of process.

At this point, I am not of course advocating a shift in balance between performance and cooperation, for I have said very little about their respective merits. This is because direct associations between mode of teaching and educational outcome are tangential for the purposes of this book. The critical issue is how children experience their peers by virtue of the modes, and whether these experiences have consequences for their development, including what they achieve in school. In other words, the interest is in indirect associations between mode and outcome, not direct ones. Chapter 4 begins the process of exploring developmental consequences, but it is not until chapter 9 that modes of teaching can be adequately appraised. For now the key point to take forward is that the characteristic form of classroom activity involves performance, and this has straightforward implications for how children experience their peers. In particular, for the children who are performing, peers constitute the audience. For the children who comprise the audience, the performing peer is collaborating with the teacher to produce a message that they are expected to learn. Occasionally, classroom activity places children in the cooperative mode, and here the implications for experiences of peers are different and more complex. Sometimes, cooperation results in relatively symmetric roles, when children debate ideas. Here children experience their peers as respondents to their own ideas, and sources of alternative ideas to which they can respond. On other occasions, cooperation results in asymmetry, when one child requests assistance and another child provides this (or fails to respond despite being asked). Children who request and receive assistance once more experience their peers as sources of alternative ideas, while children who provide assistance experience their peers as recipients. Children who request assistance and do not receive this experience their peers as non-compliant.

Chapter 4

Cooperative Interaction and Curriculum Mastery

Introduction

Classrooms are the core peer group environments, and chapter 3 considered the activities that occur within them from the perspective of defining children's peer group experiences. From that perspective, chapter 3 identified two modes of activity, the predominant "performance mode" and the peripheral "cooperative mode." The performance mode is activated on every occasion that children engage in the teacher initiation–child response–teacher feedback (or IRF) sequences that pervade classroom discourse. Initiation–response–feedback sequences place one child in the role of performer, and his peers (or, less often, her peers) in the role of audience. Thus, children experience their peers as performers, or as the audience for their own performance. The cooperative mode depends on children interacting with each other in a fashion that is not directly mediated by teachers, and this rarely happens in classrooms. When it does happen, it can take a relatively symmetric form, where children exchange views about the task in hand. Here children experience their peers as respondents to their own ideas and proponents of ideas to which they in turn can respond. Alternatively, the cooperative mode can operate asymmetrically, where one child provides the assistance that another child requires. This time children experience their peers as sources or recipients of guidance. There is no reason to think that the symmetric and asymmetric forms are sharply demarcated within the cooperative mode. On the contrary, it seems likely that children switch constantly between the two forms. This may be why, as detailed in chapter 3, researchers in the cooperative learning tradition subsume both forms within the broader concept of "promotive interaction."

With peer group experiences within the performance and cooperative modes now defined, it is appropriate to switch to the book's second aim:

examining the consequences of these experiences for children's development. The most obvious interpretation of the aim as applied to classrooms is to ask how experiences within the performance and cooperative modes impact on curriculum mastery, in other words how these experiences relate to those aspects of cognitive development that are prioritized in schools. As regards the performance mode, it is difficult to envisage direct effects, either positive or negative. From the audience's perspective, there seems little difference between conveying a historical date via "TEACHER: When was the Battle of Agincourt? PUPIL: 1415; TEACHER: Very good" and doing this via "TEACHER: The Battle of Agincourt was in 1415." From the performer's perspective, responses (and therefore teachers' feedback) are unlikely to be very different in the presence of peers than they would have been in one-to-one interaction with teachers.

I make the latter claim in full knowledge that, at one time, it would have been regarded as contentious. A venerable strand in social psychological research would once have been interpreted as suggesting that responses are affected by the presence of peers, even when these peers act merely as witnesses. As presented in Zajonc (1965), the message from the research is that peer presence boosts performance on well-learned tasks (social facilitation), and impairs performance on tasks that are not well learned (social inhibition). Social facilitation and inhibition have been demonstrated with cockroaches, ants, rats, and chickens, as well as with children. Because the focus of teaching is emergent rather than mastered tasks, the implication is that when children respond in classrooms before a peer audience, their performance will be worse than it would have been with their teacher alone. However, based on a meta-analytic review of 241 studies of social facilitation and inhibition (involving 24,000 participants), Bond and Titus (1983) demonstrate that the mere presence of others accounts for only between 0.3% and 3% of the variance in performance. The implication is therefore that responding in front of classroom peers has little impact on how children perform, and thus on what they take from their performance that is relevant to curriculum mastery.

Peer group experiences in the cooperative mode are not so easily dismissed. The role of teachers is somewhat removed, especially given the evidence presented in chapter 3 that the occurrence of the cooperative mode in classrooms as currently constituted depends (to some extent at least) on teachers refraining from direct intervention. Thus, the cooperative mode provides experiences that are more straightforwardly peer-based than those offered within the performance mode. In addition, peer group experiences in the cooperative mode involve joint activity rather than mere presence. Therefore the negligible effects of peer presence are no longer relevant. Finally, as we have seen, the social interaction that accompanies joint activity in the cooperative mode has been designated "promotive" within the formal cooperative learning movement, and so one school of thought at least regards it as helpful. Recognizing this, the bulk of the present chapter examines whether peer group experiences in the cooperative mode do in fact have beneficial consequences. Initially, the analysis is restricted to direct implications for curriculum mastery. However, as the chapter develops, the possibility of other direct consequences becomes apparent. This possibility stems from chapter 3's second major theme—the existence of systematic individual differences in experiences of classroom peer groups—and it relates to social inferences rather than academic achievement.

Concluding with an outline of what social inferences involve, the chapter raises the prospect of them having *indirect* consequences for children's development, including for curriculum mastery. Thus, the analysis of direct influences that occupies the chapter's earlier sections is only part of the story. Taking the issue forward requires detailed information about the informal dimension of children's peer groups, within and beyond the classroom. Thus, it will not be until chapters 7 and 8 that it can be discussed in depth. Nevertheless, it is raised in the present chapter and it needs to be kept in mind from the outset, if only because it turns out to apply to the performance mode as well as the cooperative. Readers may, after all, need reassurance at this point that I did not devote half of chapter 3 to specifying the performance mode, only to dismiss it in the single paragraph that appears above! Peer group experiences in the performance mode could still play a critical role in children's development (including those aspects that are focal within classrooms). It is simply that this role cannot be direct.

Piagetian Perspectives on Cooperative Interaction

As noted, peer group experiences in the cooperative mode can be symmetric or asymmetric. When experiences are symmetric, they revolve around the exchange of opinions about the task in hand, and as chapter 3 noted, the emphasis upon exchange is reminiscent of the perspective taken by Jean Piaget. Piaget's ideas about children's peer groups were discussed in chapter 1, where they were presented as a consequence of his belief (e.g., Piaget, 1932, 1985) that cognitive growth depends on existing beliefs being coordinated with contrasting perspectives. Through being coordinated, existing and contrasting ideas can be compared, and for Piaget comparison was no less than a necessary condition for cognitive growth. Peer interaction that involves the exchange of opinions about some joint activity ought to be an ideal context for triggering coordination and comparison, and this was the crux of Piaget's approach. Reservations were expressed in chapter 1 about the specific way in which Piaget theorized about peer groups, but in broad terms his ideas were accepted as plausible. Thus, the issue to be discussed below is whether contemporary research supports these ideas. This is the sense in which the section addresses Piagetian perspectives on cooperative interaction, although it needs to be remembered that Piaget's ideas were in the public domain by 1932. Therefore, they predate even Morton Deutsch's (e.g., Deutsch, 1949) foundational research, let alone its incorporation within the cooperative learning movement.

Sociocognitive conflict, transactive dialogue, and exploratory talk

It was not until the final quarter of the 20th century that Piaget's views about contrast, coordination, and comparison were examined empirically in the context of children's peer groups. Moreover, even when work began, it did not ask the directly relevant question of whether contrasting opinions, as expressed in classrooms, precipitate growth. As noted in chapter 3, evaluations of formal programs in cooperative learning have focused on outcomes rather than processes. In any event, the emphasis upon the umbrella concept of promotive interaction means that the symmetric version is seldom differentiated in research from its asymmetric counterpart. Beyond formal cooperative learning, the cooperative mode occurs too infrequently in normal circumstances to be examined in bona fide classrooms.

Thus instead of looking directly at classrooms, most studies have created the key forms of interaction through experimental manipulation in out-of-class settings, and explored the consequences in such settings. Over time, concerns about authenticity have grown, and as we shall see, there have been increasing attempts to connect with classroom realities. These attempts have been made in a fashion that tries to preserve the great strength of the experimental method, namely the potential for controlled investigation. On the other hand, no matter whether it is classroom-based or experimental, the research looks more or less exclusively at small-group rather than whole-class interaction. As noted in chapter 3, the cooperative mode has been observed (infrequently) at the whole-class level, but as far as I can see, formal evaluation has been limited to *Philosophy for Children* (e.g., Lipman & Sharp, 1978). As chapter 3 explained, *Philosophy for Children* involves children in teacher-guided, whole-class, philosophical enquiry. Research has identified positive consequences for reading, mathematics, logic, creative thinking, self-esteem, and emotional intelligence (Trickey & Topping, 2004). However, evaluation of the cooperative mode at the whole-class level is exceptional, and therefore the material that follows is limited to small groups.

Relevant research with small groups began with the work of a team led by Piaget's colleague Willem Doise. The team's starting point was the assumption that if peer interaction stimulates growth, it will be because current ideas are coordinated with contrasting alternatives. Thus, the emphasis was upon the discussion of differences during peer interaction, discussion that was termed "sociocognitive conflict" (see, e.g., Doise & Mackie, 1981; Doise & Mugny, 1984). The association of "conflict" with the Piagetian concept of contrast is not necessarily helpful, since ideas can contrast without being in direct opposition. Contrast can occur because one idea is a partial version of the other (as with "It'll float because it's light" versus "It's not because it's light, but because it's light for its size"), or because different aspects are highlighted (as with "The tea will soon cool down in a metal teapot" versus "And its sides are very thin"). Nevertheless, in the specific contexts explored by Doise and colleagues, the contrasts did usually imply incompatibility, and therefore the concept of "sociocognitive conflict" seems appropriate. Unfortunately, a broader sense of contrast has been used in subsequent research, despite in some cases continuing reference to sociocognitive conflict.

Empirical investigation of sociocognitive conflict conducted by Doise's team typically involved children aged around 6 or 7 years working in dyads or triads on age-appropriate tasks. One favored task (e.g., Doise, Mugny, & Perret-Clermont, 1975) was Piaget's classic conservation problem, where children: (a) view identical quantities with identical appearance, for example two equal-sized balls of Plasticine; (b) witness the appearance of one quantity being transformed, for example one ball rolled into a sausage; and (c) judge whether the quantities are identical before and after transformation. Another favorite (e.g., Doise & Mugny, 1979; Mugny & Doise, 1978) was Piaget's spatial transformation task, where children: (a) view a model comprising three contrasting objects, for example mountains or, as used by Doise and colleagues, buildings; and (b) construct the model as it would appear to an observer seated at a 90° or 180°

angle, or choose a photograph that depicts what the observer would see. Support for the relevance of contrasting ideas was obtained from the progress that children made from individual pre-tests administered before the group session to individual post-tests administered shortly afterwards, so long as at least one child in the group had failed the task at pre-test and at least one other child had partially succeeded. When group members had performed equivalently at pre-test, progress was reduced or non-existent. Other research (e.g., Ames & Murray, 1982; Bearison, Magzamen, & Filardo, 1986; Psaltis & Duveen, 2007) has not only replicated these results but also, through dialogue analysis, shown that progress is predicted directly by the exchange of views.

Further support for the role of contrasting opinions has emerged from research which began slightly later than the work of Doise and colleagues and used social tasks rather than conservation and spatial transformation. Again the emphasis was upon children operating in small groups rather than arrangements that approximate the classroom as a whole. For instance, working with children who, across the two studies, were aged between about 6 and 10 years, Damon and Killen (1982) and Kruger (1992) considered the relevance of dialogue to reasoning about "distributive justice." This was exemplified in a scenario where four children were described as receiving 10 candy bars for making bracelets and the task was to divide the bars fairly, bearing in mind factors like one child making more bracelets and another being poorer. Leman and Duveen (1999) recorded pairs of children working on the moral reasoning task that provided the foundations for Piaget's original theorizing about peer interaction (see Piaget, 1932). The task requires judgments of who is most naughty—a boy who breaks a large number of cups accidentally, or a boy who breaks a small number while engaging in forbidden behavior. Using a specially designed board game entitled "Conviction," Roy and Howe (1990) examined 9- to 11-year-olds' reasoning and dialogue about legal transgressions of both a minor nature (e.g., parking on a double yellow line) and a serious nature (e.g., stealing from an elderly person). In all of these studies, evidence was provided for the value of exchanging opinions, with such exchanges sometimes still referred to as sociocognitive conflict (despite the fact that the contrasts no longer typically involved opposition), but sometimes now termed "transactive dialogue." The concept of transactive dialogue was introduced in Berkowitz, Gibbs, and Broughton (1980), in the context of further research into dialogue around moral dilemmas. This research confirms the significance of contrasting opinions, although it involves undergraduate students rather than the age group of current interest.

As concerns have grown about relevance to classrooms, peer interaction has been increasingly studied around aspects of the school curriculum. Once more, results have confirmed the significance of contrasting views. Literacy and the arts have been examined (e.g., Miell & Littleton, 2004; Miell & MacDonald, 2000; Pontecorvo, Paoletti, & Orsolini, 1989), as has mathematics. With mathematics, support for an emphasis upon difference has been obtained in research on rational numbers (e.g., Damon & Phelps, 1988; Schwarz, Neuman, & Biezuner, 2000) and matrices (Blaye, 1990). These specific studies continue the emphasis upon sociocognitive conflict or transactive dialogue, while a further body of classroom-oriented research has developed the concept of "exploratory talk" as outlined initially in Barnes and Todd (1977). For Barnes and Todd, the key features of exploratory talk include the sharing of information, the explanation of opinions, and the critical examination of explanations, while as elaborated in Mercer and Littleton (2007), exploratory talk involves purposeful, critical, and constructive engagement with other participants' ideas. Although researchers interested in exploratory talk seldom align themselves with the Piagetian perspective (and, like me in chapter 1, occasionally distance themselves explicitly from some of its constructs), it seems clear that the approaches to peer interaction are compatible. Thus, it is encouraging that, in work to be revisited in chapter 9, Mercer and Littleton report positive associations between exploratory talk and performance on tests relating to science, mathematics, English language, and logical reasoning. The results were obtained from research in England with 6- to 14-year-olds, and from research in Mexico with 10- to 12-year-olds. The work is impressive, not simply because it focused on authentic curriculum topics, but also because it involved genuine subgroups in genuine classrooms.

Group work in science

The inclusion of science within Mercer and Littleton's battery of tests is significant, for science is among the most popular contexts for relating the Piagetian perspective to authentic school subjects. The reason for the emphasis is undoubtedly the evidence, summarized in chapter 2, that classroom subgroups are more frequently used in science than in other disciplines, probably because science requires apparatus, and resource shortages in schools mean that apparatus has to be shared. Thus, through showing (or exploring and failing to show) that exchanges of opinion benefit knowledge and understanding in science, researchers are providing evidence with immediate practical relevance. This is certainly one reason why I have chosen to focus on science in my own research, through a series of studies conducted over the past 20 years with children aged between 8 and 15 years. Some of these studies are summarized below, concluding with results that do not merely confirm the value of contrasting opinions but actually go beyond this.

Many of my studies involved groups (dyads, triads, or foursomes) working on tasks that address the conceptual dimension of science, for example the properties of objects relevant to floating and sinking (Howe, Rodgers, & Tolmie, 1990; Tolmie, Howe, Mackenzie, & Greer, 1993), the movement of objects as they roll or fall downwards (Howe, Tolmie, & Mackenzie, 1995b; Howe, Tolmie, & Rodgers, 1992), and the characteristics of containers that determine the rate at which hot water cools (Howe & Tolmie, 2003; Howe, Tolmie, Greer, & Mackenzie, 1995a). The tasks required groups to formulate joint predictions about outcomes, for example whether an empty aluminum box or a solid rubber ring would float or sink in a tank of water, and whether a heavy lorry rolling down a slope with a rough surface would travel a greater, similar, or lesser distance along the floor than a light car rolling down a smooth surface. Having agreed predictions, groups were invited to test these using apparatus that was provided, and to formulate joint interpretations of why things turned out as they did. Sometimes task instructions were presented via computers, but usually they were presented via workbooks, which group members took turns to read out loud. Researchers (occasionally teachers—see below) introduced the tasks and remained with the groups until task procedures were clear. Thereafter, they withdrew, and the groups worked on their own. The groups typically took about an hour to complete the task.

In all of the studies, children were individually pre-tested prior to the group tasks, sometimes by responding orally in one-to-one interviews, and sometimes by completing written tests in whole-class settings. Some studies took groups where children were known, from pre-test responses, to have contrasting views about the concept under investigation, and compared these groups with groups where children were known to have similar views. Mostly the studies considered peer interaction directly, through analysis of videotapes recorded while the group tasks were in progress. Without exception, the results provide strong evidence for the power of contrasting opinions. In particular, the children who worked in groups where initial ideas differed and/or were observed to express differences during group work performed significantly better when individually post-tested a few weeks later than during the initial pre-test. Their pre- to post-test progress also significantly outstripped the progress detected with children who worked in similar groups and/or failed to express contrasting ideas. The latter children sometimes made no pre- to post-test progress whatsoever. Contrasting opinions triggered change despite the fact that, as illustrated in Sequence 4.1 below, their scientific quality often left much to be desired. The sequence involves a group of 10- to 11-year-olds comparing how toy vehicles roll down slopes of varying surface friction, when the angle of incline is determined by the height of pegs upon which the slopes are resting.

Sequence 4.1

JONATHON: Well, the lorry's heavier, and it gives more. See like it pulls down like. If it's light, it just moves down in its own time, but if it's got a lot of things it'll make it go faster. Also, it's on the higher peg.

ANNA: But say it was like going down a water slide, and there was a great, big, heavy person getting down.

CHUNG: That's different. Skin's different to rubber, and you slide down in water.

ANNA: I know, but cars are metal.

CHUNG: It's rolling on paper, so the lorry'll hit it, and it'll stop. But it's got weight to push it in the start, so I think it'll go faster.

Of all my studies, the most telling perhaps is the SCOTSPRinG project that was introduced in chapter 3 (Howe et al., 2007). The aspect of the project that is relevant here involved recording the dialogue of 10- to 12-year-olds, while they worked through extended (3+ weeks) programs of teaching on first evaporation and condensation, and then force and motion. Classroom teachers delivered the programs. Moreover, although the programs incorporated group tasks that were modeled on the tasks used in my other research and completed in small subgroups, they involved whole-class teaching and practical demonstration in addition. The programs were, in fact, fully embedded in routine practice, and peer-based activities were only one component among many. Yet the expression of contrasting opinions during subgroup activity with peers turned out to be the single most important predictor of knowledge gain. Furthermore, this was gain that was detected not simply between pre-tests prior to the programs and post-tests a few weeks later, but also found to be sustained after an 18-month interval (Tolmie et al., 2007).

Resolving differences

Given the volume and variety of relevant research, it seems safe to conclude that, as Piaget would have anticipated, the exchange of opinions during peer interaction does support progress. Nevertheless, the expression of contrasting opinions cannot be sufficient in its own right to precipitate growth. Children must also resolve differences in a productive fashion. Recognizing this, many studies have included resolution during peer interaction among the categories that they employed when coding dialogue. Strangely, most report that resolution is a coding category that they seldom had to use, at least prior to the teenage years. With young children, differences of opinion are rarely resolved during peer interaction (Hartup, French, Laursen, Johnston, & Ogawa, 1993; Howe & McWilliam, 2001, 2006). Since resolution must occur at some point, the implication is that it takes place after the interaction is completed, that is, it involves what O'Donnell and Dansereau (1992) term "post-group reprocessing." Certainly, the ideas that children produce during post-tests a few weeks after group work with peers have sometimes been found to be superior to the ideas produced during group work itself (Howe et al., 1992; Mugny & Doise, 1978), even though post-test performance continues to be predicted by differences of opinion during group discussion. Likewise, the ideas produced at post-tests 11 weeks after group work with peers have been found to be superior to the ideas produced at post-tests only 4 weeks after (Tolmie et al., 1993), despite the fact that progress is again predicted by the expression of differences within group discussion.

Intrigued by post-group reprocessing, my colleagues and I have attempted to explain how it happens via research that considers both peer interaction *and* post-interactive experiences (Howe, McWilliam, & Cross, 2005). Our main conclusion is that it involves the productive use of post-group events, with such use being "primed" by unresolved contradiction during peer interaction. Specifically, our research involved: (a) pre-testing children aged 9 to 12 years to ascertain their initial understanding of floating and sinking; (b) grouping them into foursomes to work on tasks where, as with my earlier work, they formulated joint predictions about floating and sinking, tested these predictions, and interpreted outcomes, with their dialogue recorded throughout; (c) providing relevant demonstrations without instruction (or even discussion) two, four, and six weeks after the group task, for example evidence that all other things being equal, big things are more likely to float than small things; and (d) post-testing the children two weeks after the final demonstration. The children were more receptive to the demonstrations than control children who witnessed the demonstrations without experiencing the group tasks (and the associated dialogue), and they also performed better at post-test. Moreover, their post-test performance also surpassed children who completed the group task without experiencing the demonstrations, and children who experienced neither the group task nor the demonstrations. Strong relations were detected between post-test performance and the frequency of unresolved contradiction during peer interaction, for example asserting that "Big things float" and "Small things float" without reconciling the difference. These relations have now been confirmed with datasets addressing motion down an incline and rates of cooling, as well as with further results relating to object flotation (Howe, 2009). It is interesting that through unresolved contradiction, the sense of direct opposition discussed earlier in relation to sociocognitive conflict has resurfaced.

The evidence for post-group reprocessing is significant from several perspectives. For one thing, it suggests that teachers should be wary of effecting premature closure, through, for example, jumping in too quickly to consolidate ideas once group work is complete. This point was underlined in another study on floating and sinking with which I was involved (Tolmie et al., 1993). Mimicking characteristic teaching strategies, some participants in this study were given a quiz with feedback upon completion of group activity. Conceptual growth in participants who experienced the quiz was significantly *worse* than in otherwise equivalent participants who did not have this experience. In the present context, though, the key point to be drawn from post-group reprocessing is its message about the power of contrasting opinions. It does not merely confirm that sociocognitive conflict, transactive dialogue, exploratory talk, or whatever can precipitate growth; it also shows that these forms of social interaction are so powerful that they can sustain cognitive activity over many weeks when, as often seems to happen with children, differences are not immediately resolved. It seems then that the present section can end on a positive note. As Piaget would have anticipated, children benefit from exchanging opinions within small groups. Thus insofar as such exchanges amount to one component of what was earlier referred to as "promotive interaction," this component, at least, has proved to be aptly named.

Assistance and Cooperative Interaction

The previous section focused on the exchanges of opinion that can occur when children, working in small groups, are engaged in what has been termed the cooperative mode of classroom interaction. Noting that Piaget had claimed as long ago as the 1930s that such exchanges should be helpful for cognitive growth, the section looked for evidence in studies that, to a greater or lesser degree, have been inspired by the Piagetian perspective. A substantial body of evidence was identified, covering classic Piagetian tasks, social and moral dilemmas, and standard school subjects. The overall message is that exchanges of opinion are extremely beneficial. Exchanges of opinion were identified earlier with the relatively symmetric component of so-called "promotive interaction," but as we have seen, the concept of promotive interaction has an asymmetric component in addition to the symmetric one. This component revolves around the provision of assistance, and therefore the next question is whether it too has positive implications for curriculum mastery. The question has attracted a substantial body of research, which is summarized below. Based on the summary, an attempt is made to integrate the findings with what has already emerged relating to opinion exchange.

Helping and learning

A good place to start for research into the consequences of assistance is the review article of Webb (1989), which has been discussed several times already. As noted, Webb compared the results of 19 studies all relating to group work in mathematics and computer science, and covering more or less the full school age range. The main finding of relevance here is that knowledge gain was consistently associated with *giving elaborated explanations*, that is, explanations that are sufficiently detailed to deal comprehensively with misunderstandings. An example from a subsequent article (Webb & Mastergeorge, 2003) is: "Just, just go like this. OK, it's a first minute, put a line through it. Just put a line like this to divide them. No, the other way. And then put the additional minutes times 10, because the 11th one, the first minute costed 22 cents" (p. 81). The key point is not simply that elaborated explanations help, but the main beneficiary is the child who gives them, in other words the child who *provides* the assistance. Reviewing newer research, Webb (2009) notes that the benefits for the explainer have continued to be confirmed. However, based on research such as Webb and Mastergeorge (2003), she also shows that the recipients of explanations can sometimes be helped, so long as they make the assistance their own. This can be achieved through translation into the recipients' own words or application in problem solving.

Webb and Mastergeorge's (2003) evidence that in some circumstances recipients of assistance can be helped along with providers is encouraging for at least two reasons. First, it broadens the set of potential beneficiaries.

Second, it counters an unwelcome, alternative interpretation of the general results. This follows from evidence presented in chapter 3 that help giving is positively correlated with ability (in addition to gender). It is therefore possible that the reason why assistance is associated with learning gain in the children who provide this has nothing to do with assistance per se. Rather it is an artifact of the simple fact that high-ability children develop relatively quickly, while also happening to be the primary source of assistance. Once potential benefits for the recipients of assistance are acknowledged, the force of this alternative interpretation is diminished, given that on average the ability of recipients will be lower (see chapter 3). This said, it is unclear how often the potential for benefit is realized in practice. Webb and Mastergeorge provide little sense of the frequency with which children become effective seekers or users of assistance, nor indeed of the frequency with which other children formulate elaborated assistance. Other research gives a mixed message.

On the one hand, there is the apparent success of so-called "peer tutoring," where children are trained in the skills of tutoring and, if necessary, the subject matter to be taught, and then given opportunities to hold one-to-one tutorials with classmates. Sometimes, children are assigned to the tutor role because they are known in advance to have relatively good understanding of the subject matter, although with some approaches roles alternate, for instance with Palincsar and Brown's (1984) "reciprocal tutoring." Regardless of approach, peer tutoring is conceptualized in a fashion that closely resembles what has here been presented as help giving, and evaluations have produced consistently positive results (Goodlad & Hirst, 1989; Topping, 1992; Topping & Ehly, 1998). These evaluations cover the full school age range and a wide array of subjects (e.g., reading, mathematics, and science), and demonstrate benefits for both tutors and tutees. Significantly, given Webb's (1989) findings, the benefits seem more pronounced for tutors than for tutees.

On the other hand, there is research such as Ellis and Rogoff (1982), which compared the ability of adults and 8-year-olds to guide 6-year-olds through a classification task, and Radziszewska and Rogoff (1991), which studied the facility with which adults and trained 9-year-olds guide further 9-year-olds as they plan sequences of errands to minimize the route traveled. Child tutors were relatively ineffective at providing assistance, which resulted in low levels of task success from the recipients. Child tutors were also considerably less effective than adults, as indexed both through their tutorial behavior and through their tutees' success. When we saw in chapter 2 that adults (even mothers and teachers) struggle to emulate optimal tutoring behavior, the implications of these results with children are only too clear.

Assistance versus contrasting

One way of reconciling the various strands in research relating to help giving is to suggest that exchanges where one child provides assistance to another child can be beneficial, but the benefits are hard won. This is particularly the case for the child who is receiving assistance, given that the formulation of effective assistance is challenging. However, if this account deals with the (disappointing) results relating to recipients, it does not explain why the children who provide assistance do typically progress. Discussing the issue, Webb (1989) calls upon cognitive processes that can be triggered when explanations are formulated, for example rehearsing information, restructuring material, filling gaps in knowledge, and taking new perspectives (for similar analyses, see Bargh & Schul, 1980; Chi, De Leeuw, Chiu, & LaVancher, 1994). I find this interpretation entirely plausible, and I shall eventually accept it. Nevertheless, I need to point out first that there is another possible explanation. This is that children who provide assistance (and possibly other children too) learn via the processes of contrast, coordination, and comparison that were shown in the previous section to lie at the heart of the Piagetian perspective. In the following paragraphs, I should like to explain why the Piagetian perspective is in principle relevant to assistance, why it can be ruled out in practice, and what this means when the Piagetian perspective has proved significant in symmetric contexts.

To see why the Piagetian approach might have been relevant, consider Sequence 4.2 below from Wegerif (2000, pp. 130–131). It involves three children, who are working together on Raven's Progressive Matrices. The Matrices comprise series of problems, where two standard diagrams are presented that differ in some respect. A third diagram is also presented, and the task is to identify its partner from an array of possibilities through analogy with the difference between the standard diagrams. Sequence 4.2 relates to a problem where the standard diagrams each depicted a diamond placed inside a square. In one diagram, there was a circle inside the diamond; in the other, the diamond was blank. The third diagram showed a square containing a circle, and therefore the correct answer (number 5 in the array of choices) was a blank square.

Sequence 4.2

SUSAN: I think it's number 6. [*Number 6 is the same as one of the standard diagrams*]

TRISHA: No 'cause it's got to swing round every time, so there is a circle in it.

SUSAN: Yes, but it hasn't got a circle in there has it, and that one has.

[12 exchanges follow with little progress]

TRISHA: Look, that's got a triangle, that's got a square, look that's got a square with a diamond with a circle in, that's got a square with a diamond in and that's got a square with a circle in so that's got to be a square.

GEORGE: I don't understand this at all.

TRISHA: Because look on that they've taken the circle out yes? So on that you are going to take the circle out because they have taken the circle out of that one.

GEORGE: On this they have taken the circle out and on this they have taken the diamond out, and on this they have put them both in, so it should be a blank square because look it goes circle square.

SUSAN: It's got to be a blank square. Yeah it is.

GEORGE: Do you agree on number 5, do you agree on 5?

By virtue of explaining what in her view are the underlying principles, Trisha offers assistance during all three of her contributions. The assistance within the first contribution is off the mark, but thereafter matters improve. She certainly fulfills Webb's (1989) criteria for offering elaborated explanations, and in the process of formulating these explanations she may have engaged in rehearsing, restructuring, filling gaps, and so forth. At the same time, Trisha also experiences contrasting ideas. Her first contribution contrasts with what Susan says in the contribution that immediately follows, and also with what she herself claims in subsequent contributions. Assuming that Trisha benefited from the discussion, the benefits could in principle have been triggered through contrast rather than from the cognitive processes involved in explaining. Certainly, research discussed in the previous section (e.g., Howe et al., 1990, 1992; Mugny & Doise, 1978) shows that children with relatively good understanding can benefit from exchanges of opinion, as well as children with relatively poor understanding. Moreover, further results from the SCOTSPRinG project (Howe et al., 2007) suggest that contrast can sometimes take precedence over helping when both occur. As noted earlier, the main finding from the project was a strong, predictive relation between the expression of contrasting opinions and knowledge gain. As it happens, the expression of contrasting opinions was also correlated with indicators of assistance, but despite this, it was contrast rather than assistance that predicted the positive outcomes. This said, it is important that the results are not overinterpreted. Howe et al. do not differentiate between children with relatively good understanding and children with relatively poor understanding, and their indicators of assistance are much cruder than Webb's concept of elaborated explanation. Nevertheless, the results do signify that in circumstances where helping occurs, contrast can be what children attend to.

Actually, as regards Trisha in the sequence quoted above, it is probably impossible to decide whether Piagetian processes were or were not being used. However, George and Susan make matters clearer. In his second contribution, George translates the assistance into his own words. Thus, for George, all the ingredients are present for what Webb (2009) regards as effective help. However, there is nothing equivalent for Susan, and therefore from the data that Webb presents on the learning of help recipients (see above), it must be assumed that only George benefits from the interaction. On the other hand, both children experience contrast. In George's case, there is contrast between what he hears from Trisha and Susan, and also between what he hears and his own (unexpressed) starting position. After all, his admission that "I don't understand this at all" signals that his initial views were different from what either of the girls was saying. For Susan, the contrast is between her own initial position and Trisha's proposals, the second of which, from her concluding comment, she comes to accept. Thus, from the Piagetian perspective on contrast, coordination, and comparison, both George and Susan would be expected to gain, when it has to be assumed that the benefits are restricted to George. Of course, in the specific case of Trisha, George, and Susan, all three children may have progressed. I have absolutely no idea what happened in practice. Nevertheless, Susan illustrates what must apply in general given Webb's results: children who receive help, but do not make this help their own, do not typically progress after cooperating with peers, yet such children often experience the contrasting ideas that in other circumstances have been shown to be helpful.

The implication is, I think, that two mechanisms potentially apply when children engage with their peers in the cooperative mode, and both can provide benefits. The first involves contrast, coordination, and comparison, and in some respects it is the preferred mechanism since all children can benefit. In other words, this mechanism is fruitful for children with relatively good understanding, and for children whose understanding is relatively weak. This point is developed in chapter 9, by which time other reasons for preferring it will have been introduced. The second mechanism stems from the provision of assistance, where children who provide assistance consistently benefit. There is no reason to doubt Webb's (1989) suggestion that the benefits stem from rehearsing information, restructuring material, filling gaps in knowledge, taking new perspectives, and equivalent cognitive processes. Children who receive assistance can also benefit, so long as they make the assistance their own.

However, when assistance is passively received, the advantages appear rather limited.

The Social Impact of Classroom Interaction

The acknowledgment of two mechanisms in the preceding section is entirely consistent with the sociocultural perspective that was sketched in chapter 1. There it was emphasized that because peer groups are products of recent cultural developments, their influences cannot result from mechanisms that are specialized to the peer group context per se. Peer groups may depend more heavily than other contexts on mechanisms that are triggered by, say, contrast and coordination. However, this is merely because these mechanisms require rough equivalence of power, and this is relatively probable with peers. As chapter 1 put it, there can be no impermeable barriers that prevent mechanisms that are found with peer groups applying elsewhere. Furthermore, there can, by the same token, be no barriers that preclude non-specialized mechanisms, which happen to be strongly associated with other contexts, applying with peer groups. Chapter 1 identified instruction as a possible example of the latter type of mechanism, and certainly the descriptions of mother–child and teacher–child interaction in chapters 2 and 3 suggest that it applies in non-peer group settings.

What the material reviewed in the previous section has done is demonstrate the relevance of instructional processes like assistance and tutoring to peer groups, along with processes precipitated through contrast. Nevertheless, while the existence of two mechanisms is non-problematic, a greater challenge arises when trying to explain why one mechanism is activated rather than the other. The present section begins by discussing the challenge, highlighting the role played by children's social beliefs. It then argues that the nature of these social beliefs means that they must be drawn from how peers are experienced in classrooms. Thus, the chapter concludes by acknowledging that no matter what their implications for curriculum mastery, peer group experiences in school are profoundly significant in social terms.

Selecting mechanisms

It has been assumed throughout the chapter that when children engage with their peers in cooperative mode, symmetric and asymmetric forms of interaction typically both take place. As stated in the introductory paragraph, it is likely that children switch constantly between the two forms. Certainly, this is the assumption made by Damon and Phelps (1989) in an article that resonates with much of the present analysis. Damon and Phelps discuss cooperative learning specifically, rather than the present, broader conception of a "cooperative mode," which includes cooperative learning but is not restricted to this. Crucially, during the course of their discussion, they note that cooperative learning can have elements of both "peer tutoring" and "peer collaboration," these terms mapping closely onto the current distinction between the asymmetric and symmetric forms. Peer tutoring was in fact explicitly aligned in the previous section with the provision of assistance. The term "collaboration" has been avoided here, partly because debating opinions is not self-evidently more collaborative than providing assistance, and partly because the term has been used in other ways in the literature—for instance, compare Damon and Phelps' concept of peer collaboration with Sullivan's (1953) usage as outlined in chapter 1. Nevertheless, despite the terminological differences, Damon and Phelps confirm the basic point, that symmetric and asymmetric forms of interaction are not strongly differentiated within the cooperative mode.

The trouble is that although the two forms of interaction co-occur, data presented already show that only one is developmentally relevant at any moment in time. Moreover, which is relevant is subject to change. The SCOTSPRinG results discussed in the previous section (Howe et al., 2007) indicate that contrast, coordination, and comparison sometimes override the mechanisms associated with assistance, even when assistance is also being provided. However, the fact that children are sometimes stymied by assistance that they cannot use, despite being potentially able to benefit from contrasting opinions (as also discussed above), indicates that sometimes the mechanisms associated with assistance override contrast, coordination, and comparison. The implication is that which mechanism is selected depends on how the interaction is contextualized. Task instructions are probably important here. For instance, the tasks that I used to promote conceptual knowledge in science in the studies outlined earlier always started with children making private predictions before working together. Thus, when flotation was the topic (as, e.g., in Howe et al., 1990, 2005), children were asked to tick on cards to indicate their personal views about whether a series of objects would float or sink in a tank of water. They were then asked to share their predictions with each other, under instructions like "Talk very carefully about what everybody thinks, and decide together whether [named object] will float or sink." After the predictions were tested by immersing objects in water, further instructions followed along the lines of "Talk very carefully about why things turned out as they did. Make sure everybody says what they think." Such instructions more or less force an emphasis upon contrasting ideas. On the other hand, the manner in which formal peer tutoring programs are structured (see again Goodlad & Hirst, 1989; Topping, 1992; Topping & Ehly, 1998) seems to highlight assistance.

Nevertheless, while task instructions undoubtedly contribute on occasion, looser situations also occur where children are in a sense free to select either mechanism. Sequence 4.2 is an example, for like Wittgenstein's duck-rabbit, no particular interpretation is being imposed. Yet children must choose, and in the absence of task constraints, the only possible basis for selection is the expertise that children attribute to their peers. In other words, when children see everyone in the group as potentially having something to offer, they focus on contrasting opinions. When they believe that one individual is likely to know the answer, the emphasis shifts to assistance. In chapter 1, I suggested that reduced power differentials boost the probability of Piagetian mechanisms applying during peer interaction, when compared with adult–child interaction. I am now suggesting that even within peer interaction, power differentials apply and influence the selection of mechanisms.

Social judgments in classrooms

So children size up their classroom peers, such that when they cooperate with those peers during research experiments or occasionally "for real," their judgments influence how they learn. Moreover, since the relevant judgments in the contexts that we have been considering relate to academic expertise, they must derive from differentiated experiences of peers in classrooms. Enough has been said already to indicate that children have plenty of opportunities to have these experiences. As documented in chapter 3, there are systematic individual differences in the roles that children play when cooperating during lessons. Some children characteristically ask for help and others characteristically provide this. Over time, information about who typically plays each role and how they perform within the role will contribute to a picture of relative expertise. More importantly though, precisely the same inferences can be drawn from the systematic individual differences that chapter 3 documented with the performance mode. The responses that children give to teachers' initiations and the feedback that is characteristically provided will inform conclusions about expertise, as will habitual silence from members of the audience. The chapter started by asserting, hopefully persuasively, that children's experiences of their peers when in performance mode have little direct impact on curriculum mastery. What is being claimed now is that they have direct impact of a different kind, namely as a source of social information regarding expertise.

Moreover, while peer group experiences during schooling must be relevant to attributed expertise, they are most likely also relevant to other forms of social judgment. There is a comprehensive body of social psychological and linguistic research showing that the judgments people make and the cues they utilize are highly interrelated. It is unnecessary to go into detail about this research (for more information, see Argyle, 1988; Bradac, 1990; Brown & Levinson, 1978; Hogg & Vaughan, 2002; Howe, 1989; Telfer & Howe, 1994). Nevertheless, five points can be made. First, social judgments involve inferences about what individuals are like as people, and attitudes toward individuals based on those inferences. Second, inferences revolve around personality traits, for example honest, friendly, cold, stupid, dominant, or weak. Third, although numerous traits are called upon when making inferences, specific traits tend to be intercorrelated. For instance, people who are regarded as friendly are often regarded as honest and seldom regarded as cold. This means that statistical techniques, which examine patterns of association over repeated inferences, often unearth "implicit personality theories" where traits are clustered along a small set of dimensions. Fourth, the number of dimensions varies from study to study, but two invariably emerge. One relates to likeability, with honesty and friendliness located at the positive pole and coldness at the negative pole. The other relates to potency, with dominance located at the positive pole and weakness and stupidity at the negative pole. This is of course where academic expertise fits into the picture. Fifth, attitudes toward other people mirror the personality dimensions, for people are liked, disliked, admired, or held in contempt.

Conclusions

In sum then, peer group experiences in classrooms must inform one aspect of social judgment, namely attributed expertise. Otherwise, the switching between learning mechanisms, of which children are clearly capable, would become unintelligible. However, because the inferences and attitudes that comprise social judgment are intertwined, it is likely that peer group experiences have broader significance at the social level. As regards peer group experiences in performance mode, their direct impact on children is probably limited to social judgment. By the same token, though, the direct impact of peer group activity during schooling in general must predominantly be social. Despite the considerable academic potential that the present chapter has documented, the cooperative mode is currently a peripheral form of interaction across classrooms as a whole, with chapters 2 and 3 identifying ever-increasing restrictions on usage. Thus, any consequences of classroom peer groups must stem primarily from the performance mode. The direct consequences of the performance mode lie with social judgment.

While social judgment may be the direct consequence of the peer groups we are considering, we have already seen how the social dimension impacts indirectly on the academic. The pivotal point being made in the present section is that attributed expertise determines the developmental mechanisms that children deploy when cooperating with peers, and therefore, indirectly, what they know. With this recognized, the obvious next question is whether children's peer group experiences impact indirectly on school performance in other ways. Chapter 8 presents evidence that this is precisely what happens. It also sets the scene for revisiting the positive potential of the cooperative mode as part of chapter 9's concluding discussion. However, in order to reach the point where chapter 8's evidence is meaningful, other steps require to be taken. Specifically, we need to consider the implications of social inferences and attitudes for the informal relations that children forge with peers, within and beyond the classroom. Furthermore, we also need to examine the implications of those relations for the social and personal aspects of development. These issues are the main themes of chapters 5–7, where they turn out to be closely bound up with everything that has been addressed so far. For now, the conclusions are very simple. When children experience their peers in the performance mode of classroom activity, this has little direct impact on their curriculum mastery. The direct consequences are primarily social. Children seldom experience their peers in the cooperative mode, but when they do, this is likely to prove beneficial for curriculum mastery. The mechanisms through which benefits are obtained depend on how peer expertise is evaluated. Expertise is one of a cluster of social judgments that children can be assumed to make using classroom experiences.

Chapter 5

Friendship, Status, and Centrality

Introduction

The emphasis of the preceding chapters was the peer group context of schooling. Classrooms were conceptualized as institutionalized peer groups that are orchestrated by teachers, and that are sometimes divided into smaller subgroups. The point was made that, by virtue of teacher orchestration, the peer group context has little direct impact on curriculum mastery. This is despite its positive potential, as revealed in studies where children work cooperatively (and productively) with small numbers of peers. Nevertheless, even though peers are marginalized from the teaching and learning agenda, the fact that they are jointly engaged with this agenda means that they are not ignored. The previous chapter concluded by pointing out that, as a result of classroom activity, children make social judgments about their peers, drawing social inferences and developing social attitudes. At minimum, peers are categorized in terms of likeability and potency. Depending on categorization, attitudes evolve that include liking or disliking, and admiration or contempt.

Of course, teaching and learning activities are not the only source of social information about classmates. Chapter 3 documented extensive off-task activity when children work in classroom subgroups. This too will have social relevance. Moreover, when the Scottish scenario was sketched at the start of chapter 1, reference was made to a series of breaks during the protagonist's school day. In Scotland (and in many other countries), teaching is punctuated via "playtime" (or "recess") and "lunchtime." Activities during breaks have been observed in a number of studies, conducted primarily in the United Kingdom and the United States (e.g., Blatchford, Baines, & Pellegrini, 2003; Boyle, Marshall, & Robeson, 2003; Pellegrini, Blatchford, Kato, & Baines, 2004). In addition to documenting group composition (mainly single sex) and group activity (play, conversation, games, especially ball games with boys), the studies chart behaviors that (from research discussed at the end of chapter 4) inform social judgments. The implication is that no matter where in school children experience their peers, they are exposed to socially relevant data.

Furthermore, regardless of the contexts where data are obtained, children can be assumed to build up images of their peers, and develop attitudes toward them. This is certainly the assumption underpinning research that focuses not on the formal, educational dimension of classroom peer groups but on their informal characteristics. This research is traditionally concerned with the *friendships* that children form with classroom peers, and the *status* that they have in the eyes of those peers. Both friendship and status are conceptualized in the research as relations that depend on attitudes of liking and disliking. With this in mind, the present chapter starts by summarizing how the concepts have evolved, given their mutual dependence on a shared attitudinal dimension. One point that is emphasized is that although friendship research has been informed by research into status and vice versa (and although they are linked conceptually through their mutual reliance on patterns of liking and disliking), the two fields of research are not closely integrated. This has resulted in a tendency to emphasize mutuality and equality rather than asymmetry within friendship groups, and to restrict the contexts within which status is studied. Recently there have been attempts to address these issues, and the chapter's concluding section considers what has emerged. Interestingly, some of the recent work relies not only on liking and disliking, but also on the complementary attitudinal dimension of admiration and contempt.

Paralleling its predecessors, the chapter focuses on friendship and status as they exist in classrooms. The reason for the focus is the same as before. Just as there is relatively little relevant research into formal out-of-school activities like Brownies, junior soccer, and dance classes, so little of relevance is known about friendship and status in playgrounds, homes, and neighborhoods. At least, little is known with regard to the school-age population with which the book is concerned. On one level this restrictiveness is surprising, when developmental psychologists have typically been responsible for research into friendship and status, rather than the educationalists whose work dominated previous chapters. Therefore the scholars involved do not have any particular interest in schooling. However, schools provide convenient conduits to large samples of children, and it is for pragmatic reasons such as this that classrooms have been the focus. Thus, while a small amount of extra-classroom material has been identified and is summarized in what follows, the chapter's narrative is, once more, largely classroom based. Armed with research that addresses friendship and status from a slightly different perspective, chapter 6 discusses the implications of such "classroom specificity" in greater depth.

Children's Friendships

Research into children's friendships is a multifaceted phenomenon with numerous interweaving components. Nevertheless, two strands have been a strong and consistent feature throughout its history. The first strand comprises studies that are concerned with the *membership* of friendship groups, and the second strand incorporates work that focuses on the *qualities* that children look for in friends. The first strand can be traced to observational studies conducted in the early part of the 20th century, where the length of time that children spent playing with each of their classroom peers was used to index their friendship groups. Most of the research was conducted with preschool children, but some (e.g., Wellman, 1926) involved the school-age group that is central to this book. Results show that, rather than spending equal amounts of time with each classmate, children are disproportionately engaged with a small number, assumed to be their friends. The second strand dates back even further, with studies such as Monroe (1898) analyzing children's written descriptions of the "chum" they most like. Replies from across the elementary and high school age range reveal a preference for chums who are friendly, generous, and of the same age and sex. Both strands have generated research that is relevant to this book, and therefore the remainder of this section is devoted to a brief and highly selective overview of how they evolved and what has emerged.

Membership of friendship groups

A study with preschool children that was reported by F. Moreno (1942) led to a shift away from observational techniques in identifying friendships. In this study, the patterns of peer association displayed by 12 children were identified first through using observational methods, and second through analyzing which classmates the children nominated in interviews as the ones they would like to conduct an activity with (e.g., paint a picture). There was a high correlation between matrices drawn up to show observed play partners and ones drawn up to show nominated activity partners. Since the latter can be identified with considerably less time investment than the former, nomination has become the method of choice ever since Moreno's study. Thus, since then, friendships have characteristically been identified via the straightforward strategy of asking children to name their friends (or who they like to play with). Sometimes the maximum number of nominations is specified (typically at $N = 3$), but sometimes it is unrestricted. When the research is conducted in schools (which, as noted above, is typically the case), nomination is usually limited to members of the same school class. Occasionally, a given child's friendships are identified directly from their nominations, but more commonly identification is based on reciprocated selections, that is, the criterion of friendship is that Child 1 nominates Child 2 and Child 2 nominates Child 1.

The focus on reciprocation may be one reason why friendship has often been construed as a dyadic relation (e.g., Bagwell, 2004; Gifford-Smith & Brownell, 2003; Ladd, 2005; McGuire & Weisz, 1982; Rubin, Bukowski, & Parker, 1998). This does not mean that researchers deny the possibility of friends being clustered in larger groups, but it has led to such groups being conceptualized as combinations of fully reciprocating dyads, for example groups of three where Child 1 nominates Child 2 and Child 3, Child 2 nominates Child 1 and Child 3, and Child 3 nominates Child 1 and Child 2. Because such symmetry is unlikely in practice, researchers face dilemmas about where lines should be drawn. For instance, how should a situation be regarded where Child 1 nominates Child 2 and Child 3, but Child 2 and Child 3 each only nominate Child 1? And what should happen if Child 2 and Child 3 nominate Child 4 and are nominated by Child 4 in return, but there is only a one-way linkage between Child 1 and Child 4? Mindful of such issues, researchers have adopted a range of reasonable (albeit ultimately arbitrary) solutions. For instance, Sanson, Finch, Matjacic, and Kennedy (1998) asked Australian children aged between 10 and 11 years to indicate on 5-point scales how much they liked to play with each of their classmates. Ratings of 1 (*never*) or 2 were defined as negative ties, and ratings of 4 or 5 (*almost always*) were defined as positive ties. Using a technique called "block modeling," groupings were identified within each of three school classes, to fulfill criteria of minimizing negative ties and maximizing positive ties *within* groups, maximizing negative ties and minimizing positive ties *between* groups, and minimizing blocks containing single children. Although this resulted in fully reciprocating groupings in some cases, the degree of reciprocation was less than 50% in others.

Across the three classes, the groups that Sanson et al. (1998) identified comprised four dyads, five triads, four foursomes, and two groups of five. This is consistent with what Epstein (1985) and Hartup and Stevens (1997) conclude from reviews of relevant research, that is, friendship clusters averaging between four and six members (Epstein) and three and five members (Hartup and Stevens) throughout the school years. Both reviewers infer that this is somewhat larger than the average reported for the preschool age group, and Hartup and Stevens demonstrate that it is also smaller than the average in early adulthood. Both Epstein and Hartup and Stevens point to literature indicating that friendship groups involving boys tend to be larger than friendship groups involving girls. Girls' friendships are, indeed, more likely to be dyadic. Friendship groups involving boys plus girls are not mentioned, for the simple reason that such groups are exceedingly rare during the school years. What has sometimes been referred to as "gender homophily" has been reported on numerous occasions, but perhaps most tellingly (given the scale of the study) in a paper by Shrum, Cheek, and Hunter (1988). Shrum et al. asked 2,460 students in the age range 8 to 17 years to write the names of those students from their schools who were their "best friends" and who they "spend the most free time with." Answers to the two questions overlapped considerably, so analysis was based on best friends only. At every age level until 14 years, more than 85% of the nominations were same sex. Thereafter, same-sex nominations decreased, but even at 17 years they accounted for around two thirds of the data. Looking in greater detail at changes in gender composition between 15 and 17 years, Connolly, Furman, and Konarski (2000) indicate that mixed-sex friendship groups often arise through merger of smaller single-sex groups. Initial dating partners are often found from within mixed-sex friendships.

It is not just an old proverb but also social psychological theory (see, e.g., Buunk, 2001) which predicts that "birds of a feather flock together." As a result, research into membership of friendship groups has explored many sources of potential similarity in addition to gender. For instance, Shrum et al. (1988) analyzed their data for racial homophily as well as gender, and report a steady increase from around 67% same-race nominations at 8 years to an asymptote of more than 90% from 12 years onwards. Although racial (and ethnic) homophily have been noted in many other studies, their extent appears to vary. For example, Hamm (2000) found that, while more than 80% of the European American and African American students in her sample of 14- to 18-year-olds nominated members of their own ethnic group as closest friends, only 59% of the Asian American students did this. Heim et al. (2004) report that around 90% of the White young people in a sample of 15- to 25-year-olds and around 80% of the young people from Pakistani backgrounds claimed that all or most of their friends were from the same ethnic group. However, less than half of the young people from Indian and Chinese backgrounds did this. Working with children aged 12 to 14 years, Smith and Schneider (2000) found that, regardless of respondents' own ethnicity, only a minority of nominated friends were from the same ethnic group. On the other hand, stronger evidence for ethnic homophily was found with nominated best friends.

In addition to gender, race, and ethnicity, homophily over cognitive and behavioral characteristics has also been reported. For instance, Altermatt and Pomerantz (2003) obtained information about the academic performance of 929 American children aged 9 to 11 years. Data were collected on three occasions six months apart, and on each occasion the performances of pairs of friends were positively correlated. With a sample of 58 children, who were aged between 7 and 9 years, Erwin (1985) found more similarity in the responses to an attitude survey from pairs of friends than from pairs of children who had not nominated each other as friends. Bagwell and Coie (2004) identified 24 highly aggressive boys in a sample of 10-year-olds, by asking all pupils in a series of school classes to identify who in their class starts fights, says mean things, teases others, and so forth, and then summing scores across class members. The rated aggression of the boys whom the aggressive boys nominated as friends was significantly higher than that of classmates whom they did not nominate. Haselager, Hartup, van Lieshout, and Riksen-Walraven (1998) compared 192 Dutch children whose average age was around 11 years with, on the one hand, their friends, and, on the other, classmates whom they had not nominated (or been nominated by) as friends. Using ratings supplied by the whole class, target children, friends, and non-friends were assessed for prosocial tendencies (cooperative, helpful, has friends), antisocial tendencies (bullies, disrupts, starts fights), shyness/dependency, and depression. Target children were more similar to friends than to non-friends on all four dimensions, although the similarity was particularly marked for antisocial tendencies. This latter finding was confirmed by Hamm (2000) in the study mentioned above. In all three ethnic groups, there were significant positive correlations across friendship pairs for reported substance use and academic "orientations" (school performance, aspirations, and motivation). However, the correlations were stronger for substance use than for orientations. Finally, in one of the few studies to be conducted in a non-school setting, Savin-Williams (1979) reported that friends attending a summer camp were similar in dominance rankings.

With gender homophily, it can be assumed that birds of a feather are flocking together despite opportunities to act differently. As noted in chapter 2, the modal classroom is mixed sex, and therefore in theory children have as much chance to affiliate with the opposite sex as with their own sex. With the other characteristics, the situation is less clear cut. As also noted in chapter 2, classrooms are often regrouped for specific subjects with reference to ability. When subgroups are used for purposes of teaching, these too are often homogeneous with respect to ability. Therefore, as pointed out elsewhere (Hallinan & Sorensen, 1985; Neckerman, 1996), the correspondence among friends over school performance may result, in part at least, from equivalently achieving pupils being brought together. As regards racial/ethnic homophily it appears most prevalent when the population being sampled is reasonably large. It seems less frequent with small minorities. For instance, White youngsters and youngsters from Pakistani backgrounds are relatively numerous in the Glasgow schools and colleges where Heim et al.'s (2004) research was conducted, and these were the groups who displayed homophily. However, the number of young people of Indian and Chinese origin is much lower, and homophily was, as noted, also lower. Toronto, where Smith and Schneider (2000) found limited evidence for homophily, is an extremely cosmopolitan city, with large numbers of small minorities. Thus, with racial/ethnic homophily, the implication is preference for one's own group (as with gender) but willingness to make do with other groups when circumstances dictate.

The qualities of friends

No matter what their origins, the results summarized above paint a picture of considerable homogeneity within friendship groups, with friends resembling each other over a wide range of demographic, cognitive, and social characteristics. The homogeneity is not perfect; even gender homophily does not reach 100%. Nevertheless, it is substantial, and therefore it might also be expected to feature in the second major strand within friendship research. This is the strand concerned with the qualities that children look for in friends. As noted, the strand can be traced back to research conducted over a century ago, and for most of the intervening period, data have been collected in the same way. Children are asked to write down, or state in interviews, what they expect in friends. Responses are categorized, and conclusions are drawn from the frequency with which categories are used. Particular emphasis has been placed upon changes in category usage as a function of children's age.

Work conducted in the 1970s by Bigelow provides a good example of the approach, namely the study reported by Bigelow and LaGaipa (1975) with 480 Canadian children aged 6 to 14 years, and its follow-up reported by Bigelow (1977) with a similar-sized sample of Scottish children of equivalent age. In both studies, children were asked to write essays about what they expect in friends that is different from what they expect in acquaintances. Responses were coded using 21 categories, with the onset of each category identified as the age level at which its usage became significantly different from zero. With minor exceptions, age of onset was consistent across the two studies, and varied as a function of category type. The youngest children had what Bigelow (1977) terms a "reward–cost" perspective on friendship: friends are in close physical proximity, share in the child's activities, and provide help when needed. Between 9 and 11 years, a "normative" perspective was detected, with friends identified as accepting, loyal, genuine, non-judgmental, and highly admired. By early adolescence, expectations were more "empathic," with an emphasis upon opportunities for self-disclosure, and shared interests and values. Commenting on Bigelow's results, Hartup (1978) characterizes the progression as from egocentrism to sociocentrism, and from sociocentrism to empathy, and summarizes other research (e.g., Selman & Jaquette, 1977) that obtained equivalent results.

Since the early 1980s, attempts have been made to explore children's expectations about friendship using methods that are more structured and less open-ended than in earlier work. For example, Hindy (1980) devised cartoons depicting threats to what he called the unilateral physicalistic, reciprocal physicalistic, and reciprocal emotional bases of friendship. These categories are close to Bigelow's reward–cost, normative, and empathic constructs. Unilateral physicalism was threatened, for instance, via a cartoon showing Mary throwing a toy at Jane, Jane saying "I don't like the way you play," Mary responding "We don't have to play together," and Jane retorting "Maybe we won't—we're starting different schools tomorrow anyway." Children (N = 278) aged 6 to nearly 15 years were asked to predict outcomes using simple yes/no responses. Furman and Bierman (1983) used a set of 10 pictures, which portrayed sharing, sitting beside, common activities, similar physical characteristics, and so forth. They asked 64 children in the 4- to 7-year age range to select those pictures where the depicted actors would probably become friends. The pictures were also presented in pairs, with the children asked to select the picture in each pair that showed the behavior of greatest importance to friendship. Berndt and Perry (1986) identified the close friends of 122 children aged 8, 10, 12, and 14 years, and presented

30 yes/no questions about these friends to each child in turn. Questions tapped the main dimensions of friendship established in previous research, and included "Do you ever spend your free time with [name of friend]?" and "When you have a problem at home or at school, do you talk to [name of friend] about it?" Bukowski, Hoza, and Boivin (1994) have developed a "Friendship Qualities Scale," which taps the key dimensions using a psychometrically robust questionnaire.

In general, the introduction of structured methods has confirmed rather than challenged the picture obtained from earlier research. Children still appear to move from a reward–cost/egocentric perspective through a normative/sociocentric perspective to an empathic perspective. Newer methods have perhaps flattened the age differences, suggesting that the ages at which children progress are younger than previously thought, and that the range of responses at each age level is broader.

The methods are also quicker to administer than their predecessors, and permit more sophisticated statistical analyses. However, the basic message survives from the earlier work, and since this message can, as a consequence, be regarded as grounded in a multiplicity of methods, it seems compelling. Children expect their friends to be playmates, helpers, admirable, accepting, loyal, genuine, non-judgmental, trustworthy, and sharing interests and values, with the relative emphasis upon these characteristics changing with age. This said, the documentation of age differences does not preclude other influences, and one weakness of the research to date is that age has been the overwhelming focus to the exclusion of other variables. In fact, gender is the only other factor to have received systematic attention. Many of the studies summarized above compared the responses of boys and girls within age groups. Few gender differences have been reported with young children, although several studies (e.g., Berndt & Perry, 1986; Douvan & Adelson, 1966; Furman & Buhrmester, 1985) indicate divergence that starts in adolescence. The suggestion is that adolescent girls are more genuinely empathic than adolescent boys, emphasizing emotional support during crises, and the keeping of confidences. For adolescent boys, the key factors are being easy to get along with, doing favors, and backing up against adult authority.

Similarity and complementarity

Actually, no matter how many variables supplement and/or interact with the effects of age in determining expectations, the fact that expectations take the form that they do itself raises issues. Children may talk in terms of rewards and costs, normative behaviors, and empathic relations. However, with the exceptions of shared interests and values (which only become important in adolescence) and, arguably, potential as playmates, children seldom say that what they are looking for in a friend is "someone like me." Apart perhaps from the pioneering study of Monroe (1898) where, as noted earlier, children reported looking for chums of the same age and sex, the emphasis seems to be upon complementarity, and positive characteristics of an absolute kind, rather than similarity. Therefore, there are difficulties in squaring the homophily documented earlier in this section with the expectations that have emerged, and it is far from obvious how these difficulties should be resolved. One scenario is that immediately obvious characteristics like gender and race influence whom, within the "pool" of possible friends, children initially target. In other words, these characteristics are relevant during the first stage of what is widely recognized as a multistage process (Levinger & Levinger, 1986; Newcomb & Bagwell, 1995), the stage when friendships are being initiated. The extent to which targeted individuals measure up to expectations influences the course of subsequent stages, for example whether the relation will continue and deepen, and whether it will eventually deteriorate and end. Measuring up to expectations depends in part on similarities in the less obvious cognitive and social characteristics like academic prowess and susceptibility to aggression. The implication is therefore that similarity and expected qualities operate in an interdependent fashion, with their force varying as a function of the stage that the relation has reached.

Although other scenarios can probably be proposed, the suggested relation between similarity and expectations is consistent with two pieces of evidence. First, it implies stronger similarities within friendship groups over characteristics that are relevant during the initiation stage than over characteristics that are relevant later, since the effects of the latter are indirect. Based on a review of studies that were then available, Hartup (1983) concludes that "behavioral and attitudinal similarities are not as great as similarity between best friends in sex, age and race" (p. 141). Second, the suggested interplay between expectations and cognitive/social similarity is consistent with further data obtained by Hamm (2000) in the study outlined earlier. Across her sample of African American adolescents, Hamm found that the similarity between friends over academic orientations increased as levels of parental education increased. It can perhaps be assumed that the higher the level of parental education, the more their sons and daughters will value intellectual pursuits, and common values have indeed already emerged as a friendship expectation at the adolescent stage. As a result, Hamm's data are consistent with the relevance of academic similarity to friendship being dependent on underlying expectations about the friendship relation, namely shared values.

At first sight, research by Thomas and Berndt (2004) might be regarded as counterevidence to the proposed model. Based on data relating to 153 children whose average age was just over 13 years, Thomas and Berndt also obtained a positive correlation between the academic "adjustment" (performance and motivation) of pairs of friends. However, they found no association between academic adjustment and the extent to which friends had the qualities expected of them, as assessed following the approach taken by Berndt and Perry (1986) that was described earlier. On the other hand, Berndt and Perry's approach covers many qualities besides academic values, and therefore the key relationship may have been eclipsed. Furthermore, Thomas and Berndt related individual academic adjustment to the qualities expected of friends, when arguably the relevant relation is between degree of similarity across friends and expected qualities.

Peer Status in Formal Groups

With a provisional model of how the two strands within friendship research might be integrated, we can turn now to the second major tradition of relevance to the chapter, the tradition that addresses peer status. Like friendship, research into status has a long history, and indeed in the early days it was closely aligned with attempts to map friendship. When scholars like F. Moreno (1942) asked children to nominate preferred activity partners (as detailed earlier), they did not use the data simply to specify friendship patterns. They were also interested in relative status. However, they defined status in a fashion that almost guaranteed that the traditions would move apart, and the present section will start by explaining why this happened. The section will then trace the evolution of contemporary approaches to peer status, addressing issues relating to how status is currently conceptualized, and how it is assessed. As will become clear, there have been two significant changes over the years. First, contemporary researchers usually recognize five status categories, which is somewhat more than in the early research. Second, consideration is now given to which children are nominated as disliked (or disliked as activity partners), as well as to which children are identified as liked. Nevertheless, the schism between research into friendship and research into status has continued, and it is only recently that attempts have been made to bring the two traditions together.

Sociometric relations

To identify friendships among children, the focus is on the *content* of peer nominations, that is, which children a given child nominates, and whether these nominations are reciprocated. However, it is also possible to use nominations in a more quantitative fashion, to ask, for instance, about how many nominations a given child receives. Both forms of nomination were of interest to J. Moreno (e.g., 1934), via the analyses he conducted of "sociometric relations" (his term for nomination patterns) as typically represented in what he referred to as "sociograms." An illustrative sociogram is presented in Figure 5.1. This figure is intended to represent the sociometric relations within a class of 10 children, although it could in principle represent the relations within a factory with 10 employees, as well as many other scenarios. Assuming that each of the numbered circles represents one child and the arrows represent nominations (and therefore sociometric relations), Child 1, Child 2, Child 3, Child 4, and Child 5 are clearly members of a friendship group. Their nominations are not fully reciprocating, but the approximation to reciprocation is sufficiently high for the "compromise" methods discussed in the previous section (e.g., Sanson et al., 1998) to identify them as a group. However, Child 5 not only receives a relatively large number of nominations from within the group, but is also nominated from outside the group, leading overall to the largest number of nominations in the class. This indicates that Child 5 is a sociometric "star," with a status

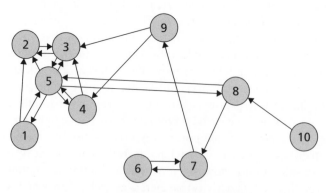

Figure 5.1 Sociogram illustrating classroom relations.

that contrasts in particular with that of Child 10. Child 10 nominates Child 8 but is not nominated by any member of the class, indicating "isolate" status.

The distinction between the way in which sociometric relations were used in J. Moreno's work to identify friendships and the way in which they were used to identify status was recognized almost immediately. Bonney (1943), for instance, drew a clear line between "reciprocated friendships" and "general social acceptance." In the present context, the key point about the distinction is that the peer groups in which children were linked through friendship were not the groups in which they were linked through status relations. For J. Moreno and his contemporaries, friendship groups were informal subgroups within formal structures. Status relations, on the other hand, were informal relations across formal structures. Thus, if the formal structures were classrooms, which even in the 1940s was normally the case when children were involved, friendship groups were classroom subgroups, cutting across whatever subgroups might be used for teaching purposes. Status groups were whole classes, and therefore equivalent to the formal structure used for teaching. In principle, there appear to be other possibilities, for instance perhaps children have differential status within friendship groups. Later in the chapter, these possibilities are discussed in greater detail. For now, it is important to be clear about the way in which J. Moreno and his contemporaries conceptualized status and how they differentiated status from friendship, for the approach is not merely of historical interest. It has in fact informed most of the research conducted since then, and it continues to be influential to this day. As signaled already, the main changes have been in the categories used to represent status, and the methodologies used to assign children to categories.

Assigning status

Throughout the 1940s and 1950s, the normal approach to assessing peer status among children was the one sketched already, namely asking children to nominate those classmates whom they liked (or liked to work or play with). Children receiving large numbers of nominations were, on the other hand, soon characterized as "popular" rather than as stars, and children receiving few nominations were increasingly regarded as "rejected" rather than as isolates. Other children were typically designated as "average." However, by the late 1950s (e.g., Gronlund, 1959), it was recognized that just because a child is not identified as liked, it does not necessarily mean that this child is actively disliked. The child may be overlooked, or "neglected." As a result, researchers increasingly looked at both liking and disliking when determining status. This not only resulted in the differentiation of rejected children (disliked by many, liked by few) from neglected children (liked by few, disliked by few); it also led to a distinction between popular children (liked by many, disliked by few) and controversial children (liked by many, disliked by many).

For instance, the popular, rejected, neglected, and controversial categories were all used by Coie, Dodge, and Coppotelli (1982), together with a fifth "none of the above" category, which they labeled "average." Coie et al. based their analysis on nominations provided by 848 children aged about 9, 11, or 14 years, with each child being asked to nominate three classmates whom they liked most (LM), and three whom they liked least (LL). The number of LM (and then LL) nominations that each child received was totaled, and standardized to take account of variations in class size across the sample. Each child's standardized LM and LL scores were also used to compute their social preference score (LM − LL) and social impact score (LM + LL). The popular group were children with social preference scores above 1, LM scores above 0, and LL scores below 0, namely high social preference and LM, and low LL. The rejected group had social preference scores below −1, LM scores below 0, and LL scores above 0, namely low social preference and LM, and high LL. The neglected group had social impact scores below −1, and LM scores of 0, namely low social impact and medium LM. The controversial group had social impact scores above 1, and LM and LL scores above 0, namely high social impact, LM and LL. Children who did not comply with any of these four profiles were classified as average.

The fivefold classification scheme (popular, rejected, neglected, controversial, average) adopted by Coie et al. (1982) has become standard within the literature, as has the use of liking and disliking for assignment to categories. However, the manner in which liking and disliking are employed varies: LM, LL, social preference, and social impact are not invariably used, and when they are used, it is not invariably in accordance with Coie et al.'s approach. Moreover, questions have been raised about the use of nominations to assess liking and disliking. It is generally recognized (see Hymel, Vaillancout, McDougall, & Renshaw, 2002; Maassen & Verschueren, 2005; Terry & Coie, 1991) that nominations have the advantages of being quick to collect, imposing limited cognitive demands upon children (since only a small number of classmates have to be focused on), and allowing straightforward identification of the five status categories. However, precisely because children focus on small numbers of classmates when nominating, they may overlook individuals who are actually important to them. Moreover, some researchers have argued that nominations are unethical, because they require children to indicate peers whom they dislike. (I have direct personal experience of local authority permission to conduct research being refused on precisely these grounds.) Yet there is no evidence of adverse effects from using nominations. For instance, negative behavior toward rejected children does not increase after obtaining nominations (see again Hymel et al., 2002; Maassen & Verschueren, 2005; Terry & Coie, 1991). Finally, nominations treat liking and disliking as categorical variables, when as we have seen they are actually poles of a single attitudinal dimension. The dimension also permits positions of neutrality, which are not recognized in nominations.

The main alternative to nomination in the assessment of status involves the use of rating scales, which are, of course, intrinsically dimensional. Typically (see, e.g., Asher, Singleton, Tinsley, & Hymel, 1979), children are presented with the listed names of classmates, with smiling, neutral, and glum faces against each name. They are asked to circle the face that indicates how much they like/like to play with each named individual. Variants of the approach include Maassen and Verschueren's (2005) use of scales running from +2 to −2. By not mentioning dislike explicitly, ratings may overcome the supposed ethical objections to nominations. It also seems less likely than with nominations that children will overlook key individuals, since they will be presented with the "aide-mémoire" of a list. Furthermore, ratings support more sophisticated statistical techniques than do nominations (Cillessen & Mayeux, 2004). Finally, as Maassen, van der Linden, Goossens, and Bokhorst (2000) note, they allow for fine-grained distinctions, for example between most popular, second most popular, and so forth, although there is no evidence that these are particularly useful distinctions to make.

On the other hand, the differentiation of controversial children from popular is harder to achieve with ratings than with nominations, as is the differentiation of neglected children from rejected. Furthermore, the reliability of ratings is reduced if significant numbers of children are omitted from the list to be rated (see Hymel et al., 2002). Since children ought to be omitted if parents refuse consent to participate, this is a non-trivial issue. Some researchers have also expressed concerns about the implications for use of ratings of gender homophily as discussed in the previous section. When children have limited cross-gender contact, it may distort the picture if they are obliged to rate the whole class. Restriction to same-sex names has sometimes been advocated. However, as we have seen, racial/ethnic homophily is also prevalent, and most researchers would find restrictions along these lines (although methodologically just as defensible as gender restrictions) as abhorrent from every other perspective. Fortunately, then, reasonably close agreement has been found between status categorizations derived from within-gender ratings and those derived from whole-class ratings (Terry & Coie, 1991).

It would be reassuring to be able to say that, despite their pros and cons, nominations and ratings lead to broadly similar conclusions about peer status. However, this is only partially the case. Rough interchangeability can probably be assumed with identifying popular or rejected children. Here Gifford-Smith and Brownell (2003) believe that the differing methods achieve comparable results, and Ladd (2005) concludes that there is no difference so long as researchers obtain at least four nominations. On the other hand, there appears to be much less convergence over assignment to the neglected, controversial, and average categories, probably because of the contrived way in which these categories have to be derived from ratings. Faced with divergence, Terry and Coie (1991) conclude that the decision between nominations and ratings ultimately has to boil down to research goals, an analysis that does not seem entirely satisfactory if the desire is for *valid* assessment. Perhaps the way forward is via some hybrid measure. For instance, Asher and Dodge (1986) used a combination of positive nominations (i.e., liking, but not disliking) plus rating scales. They claim 91% agreement between nominations alone and positive nominations with ratings over assignment to the rejected category, but then it is the neglected, controversial, and average categories that have proved problematic, not the rejected. Moreover, Terry and Coie (1991) found the agreement between nominations alone and positive nominations with ratings to be far lower than 91% over rejections, albeit still positive and statistically significant.

Beyond the classroom

Over the years, then, consensus has been achieved about how peer status should be conceptualized: as popular, rejected, neglected, controversial, and average. While debate continues about how status categories should be identified, a range of extensively used techniques is now available. Both nominations and ratings are regarded as psychometrically reliable (Hymel et al., 2002). Of course, most of the relevant research (including virtually everything that was cited above) has been conducted in classrooms, and there must be concerns about generalization to other contexts. Nevertheless, the few out-of-class studies that exist give grounds for optimism. For instance, Criss, Shaw, Moilanen, Hitchings, and Ingoldsby (2009) have explored the relations forged among groups comprising 10–12 children (with a total of $N = 146$ across groups), who were attending two-week summer camps in the United States. Children were asked to rate each group member as 0 (*don't like*), 1 (*like OK*), or 2 (*like a lot*), and to nominate whom they liked most and least, and who was their best friend. Despite the camps' relatively short duration, Criss et al. were able to discern both emergent friendship patterns and the standard status distinctions. However, summer camps, like classrooms, are formal structures, and therefore Criss et al. are only endorsing the relevance of status categories like popularity, rejection, and so on across formal peer groups. As noted already, it is possible that some children have differential status within informal peer groups like friendships, and moreover that something important is being overlooked through ignoring these differences.

Differential status within informal peer groups will only be an issue for those children who belong to such groups. In the classroom context depicted in Figure 5.1, the only peer group that Child 10 belongs to is the class as a whole, that is, the formal group. Thus, there is probably little to be said about individuals like Child 10, at least as regards their classroom groupings, beyond the fact that they are rejected or neglected, and do not have many friends. In other words, the framework sketched so far, and particularly the separation in research between status and friendship, may be adequate to capture the situation of children who were originally called "isolates." Less clear is the situation for "stars" like Child 5. Is it sufficient to identify such children as popular (or perhaps controversial) across the class or summer camp as a whole and to note that they are in possession of many friends, or does their status within the friendship group also have to be acknowledged? Moreover, whatever the relevance of status for informal groups which are located within formal structures, what about informal groups that do not lie within these structures, for example neighborhood friendships including perhaps gangs? Addressing this latter issue raises methodological as well as conceptual challenges, for both the nomination and the rating techniques require that all respondents consider the same set of peers. The framework provided through formal structures like classrooms is a powerful device for ensuring that this happens. Challenging or not, though, the issue of status within informal peer groups needs to be addressed, and although research is currently sparse, relevant material does exist.

Status in Friendship Groups

The pioneering studies concerned with status in informal peer groups are ethnographic in character, relying upon participant observation and interviews rather than nominations and ratings. The present section starts by outlining one example, and it will soon become clear that despite the continuing emphasis upon classroom friendships, the work has a rather different flavor from the material considered above. Thus, it amply illustrates a further point that is developed below, namely the difficulties that scholars have experienced with integrating ethnographic studies with other research and using these studies to resolve the key issues. These issues include ascertaining the added value of studying status within friendship groups with children who have already been established to have high status at the classroom level, and to possess many friends. It is only recently that methodologies have been adopted which allow ethnographic insights to be combined with those resulting from alternative approaches. The second half of this section summarizes a selection of studies that have used these methodologies, and synthesizes their conclusions.

Ethnographic approaches

The selected example of ethnographic research is reported in Adler and Adler (1995, 2003), but see, for example, Eder (1995) for complementary material. Adler and Adler's work was conducted in the United States and focuses on children aged between about 9 and 12 years, recruited from public and private schools, but generally from middle-class backgrounds. Through a mixture of extended observation and semistructured interview, Adler and Adler construct a picture of classroom relations, which assigns each child to one of four major roles. Some children are deemed to be members of "popular cliques," which, according to Adler and Adler, are usually the largest group in the classroom, and can account for as many as 33% of the children. Clique size is said to increase with age. Figure 5.1 contains what would be regarded as a popular clique, namely the group comprising Child 1, Child 2, Child 3, Child 4, and Child 5. Other children are viewed as belonging to "middle friendship" groups. These groups are reported to each have fewer members than popular cliques, but in total to encompass around 50% of the class. The dyadic relation between Child 6 and Child 7 in Figure 5.1 epitomizes a middle friendship group. Adler and Adler identify the remaining children as "isolates" (as characterized by J. Moreno (e.g., 1934), and discussed earlier), or as "wannabes" who hang around popular cliques without being members. While Child 10 in Figure 5.1 typifies an isolate, as noted already, Child 9 would be defined as a wannabe. Adler and Adler's key point is that popular cliques are highly stratified, comprising leaders who exert power over group activities and membership, second-tier members who are the leaders' best friends, and so on. The bases of leadership include athleticism, coolness, toughness, and precocious cross-gender behavior for boys, and high socioeconomic status, good looks, stylishness, and precocious cross-gender behavior for girls. Leaders are admired rather than liked. By contrast, middle friendship groups are quieter, more intimate, and more reciprocal than popular cliques, and their structures are less hierarchical.

Thus, through their conception of popular cliques, Adler and Adler (1995, 2003) highlight strong status differentials within friendship groups. However, in doing this, they also challenge assumptions underpinning the research that was discussed earlier in the chapter. For instance, in contrast to this other work, Adler and Adler acknowledge the point made at the start of the chapter, that social attitudes cover admiration and contempt as well as liking and disliking. Leaders, they suggest, are admired. If admiration is indeed relevant (or even if one merely suspects that it might be relevant), it becomes inappropriate to identify peer relations using measures (whether nominations or ratings) that depend purely on liking and disliking. Measures that recognize both attitudinal dimensions, or even better bypass attitudes altogether, might be preferable, and as it happens such measures have been available since the late 1980s. The original, and most frequently used, approach involves social cognitive maps, as outlined in Cairns, Cairns, Neckerman, Gest, and Gariépy (1988). Essentially, this approach sidesteps the attitudinal issue by asking respondents to identify individuals "who hang around together a lot," and "who are not members of any groups." Responses relating to each individual are aggregated across respondents. For instance, individuals are typically regarded as belonging to a group if at least 50% of respondents have placed them there.

Concerns about the accuracy with which young children can describe overall patterns (including clusters that they are not directly involved with) have led Bagwell, Coie, Terry, and Lochman (2000) to modify the approach, so that respondents only report on who they themselves hang around with. Again, groups are identified by aggregation. In most circumstances, the two approaches produce comparable results (Gifford-Smith & Brownell, 2003), although the reliability of both depends on the frame of reference. Reliability is higher, for instance, when the exercise relates to "children in your class who hang around together" as opposed to "children in your neighborhood." On the other hand, social cognitive maps are less affected than Bagwell et al.'s approach by failure to obtain data from all potential nominees, due, for example, to absence from school, or refused permission to participate. In any event, the implication from Adler and Adler's work is that one or other approach should be used in preference to nominations and rating when identifying children's relations.

In addition to intimating a need for alternative instruments, Adler and Adler's (1995, 2003) work raises conceptual issues. First and foremost, it suggests inadequacies in the picture of similarity and complementarity that is painted in the traditional friendship research, that is, the work that was summarized earlier in the chapter. The picture can be mapped with relative ease onto Adler and Adler's image of middle friendship groups, and it may be because of such groups that research into children's friendships has obtained its typical results. After all, Adler and Adler acknowledge that middle friendship groups account for around half of the children in a class, sufficient to explain the degree of similarity between friends over cognitive and social characteristics that was documented earlier. As regards similarity over demographic characteristics, Adler and Adler indicate that gender homogeneity, in particular, is also typical of popular cliques. However, in other respects the themes of earlier research break down when it comes to popular cliques. Leaders differ from followers at the cognitive and behavioral level rather than resemble them, and the relevant qualities appear to be ones that result in admiration of leaders by followers, and reflected glory from leaders to followers. Even if this can be construed as complementarity, it is complementarity of a very different type from what was considered earlier.

Furthermore, in addition to challenging widely held conceptions of friendship, Adler and Adler also introduce an alternative perspective upon status categories. Perhaps the most significant claim here is the distinction between isolates and wannabes, compared with the earlier distinction between rejected and neglected status. The former distinction revolves around the presence or absence of aspirations toward popular cliques, while the latter depends on the degree to which individuals are or are not disliked when few children actually like them. In addition, Adler and Adler have a unitary conception of clique leaders, rather than differentiating between popular and controversial individuals.

The concept of centrality

Of the issues raised by Adler and Adler (1995, 2003), the implications for identifying relations and for conceptions of friendship appear compelling. Social attitudes are multidimensional, and therefore instruments that are restricted to liking and disliking will most likely miss something. Some friendships rely on mutuality and complementarity, but this is unlikely to be true of all friendships. Less clear are the strategic implications of adopting a broader perspective on friendship. In particular, is it really important to acknowledge stratification within informal groups? Although stratification undoubtedly occurs, does it have to be recognized within research designs? As noted already, any strategic significance is probably limited to children who are actually members of informal groups. Nevertheless, even here, it is unclear whether status within such groups adds anything to, say, popularity and numbers of friends. It is possible, for instance, that the concepts are so closely correlated that measuring one in effect measures them all. This is an empirical issue that warrants research, and it has begun to be addressed.

For instance, Lease, Kennedy, and Axelrod (2002) asked 487 children aged 9 to 13 years to identify: (a) the three most popular children and the three least popular children from listed classmates; (b) the child in all possible same-sex pairings who has the most influence or power over the other child in the pair; and (c) the three children they like most, and the three they like least. The first two indices were used to identify children of high "perceived popularity," a construct that was explicitly related to Adler and Adler's leaders of popular cliques. The third index was used to identify "sociometric popularity," that is, popularity as used in the previous section. Lease et al. also obtained assessments of each child's personal characteristics (e.g., helpfulness, snobbery, influence, admirableness, leadership, control, spending power) from classmates and teachers. As Adler and Adler would have anticipated, children whose perceived popularity was high were rated as cool, athletic, bright, prosocial, attractive, and with high spending power. More importantly in the present context, perceived and sociometric popularity turned out to be correlated at about +.60, which suggests that these are similar but not identical constructs. Consistent with Adler and Adler, social dominance was also associated with perceived popularity, but statistical estimates of its contribution show that it only partially accounts for the imperfect relation between perceived and sociometric popularity. Another factor that Lease et al. acknowledge as potentially relevant is controversial status. Controversial children would have been excluded from the sociometrically popular group, since Lease et al. used standard categorization principles to identify popularity and, as explained in the previous section, these principles differentiate between controversial and popular children. However, controversial children might have been included in the perceived popular group.

One limitation of Lease et al.'s (2002) research is that it does not examine children's positions within friendship groups. Despite the explicit association with Adler and Adler's (1995, 2003) work, "perceived popularity" is as much a classroom-level construct as sociometric popularity. Building upon an approach taken by Bagwell et al. (2000) and Cairns et al. (1988), Gest, Graham-Bermann, and Hartup (2001) have attempted to address this by assessing children's *centrality* within classroom friendships and comparing this with popularity (and controversial status) across the formal superstructure. Number of friends was also taken into account. Essentially, Gest et al. asked 239 children aged 7 or 8 years who in their school "hang around together a lot," used this information to identify groups, and computed centrality with reference to the number of times that a given child was identified as belonging to some group. Popular/controversial status was determined via the standard approach described in the previous section, using nomination data. Basically, each child indicated the three individuals whom they liked best and the three whom they liked least. Friendship patterns were ascertained from reciprocated nominations as best friends. Centrality, popular/controversial status, and number of friends were all interrelated, although the relations were far from perfect. Centrality was predicted by high levels of likeability, leadership qualities, and aggression/disruption, as assessed by classmates. However, only likeability looks to have been positively related to popular and controversial status, and only leadership was associated with number of friends.

Insofar as centrality can be regarded as a proxy for within-friendship status, the results obtained by Gest et al. (2001) suggest that examining status at this level may add something to what can be inferred from status across broader formal structures. Centrality is positively related to popular and controversial status, but the relation is imperfect. At the same time, the concept of centrality and the methods used by Gest et al. in its assessment could probably also be used in contexts where informal groups are not embedded in formal structures, for instance when examining neighborhood groups. This has yet to happen, for even though novels like *Lord of the Flies* paint vivid pictures of power and status in children's groups when there is no formal backcloth, there is little systematic research. What research exists focuses on adolescent gangs, and actually finds looser leadership structures than with classroom cliques. For example, Decker and Curry (2000) interviewed 96 students aged 12 to 15 years, who were selected from a larger sample because they were currently members of gangs, currently associated with members of gangs, or once (but no longer) members of gangs. One topic covered during the interviews was gang leadership, where it transpired that few respondents could identify leaders. When leaders were recognized, it was in relation to specific activities, and not enduring roles. Moreover, ex-members were more likely to identify leaders than current members.

Conclusions

Nothing in the above establishes centrality as a developmentally significant construct that researchers should always take account of. Establishing developmental significance requires analysis of the consequences for children of occupying central and non-central positions within peer groups, and such consequences are considered in subsequent chapters. Nevertheless, the fact that centrality in informal groups is only partially predictable from status across formal frameworks suggests that both constructs should be taken into account, along with friendship, when exploring consequences. Moreover, the introduction of centrality does seem to add something to the traditional constructs at the conceptual level. As we saw in earlier chapters, the teacher focus of classrooms makes it easy to forget that classrooms are in fact peer groups. Therefore, to the extent that peer status is considered only across institutionalized groups like classrooms, the fact that status is something that children possess within peer groups can be overlooked. Status can, as a result, be treated almost like a personality trait that characterizes children as individuals rather than as something that typifies them as members of groups. The concept of centrality redresses this by highlighting the group context. Similarly, without acknowledging that group members can have differential status within informal groups, there is a danger of overemphasizing mutuality and equality in the context of friendship, and attributing flat structures when a degree of hierarchy ought to be acknowledged.

In general then, three constructs are arguably worth recognizing when thinking about the informal dimension of children's peer groups: status across formal groups, friendship, and centrality within informal (predominantly friendship) subgroups. The first two constructs have featured in research from the earliest days, but they have been progressively refined and embellished as results have become available. The concept of centrality is relatively new, but in some respects it is the linchpin that brings the other two together. It also permits terminological simplification, assuming that the meaning of the three constructs is now reasonably clear. If centrality is restricted to status within informal subgroups (in accordance with the literature), it might be permissible to use "status" as shorthand for status across formal groups, that is, to limit the term to its traditional sense. This is not, it must be emphasized, because the traditional sense of status is the only meaningful one. It is a weakness of the literature to have assumed this to be the case, and to overlook subgroup status. Rather, it is because using centrality to refer to subgroup status allows restricted use of status itself.

Accepting the terminological distinctions, the key point to emerge from the chapter about status is that, characterized as an informal dimension of formal peer groups, it revolves around children being described as popular, controversial, rejected, neglected, or average, depending on how much their peers like and dislike them. Although virtually all research into status differentiation with children has taken place in classrooms, there is no reason to think that it would not be observed in other contexts, for example formal out-of-school activities. This is particularly the case considering that Criss et al. (2009) found differentiation after only two weeks in summer camps, implying that there is something compelling about its appearance. Friendships emerge in formal settings (and again these settings have been the locus of most research), but they are continued, extended, and otherwise modified elsewhere. As the primary informal grouping, friendships need, from research just presented, to be conceptualized along two dimensions—liking/disliking and power. It seems likely that the degree to which friendship groups display the traditional qualities of similarity and complementarity is inversely related to the extent of power asymmetries. Power within informal subgroups can be indexed by centrality measures, and is related to status across the broader formal context. However, the imperfect nature of the relation means that the constructs are not interchangeable. So status, friendship, and centrality are all worth considering, and this is presumed when, in the chapters to follow, we move toward understanding the implications of informal peer group experiences for children's development.

Chapter 6

Individual Differences in Informal Experiences

Introduction

Chapter 5 added an additional strand to the analysis of children's peer group experiences, by recognizing that these experiences have an informal dimension as well as a formal. In particular, the chapter showed how informal subgroups emerge within the overall classroom peer group, and, although research is limited, also within formal out-of-school organizations. Informal subgroups can usually be characterized as *friendships*, and traditionally friendships have been conceptualized as dyadic, reciprocal, and equal. However, as stressed in chapter 5, larger groups are common, and many friendship groups, regardless of size, have identifiable leaders. Contemporary research often indexes leadership within informal subgroups via measures of *centrality*. At the same time, chapter 5 also showed how formal groups like single classes of pupils or particular teams of soccer players typically involve informal relations as well as formal. Specifically, members of formal groups acquire peer *status* as popular, controversial, neglected, rejected, or merely average. Thus, chapter 5 identified three key constructs for examining children's informal experiences of peer groups: (a) friendship; (b) centrality, which is tantamount to position within informal groups; and (c) status, which represents informal position across formal groups.

Friendship, centrality, and status can be assumed to be relevant in all societies (or parts of societies) that institutionalize peer groups, for instance in all contexts where schooling is legally required. Therefore, they can also be assumed to reflect the experiences, in some sense at least, of all children within those societies or parts thereof. However, within this commonality, there are obvious differences. Children vary in the number of friends that they have, and in the positions that they attain. Thus, while some children experience friendship as a rich array of relations in which they themselves are included, others experience it largely through observing relations in which others are involved. Likewise, while some children experience popularity (or rejection) as personal characteristics, others experience these statuses as characteristics that can be attributed to someone else. The key question in the context of this book is whether this variation is developmentally significant, and answering the question obviously involves relating variations at one time point to developmental outcomes at a later time point. However, while this is necessary, it is not sufficient. Unless account is also taken of the reasons why experiences vary, it will be unclear whether observed associations between variations and outcomes stem from differences in peer group experiences per se or from the qualities that produce the differences. Accordingly, the present chapter starts by asking why it is that children vary in their informal experiences of peer groups.

Just because a given child has many friends and/or high peer status in one setting, it does not necessarily follow that this child has many friends and/or high status in a different setting. Equally, just because the child had many friends and/or high status at one point in time, this is not inevitably the case at earlier or later time points. Stability across place and time in informal peer group experiences is a further consideration of great relevance when charting developmental outcomes. After all, if experiences across a range of settings can be predicted (to an acceptable degree at least) from experiences within one key setting, it may be unnecessary to collect data in more than one setting. Given the classroom focus of much relevant research, this could be significant. Likewise, the challenge of relating peer group experiences to developmental outcomes is much greater if these experiences are themselves changing over time than if they remain constant.

With the factors that predict peer group experiences clarified in the early part of the chapter, it becomes possible to formulate hypotheses about the extent of stability across place and time. The chapter concludes by developing and testing such hypotheses. Inevitably the discussion is handicapped through the dearth of directly relevant research. We need research from beyond the classroom to know for certain that the restriction to classrooms is justifiable! Nevertheless, the analysis of contributory factors earlier in the chapter permits deeper probing of stabilities and instabilities than would otherwise have been the case. For instance, the small number of studies that correlate numbers of school friends with numbers of out-of-school friends can be supplemented with studies that clarify why some children have lots of school friends and some children have few. Based on the factors that the latter studies identify (and particularly their own stability across place and time), the correlation between numbers of school and out-of-school friends can be anticipated, albeit with due circumspection. Overall then, the chapter has two reasons for focusing on the factors that determine why children vary in their informal experiences of peer groups: (a) to allow the influence of these factors to be controlled in analyses of developmental outcome; and (b) to allow deeper analysis of stabilities than could otherwise be achieved.

Varying Experiences of Status

Like many of the themes developed in the previous chapter, the issue of why children differ in their informal experiences of peer groups has a long history. During the 1930s and early 1940s a series of studies was conducted, usually with children attending nursery schools, which examined how child characteristics vary with peer status and/or friendship patterns. Status and numbers of friends were identified using the nomination approach pioneered by F. Moreno (1942; see chapter 5), and then related to observed or reported classroom behavior and/or responses to the personality and intelligence tests that were then available. A picture was painted of high peer status and large numbers of friends being positively associated with active participation in classroom routines, compliance with teachers' demands, helpfulness toward classmates and respect for their property, relatively high intelligence, good looks, and qualities of leadership (Bonney, 1943; Koch, 1933; Lippitt, 1941). Low peer status and absence of friends were found to be positively associated with aggression, boastfulness, and resistance toward classmates or with quietness, listlessness, and lack of interest in classmates (Koch, 1933; Northway, 1944). The characteristics that were positively associated with high status and large numbers of friends were negatively associated with low status, and vice versa.

Reviewing the early work, Ladd (2005) judges that the conclusions were "novel, theoretically provocative, and prescient in the sense that they anticipated future discoveries" (p. 45), but also draws attention to flaws in the methodology. In many respects, Ladd's analysis provides an overview of what emerges in the early part of the present section. The research to be discussed covers school-age rather than preschool samples, and it demonstrates both methodological innovation and conceptual change. Nevertheless, it addresses characteristics that can be related directly to the ones that were highlighted in the early work, and it indicates parallel relations with high and low status. At the same time, contemporary research also shows that the characteristics provide no more than a partial explanation of emergent peer status, and as additional factors are introduced later in the section it becomes clear that they carry implications for friendship as well as status. They probably carry implications for centrality too, but the concept is too new to have attracted much research. In any event, the upshot will be confirmation of the "prescience" of the original research, but at the same time qualification.

Sociability, aggression, and withdrawal

For many researchers, the characteristics flagged in the early studies typify three broad categories: (a) sociability, (b) aggression, and (c) withdrawal. The associates of high peer status and many friends that emerged in the early work can be drawn together under the sociability construct, aggression is suggested by one of the clusters of characteristics that the studies associate with low status and the absence of friends, and withdrawal is indicated by the second cluster. A review article by Newcomb, Bukowski, and Pattee (1993) played a pivotal role in cementing the distinction between sociability, aggression, and withdrawal, but the contrast has also been made in many other contexts. The review article also introduced the distinction between "narrow-band" categories within the three-way "broad-band" superstructure, but while the superstructure is typically taken for granted, conceptualization at the narrow-band level continues to evolve. Furthermore, regardless of categorization, there have been refinements in the methods by which characteristics are assessed. These developments are sketched below, before an examination of how the characteristics relate to status, and in the next section, to friendship and centrality. There have of course also been changes in the approach to status, friendship, and centrality, but these changes were detailed in chapter 5 and do not require further analysis.

As regards sociability, Newcomb et al. (1993) saw it as comprising seven narrow-band categories: (a) social interaction (i.e., engagement in social play); (b) communication skills (e.g., conversation, questioning, instructing); (c) problem solving (e.g., conflict resolution, persuasion); (d) positive social actions (e.g., helpful, supportive, empathic, cooperative behavior); (e) positive social traits (e.g., honesty, happiness, and a sense of humor); (f) friendship relations, having friends, and living up to expectations (as specified in chapter 5); and (g) positive interaction with adults. Although studies vary in the emphasis that is placed upon each of the seven categories, there is relatively little disagreement about their relevance to the core sociability construct. Moreover, when the categories have all been included in assessment instruments—for example Greener's (2000) *Peer Assessment of Prosocial Behaviour*; Masten, Morison, and Pellegrini's (1985) *Revised Class Play*; Pekarik, Prinz, Liebert, Weintraub, and Neale's (1976) *Pupil Evaluation Inventory*—they have produced strongly intercorrelated indices of children's behavior.

On the other hand, while the concept of sociability is relatively consensual, disagreement has arisen over the concepts of aggression and withdrawal. For Newcomb et al. (1993), aggression could be characterized via the narrow-band categories of disruptive behavior, physical aggression, and negative behavior (the latter including verbal abuse and displays of negative emotion). Subsequent research (see, e.g., Deptula & Cohen, 2004; Hawker & Boulton, 2000) has often subsumed "disruptive behavior" into what amount to the second two categories, and at the same time identified what can be regarded as subtypes of "negative behavior." These subtypes include indirect aggression (enacted through third parties so that perpetrators cannot be identified by victims), relational aggression (harms/intends to harm relationships), and "other verbal." Distinctions have also been made between proactive and reactive aggression (unprovoked or provoked; e.g., Crick & Dodge, 1996; Lancelotta & Vaughn, 1989) and instrumental and hostile aggression (with or without perpetrator gain; e.g., Atkins, Stoff, Osborne, & Brown, 1993). When aggression is repeated and involves power asymmetries between perpetrator and victim, it is frequently referred to as "bullying" (e.g., Olweus, 1993). As regards withdrawal, Newcomb et al.'s (1993) initial narrow-band categories (loneliness, anxiety, depression) could be regarded as emphasizing possible consequences rather than indicative behaviors. Recent work (e.g., Harrist, Zaia, Bates, Dodge, & Pettit, 1997; Rubin & Coplan, 2004) has typically differentiated children who are withdrawn because their peers actively exclude them (i.e., "active-isolates"), from children who "select" withdrawal. The latter children are often divided into those who prefer to play alone ("unsociable"), and those who would like to play with others but are inhibited through, for example, shyness ("passive-anxious"). Occasionally, attention is paid to the kinds of activity that children engage in when withdrawn (e.g., Hart et al., 2000).

No matter how sociability, aggression, and withdrawal are conceptualized, researchers are confronted with a number of issues when they try to assess them. Perhaps the most basic question is whether assessments should be made through observing children's behavior directly, or through soliciting reports from children's acquaintances. Behavioral observation is time consuming, and it will not tap all of the finer distinctions that were outlined above. For instance, while characteristics of sociability like social interaction, communication, and problem solving could in principle be established through observation, social traits and friendship expectations might prove more challenging. Thus, even though reports are one degree removed from what children actually do, they are probably to be preferred over observation to the extent that the two approaches produce comparable data. The issue of comparability is addressed in Newcomb et al.'s (1993) review, for in addition to summarizing what 41 published studies had to say about the sociability, aggression, and withdrawal of popular, controversial, rejected, neglected, and average children, the review pays attention to the information source on which findings are based. By and large, observation and report data do paint similar pictures, although the similarities are greater for popular and rejected children than for controversial and neglected children. This of course could reflect the difficulties with *identifying* controversial and neglected children that were discussed in chapter 5 rather than anything specific to behavioral characteristics. On the other hand, even when observation and report data do point in the same direction, report data typically indicate greater variation in sociability, aggression, and withdrawal across status categories than do observations. Therefore, observational data can be interpreted as providing relatively conservative estimates of behavioral differences.

In reality (and no doubt inspired by Newcomb et al.'s (1993) broadly encouraging findings), the majority of recent studies are based on report data. As is also the case for peer status (see chapter 5), reports of sociability, aggression, and withdrawal have been obtained through nominations and ratings. For instance, sometimes reporters are asked to identify children (usually to a maximum of three, and normally to be selected from members of a classroom) who fit descriptors like "shares things with others," "starts fights," and "stands back and watches others play" (e.g., Greener, 2000; Masten et al., 1985; Pekarik et al., 1976). The number of times that each child is nominated for the descriptors relevant to sociability is totaled to produce that child's "sociability score," and likewise for aggression and withdrawal. On the other hand, sometimes reporters are asked to rate children against similar descriptors utilizing scales, with 3-point scales being most commonly used (e.g., Achenbach & Edelbrock, 1986).

Whichever approach is used, there are further issues surrounding *who* should make the assessments. Given that the focus is on peer group experiences, it might seem as if peer assessments should be prioritized.

However, peers will be providing the data from which status, friendship, and centrality are determined. Therefore, if their responses are also used to assess sociability, aggression, and withdrawal and assessments are then related to status and so on, there may be problems from what is technically referred to as "shared method variance," that is, from inflated correlations between scores due to their common source. Recognizing this, many researchers have preferred to use teachers' reports or, less frequently, parental reports and even self-reports. As well as comparing observation with report data, Newcomb et al. (1993) also contrast peer reports, reports from adults (teachers or parents), and self-reports from the children being studied. Consistent with the effects of shared method variance, the differences between popular, controversial, rejected, and neglected children are most pronounced when the reports came from peers. However, the general direction of effects is similar regardless of source, and this also seems to be the message from subsequent studies (e.g., Greener (2000) comparing peer, teacher, and self-assessments; Rodkin, Farmer, Pearl, & Van Acker (2000) comparing reports from teachers and peers). In an ideal world, researchers should probably obtain reports from several types of respondent, for example peers *and* teachers. Nevertheless, it looks as if reports from one type alone will usually prove meaningful.

Behavioral characteristics and status

As noted, Newcomb et al. (1993) were interested in variations in sociability, aggression, and withdrawal across the standard status categories. The 41 studies that they reviewed covered children from 5 to 12 years of age, and indicated that: (a) levels of sociability are highest in popular and controversial children, next highest in average children, and lowest in rejected and neglected children; (b) levels of aggression are highest in rejected and controversial children and lowest in popular and neglected children, with average children again in the middle; and (c) levels of withdrawal are higher in rejected children than in any other group, and higher in average children than in popular children (with no other status differences detectable for withdrawal). Similar conclusions were drawn more or less contemporaneously in Cowie, Smith, Boulton, and Laver (1994), and a little later in Rubin et al. (1998), based in both cases on further comprehensive reviews.

The implications of the reviews are that popular and controversial children can be differentiated from the other groups by virtue of their high sociability and low withdrawal, and as Rodkin et al. (2000) seem to confirm, they can be differentiated from each other by virtue of low and high aggression, respectively. Neglected children appear to be uniquely low in sociability, aggression, and withdrawal, although other work has suggested that they show at least moderate levels of withdrawal (e.g., Coie & Dodge, 1988; Nabuzoka & Smith, 1993). The study of nearly six hundred 5- to 8-year-olds reported in Harrist et al. (1997) indicates high levels of what earlier was called the "unsociable" style of withdrawal among neglected children. While rejected children are low in sociability, they seem to be high in both aggression and withdrawal. The somewhat paradoxical nature of this latter result has stimulated further research (e.g., Cillessen, van IJzendoorn, van Lieshout, & Hartup, 1992; Haselager, Cillessen, van Lieshout, Riksen-Walraven, & Hartup, 2002; Hymel, Bowker, & Woody, 1993), and the existence of three rejected subgroups is now generally acknowledged: rejected-aggressive, rejected-withdrawn, and rejected-aggressive-withdrawn. Research by Lancelotta and Vaughn (1989) with 98 children aged 8 years to nearly 11 years suggests that provoked, unprovoked, verbal, indirect, and "outburst" aggression are all associated with rejection, while Harrist et al. (1997) indicate that among withdrawn children, only active-isolates are likely to be rejected. As noted above, the conceptualization of "active-isolation" seems to imply rejection almost by definition, and therefore this result is probably to be expected.

Faced with the contemporary picture (which is summarized in Table 6.1), it is easy to see why Ladd (2005) described the studies conducted in the 1930s and 1940s as "prescient" in their anticipation of future results. Nevertheless, like those early studies, the research surveyed so far does not warrant conclusions about how status differences are to be *explained*, and therefore does not resolve the section's central concern. In particular, it is unclear whether it is because children vary in sociability, aggression, and withdrawal that they achieve varying status. It is perfectly possible that it is because they achieve varying status that they display these

Table 6.1 Peer status and child behavior: characteristic associations

	Popular	Controversial	Rejected	Neglected	Average
Sociability	High	High	Low	Low	Moderate
Aggression	Low	High	High	Low	Moderate
Withdrawal	Low	Low	High	Moderate	Low

contrasting characteristics. For instance, the aggressive and withdrawn behavior of rejected children may *result* from their rejection rather than operate as contributory factors. We should have greater confidence in sociability, aggression, and withdrawal as contributors to peer status (rather than, or in addition to, the reverse) if variations in these characteristics at one point predict status at a later point, particularly if status at the first point and sociability, aggression, and withdrawal at the later point are also considered. At present, studies that fulfill these requirements are limited in number, and focused on the aggression–rejection relation. Nevertheless, among these studies, aggression has consistently been found to predict subsequent rejection (see, e.g., Chen, Rubin, & Li, 1995; Dodge et al., 2003; Ladd & Burgess, 1999; Little & Garber, 1995). Moreover, the relevant work includes large samples of children (at least 300 in each of the studies), covers a wide age range (from 5 to 12 years), and involves lengthy time intervals between first and final observations (up to five years).

Behavioral characteristics in context

Despite the restriction to the aggression–rejection relation, it is now widely accepted from research like that summarized above that children's varying propensities to sociability, aggression, and withdrawal play a key role in determining their peer status. Indeed, because of this, research indicating that status varies with demographic characteristics has also sometimes seemed interpretable. For instance, it has long been recognized that children with registered learning difficulties who are placed in mainstream schools (as many are) are disproportionately susceptible to peer rejection (Asher, 1983; Frederickson & Furnham, 1998; Kuhne & Wiener, 2000; LaGreca & Stone, 1990; Nabuzoka & Smith, 1993). There is little reason to think that children with learning difficulties display relatively high levels of aggression (Bender, 1985; Nabuzoka & Smith, 1993; Taylor, Asher, & Williams, 1987), but there is considerable evidence of their propensity toward social withdrawal (Gresham, 1982; Guralnick, 1990; Guralnick & Paul-Brown, 1984; Kemp & Carter, 2002; Nabuzoka & Smith, 1993; Taylor et al., 1987; Thomson, 1993). Thus, the documented association between rejection and withdrawal has been called upon to account for the status of children with learning difficulties (Nabuzoka & Smith, 1993; Taylor et al., 1987).

Likewise, boys have generally been found to be more aggressive than girls (Archer & Lloyd, 1985; Card, Stucky, Sawalani, & Little, 2008;

Maccoby & Jacklin, 1974; Pettit, Clawson, Dodge, & Bates, 1996). Exceptions have been reported with some forms of what earlier was called "negative behavior," although initial reports of higher frequency in girls (e.g., Crick & Grotpeter, 1995) have now been superseded by evidence of virtually no gender difference (e.g., Card et al., 2008). In any event, the frequency with which individuals engage in one form of aggressive behavior is typically correlated with the frequency with which they engage in other forms (to the extent of +.76 in Card et al.'s data), and across the forms as a whole boys are predominant. When gender differences in peer status are detected (and this is not consistently the case; see Warden & Mackinnon, 2003), they are in the direction of girls being disproportionately popular and boys being disproportionately rejected (Eisenberg, Pidada, & Liew, 2001; Greener, 2000; Pettit et al., 1996). Thus, in research with 5- to 9-year-old children, Howe and McWilliam (2006) found that 23 of the 26 popular children in their sample were girls, and 28 of the 39 rejected children were boys. The most obvious interpretation of such results is to view them as a specific exemplar of the rejection–aggression relation.

Nevertheless, while some reported associations between peer status and demographic characteristics seem interpretable when sociability, aggression, and withdrawal are taken into account, others are more challenging. For instance, Kistner, Metzler, Gatlin, and Risi (1993) found that, among a sample of 532 children aged 9 to 11 years, peer status was dependent on the match between the children's own race and the racial composition of their classrooms. Black children in majority Black classrooms and White children in majority White classrooms were more popular and less rejected than Black children in majority White classrooms and White children in majority Black classrooms. Parallel results are reported in Jackson, Barth, Powell, and Lochman (2006), based on a study of 1,268 children aged 11 years. Because 94% of the sample was Black or White (with the remainder covering a range of racial/ethnic groups), the analysis focused on a Black–White comparison. It was found that across the 57 participating classrooms, the proportion of Black children ranged from 3% to 95%. Black children's popularity (as assessed via social preference—like most, and like least; see chapter 5) increased steadily from initially low levels as the proportion of Black children increased. Their popularity overtook that of White children once they achieved at least a two-thirds majority. White children's popularity was relatively high when they were in the majority, regardless of the majority size. However, their popularity decreased steadily with the proportion of Black children, once Black children were in the majority.

It is just about possible to see how the results obtained by Kistner et al. and Jackson et al. could be interpreted in terms of varying behavioral characteristics. Nevertheless, a behavioral account seems extremely implausible. Similarly challenging is evidence from Stormshak et al. (1999) that peer status is influenced by the degree of correspondence between children's own tendencies toward aggression or withdrawal and the overall levels of aggression or withdrawal in their classrooms, with the nature of the influences varying with gender. Based on data obtained from 2,895 children who were aged about 6 years, Stormshak et al. found that when overall levels of aggression were low, aggressive boys were typically rejected, but when overall levels were high, they were disproportionately likely to be popular. On the other hand, aggressive girls were rejected regardless of classroom climate. When overall levels of withdrawal were high, withdrawn boys were more popular than outgoing boys, while withdrawn girls were less popular than outgoing girls. When overall levels of withdrawal were low, withdrawal was unrelated to peer status for either sex.

One possible explanation of the results obtained by Kistner et al. (1993), Jackson et al. (2006), and Stormshak et al. (1999) lies with the account provided in chapter 5 for the composition of friendship groups. There, it was suggested that immediately obvious characteristics like gender and race influence whom children target as possible friends. The extent to which targeted individuals measure up to relevant expectations and values shapes the subsequent development of the relationship, for example whether it continues and deepens, or whether it deteriorates and ends. Measuring up to expectations depends in part on similarities in cognitive and social characteristics. If the account applies to friendship, it ought also to have some relevance to status, since both are dependent on patterns of liking and disliking. It certainly offers a straightforward explanation of Kistner et al.'s and Jackson et al.'s results: when a child's race corresponds with the majority race, that child will be identified as potentially likeable by a larger number of classmates.

Less obviously, the account also offers an interpretation of Stormshak et al.'s data, given that aggression and withdrawal are social characteristics and therefore their impact is, by hypothesis, dependent on expectations and values. In particular, it is possible that, in boys, high levels of classroom aggression and withdrawal (the latter interpreted as "coolness") coincide with a pervading climate of anti-educational values. As a result, aggressive and/or withdrawn boys in those classrooms achieve high status because they lead the class in expression of values. Girls are relatively unlikely to hold anti-educational values regardless of classroom climate. Therefore, aggression is seldom valued in girls, and withdrawal typically signals lack of engagement in classroom discourses (both formal and informal) rather than coolness. Although different in detail from the account that Stormshak et al. themselves put forward, this interpretation concurs with the broad thrust of what they propose, as well as linking status with friendship. Certainly, some account that calls upon values and expectations would appear to be needed to deal with the differing patterns for boys and for girls.

The general point from the preceding paragraphs is that sociability, aggression, and withdrawal are certainly relevant to emergent peer status, but the manner in which they are relevant is not straightforward. First, as Table 6.1 highlights, it is the patterning of sociability, aggression, and withdrawal as a whole that predicts peer status, and not one of the characteristics taken separately. Second, there are subtypes of rejection, associated with contrasting patterns of aggression and withdrawal. Third, status depends on institutional demographics, for instance the racial mix of classrooms. Fourth, the significance of sociability, aggression, and withdrawal also depends on the institutional context, specifically its norms and values. Moreover, it is not simply institutional norms and values that are important, as documented in Stormshak et al. (1999), but also institutional practices. Research reported by McAuliffe, Hubbard, and Romano (2009) shows that when the aggressive children in a sample of 7- to 8-year-olds ($N = 127$) received disproportionate amounts of corrective feedback from teachers, they were even more likely to be disliked by their peers than would have been predicted from their aggression alone.

McAuliffe et al.'s research is highly significant in the context of this book, for it demonstrates direct links between liking (and, by implication, peer status) and the teaching practices discussed in chapter 3. After all, feedback from teachers is an integral component of the IRF (initiation–response–feedback) sequences that dominate classroom interaction and produce what chapter 3 described as "performance" characteristics. Thus, by encouraging the performance mode, teachers are influencing the status distribution within their classrooms. Moreover, given they are doing this in the manner that McAuliffe et al. describe, they must also be doing it in other ways too. Compared with the alternative cooperative mode (which chapter 3 showed to be used infrequently), the performance mode minimizes questioning, instructing, persuasion, helpfulness, and of course cooperation, the very behaviors that research discussed in the present chapter aligns with sociability. Likewise, compared with the cooperative mode, the performance mode maximizes a form of withdrawal, namely passive witnessing by the pupils who are not currently responding to the teacher's initiation. In chapter 1, I signaled that links would be made between formal and informal peer group experiences. The interdependency of teaching practices and displays of sociability, aggression, and withdrawal is an instance where such links are required.

Friendship and Status Compared

One of the factors used toward the end of the previous section to make sense of status was a model that was derived from research relating to friendship. Therefore, if sociability, aggression, and withdrawal are relevant to status, albeit contextualized as outlined above, they may also be relevant to patterns of friendship. Relevance is, of course, what the very early work, summarized at the start of the previous section, appears to suggest: considerable overlap between the characteristics that vary with status and the characteristics that vary with numbers of friends, and both sets of characteristics including sociability, aggression, and withdrawal. On the other hand, this early research also indicates parallels between the *manner* in which the characteristics apply with status and the manner in which they apply with friendship, but once expectations and values are taken into consideration as suggested in the previous section, this may not be the case. The values and expectations that children hold for the institutional contexts that are relevant to status may not correspond precisely with the values and expectations that they hold for informal groupings, even when those groupings are formed in institutional contexts. Furthermore, there may be differences between children in the degree of correspondence. The paragraphs that follow review research that relates to these issues.

Sociability and friendship

In the mid-1990s, Newcomb was first author on a second review, which complements the Newcomb et al. (1993) article that proved so useful above. This second review (Newcomb & Bagwell, 1995) surveyed the literature that was then available to establish what were described as "the behavioral and affective manifestations of children's friendships" (Newcomb & Bagwell, 1995, p. 306). Newcomb and Bagwell identified 82 studies that compared pairs of friends with pairs of non-friends, taking account of whether the friends were unilaterally or reciprocally nominated (as distinguished in chapter 5), and whether the non-friends were disliked acquaintances, acquaintances who were not specifically disliked, or strangers (termed "disliked," "acquaintances," and "strangers," respectively). The studies covered children from preschool age through to early adolescence.

Compared with non-friends, Newcomb and Bagwell found friends to: (a) display more positive engagement, as revealed in higher frequencies of social contact, conversation, cooperation, and positive affect; (b) show superior conflict management, by virtue of more frequently ensuring that disputes are resolved; (c) perform better on collaborative tasks; and (d) manifest "relationship properties" of equality, closeness, loyalty, mutual liking, lack of dominance, and similarity. The differences were found with both unilateral and reciprocal friends, although they were typically stronger with reciprocal friends. They were also found regardless of whether non-friends were disliked, acquaintances, or strangers, although strangers elicited the sharpest differences from friends. The differences were apparent at all ages studied, although the contrasts between friends and non-friends over positive engagement and relationship properties became more pronounced with age. Methodological variations operated in much the same way that Newcomb et al. (1993) detected for status (see above). In other words, studies that asked children to report on their friends obtained more marked differences than studies that relied upon behavioral observation, but the overall patterns emerged regardless of research procedures.

Looking back over earlier publications, Newcomb and Bagwell (1995) began their review by suggesting that "For the most part, previous authors have described friendship as a universal good marked by some interpersonal conflict" (p. 306). They indicated that they would be demonstrating variations in the positive aspects of friendship and clarifying the role played by conflict management. However, while they did indeed develop both of these themes, it will be clear from the summary presented above that they confirmed, rather than challenged, the sense of "universal good." Moreover, the universal good that they depict seems to be one that would be promoted by sociability, with its emphasis upon positive interaction, good communication, and problem solving, and inhibited by aggression and withdrawal. Thus, there is an implication that highly sociable children have more friends and/or more sustained friendships than less sociable counterparts, while highly aggressive and/or highly withdrawn children show the reverse pattern.

Evidence supporting the above implications can be found. For instance, in the study summarized in chapter 5, Gest et al. (2001) found that children with relatively large numbers of friends were more prosocial and good humored than children with relatively small numbers of friends. They were also less likely to tease or boss other children about. Working with an Indonesian sample comprising 961 children aged 8 to 11 years, French, Jansen, Riansari, and Setiono (2003) observed that the children who lacked friends were nominated relatively frequently by both teachers and classmates as highly aggressive and highly withdrawn. On the other hand, it is important to note that French et al.'s friendless group was identified as both aggressive *and* withdrawn. Once the characteristics are separated, the picture is less clear cut. For instance, while Feltham, Doyle, Schwartzman, Serbin, and Ledingham (1985) found similar results to French et al. for children who displayed both aggression and withdrawal, they report that the children in their sample who were merely aggressive had as many friends as other children. Ray, Cohen, Secrist, and Duncan (1997) detected no differences in numbers of friends between aggressive and non-aggressive children.

Aggression, friendship, and centrality

It seems, then, that while sociability may promote friendship, aggression is no barrier, unless it is combined with withdrawal—in which case, the rosy picture of friendship groups painted in Newcomb and Bagwell's (1995) review requires qualification. The picture may be true for some friendships, perhaps even the majority, but it does not apply to all. One reason why Newcomb and Bagwell did not detect the full story may be their focus on dyads, for as became clear in chapter 5, smaller groups are especially likely to display mutuality, cooperation, and so on. Certainly, when Estell, Cairns, Farmer, and Cairns (2002) mapped classroom friendships regardless of size, they unearthed considerable heterogeneity. Estell et al. used the social cognitive mapping technique, which was described in chapter 5, to document the friendships that existed across samples of African American children aged 6 to 7 years (92 children in total). They also obtained ratings of each child's interpersonal competence, academic performance, and aggression. They found four types of group: (a) high competence, where members were popular, non-aggressive, and academically successful (and most likely akin to the groups described by Newcomb and Bagwell); (b) competent-aggressive, where members were popular, aggressive, and academically successful; (c) low academics, where members were moderately popular, non-aggressive, and academically weak; and (d) aggressive-weak, where members were highly aggressive, disliked, academically weak, exclusively male, and deemed to be at risk of long-term problems.

Beyond the classroom, groups with Estell et al.'s fourth set of characteristics exist in the form of gangs. In a study of 142 boys who were assessed when they were 10, 11, 12, 13, and 14 years of age, Craig, Vitaro, Gagnon, and Tremblay (2002) found that gang members were rated by teachers as engaging in more fights, showing less anxiety, and being more hyperactive than non-gang members. Classmates rated gang members as more aggressive and less withdrawn than non-gang members. Moreover, these characteristics were, if anything, especially true of boys who remained in gangs over extended as opposed to short periods, suggesting that high aggression, in this context at least, did not impose barriers against long-term relationships.

Furthermore, when aggressive children are involved in groups, they do not necessarily occupy positions at the periphery. Estell et al. (2002) found that 67% of the children whom they identified as both interpersonally competent and aggressive were central members of their groups. Centrality was computed as outlined in chapter 5, namely with reference to the number of times that a given child was identified as belonging to some group. Chapter 5 has already explained that Gest et al. (2001) observed something similar: centrality in their sample of 7- to 8-year-olds was associated with being simultaneously likeable and aggressive. Earlier in the present chapter (see Table 6.1), it became clear that high sociability and high aggression are characteristic of children whose peer status is controversial. Therefore, it is little surprise to find Bagwell et al. (2000) reporting that, in their sample of 10-year-olds, controversial children were relatively likely to occupy central positions in groups, and the children who occupied central positions were relatively likely to be aggressive. In qualification, it needs to be noted that this aspect of Bagwell et al.'s analysis was restricted to what they call "deviant cliques," that is, groups whose members had been identified as "getting into trouble." Nevertheless, Estell et al. and Gest et al. do not restrict their samples. Therefore, taken as a whole, the research confirms the suggestion made in chapter 5 that leadership of hierarchically structured groups is typically the prerogative of the controversial members of the class.

In their analysis of cliques, Adler and Adler (1995, 2003) demonstrate how clique leaders bolster their positions by drawing in new members or promoting lesser members, and by engaging these allies in deriding individuals who are seen as threats. In a study of African American teenagers in New York, Labov (1972) showed how prestige in neighborhood gangs was associated with skill in creating "ritual insults," as exemplified in Sequences 6.1 and 6.2 below (from Labov, 1972, p. 132 and p. 145). Derision and insults seem simultaneously to display both sociability and aggression, and therefore jointly they may clarify why individuals with propensities toward these characteristics come to occupy central positions.

Sequence 6.1

ROGER: Hey Davy, you so fat you could slide down the razor blade without getting cut . . . An' he so thin that he can dodge rain drops.
BOOT: Eh eh, your mother's so skinny she could split through a needle's eye.
BOOT: Your mother's so skinny, about that skinny, she can get in a Cheerioat and say "Hula hoop, hula hoop!"

Sequence 6.2

JOHN L: Who father wear raggedy drawers?
WILLIE: Yeh the ones with so many holes in them when-a-you walk they whistle?
REL: Oh . . . shi-it! When you walk they whistle! Oh shit!

In sum then, sociability, aggression, and withdrawal are all relevant to friendship, just as they were previously found to be relevant to status. They are relevant to the relations that children develop, and to the positions that they hold within friendship groups. Sociable children typically have relatively large numbers of friends, as well as being popular across the formal groups within which friendships are often embedded. Withdrawn children often have relatively few friends, particularly if they are also aggressive. This mirrors the tendency of withdrawn children to acquire neglected or, if they are also aggressive, rejected peer status across formal groups. Unless they are also withdrawn, aggressive children do not necessarily lack friends, particularly if they meet other aggressive children in contexts where aggression is valued (or, at the very least, not explicitly frowned upon). In such contexts, aggressive children who also have relatively high social skills often emerge as leaders within friendship groups, implying overlap between centrality in groups involving aggressive children and controversial peer status.

On the other hand, even in contexts where aggression is expected and/or tolerated, it will not typify every child, or be universally valued. It is quite possible, therefore, that non-aggressive children, perhaps especially girls from material presented toward the end of the previous section, will emerge as popular across aggressive contexts as a whole. This may be one reason why research summarized in chapter 5 indicates positive but imperfect relations between centrality, status, and numbers of friends. It is also one reason why this section has to conclude with further qualification of Ladd's (2005) comment about the "prescience" of research conducted in the 1930s and 1940s. The behavioral characteristics identified in early research are relevant to status and friendship and seemingly also to centrality although research is less extensive here. The manner in which the characteristics are relevant overlaps with what emerged from the early work. Nevertheless, the overlap is less than perfect.

Continuity and Change

The research that was reviewed in the previous sections explains why children differ in their informal experiences of peer groups, but it does not necessarily mean that children differ in the same way in all contexts and at all times. Yet it provides clues as to the extent of consistency across place and time, because it suggests that this depends on stabilities and instabilities in: (a) propensity toward sociability, aggression, and withdrawal; and (b) the values, expectations, and cultural practices that influence how the characteristics are displayed and how they are interpreted. As regards sociability, aggression, and withdrawal, it is relevant that in the late 1960s, Mischel (e.g., 1968) challenged the idea of a fixed "personality," involving characteristics that apply in every situation that individuals encounter. He drew attention instead to the context dependency of social behavior, implying variability and not stability. While Mischel is now widely believed to have overstated the degree of contextual variability (see, e.g., Kenrick & Funder, 1991; Roberts & Caspi, 2001), it is recognized that stabilities and instabilities need to be examined empirically on a case-by-case basis.

With sociability, aggression, and withdrawal, a great deal of research has already been conducted into their stability (for reviews, see Hay, Payne, & Chadwick, 2004; Rubin & Coplan, 2004). The consensus is high degrees of consistency as children develop, and also across settings at any particular age level. This is not to say that there are no changes with age. On the contrary, there are shifts over time in the form that sociability, aggression, and withdrawal take, and the frequency with which the characteristics are displayed also alters. Thus, while preschoolers can hold disputes every few minutes (Shantz, 1987), many involving hitting and snatching, the incidence of such exchanges is much reduced with older children. Despite this, the children who, at one age level, display high sociability, aggression, or withdrawal relative to their peers are likely to be the children who do this at other age levels. In other words, the relativities remain stable, while the absolute levels change. When all three characteristics almost certainly have biological underpinnings (Rothbart & Bates, 1998), the stability is not necessarily surprising.

As regards the values, expectations, and practices within which sociability, aggression, and withdrawal are contextualized, there is evidence for continuity and discontinuity. As detailed in chapter 3, the performance mode of teaching pervades classroom practice with all aspects of the curriculum, at all age levels, and in all corners of the world. Insofar as the performance mode encourages withdrawal, constrains sociability, and magnifies the effects of aggression (as argued earlier), its own consistency is a force toward stability over sociability, aggression, and withdrawal, and therefore the peer group experiences they are associated with. On the other hand, it is almost certain that the values and expectations, which render sociability, aggression, and withdrawal meaningful, change over time. After all, as we saw in chapter 5, children's expectations of friendship move with age from an "egocentric" perspective (Hartup, 1978) through a "sociocentric" perspective toward an "empathic" perspective. More prosaically perhaps, there is evidence that very young children scarcely notice peer withdrawal, even when they are attuned to sociability and aggression (Rubin et al., 1998). This too implies discontinuities in how peers are regarded and how they are treated.

Taking everything into account, the pointers are toward continuities of peer group experiences at specific age levels. All of the forces toward discontinuity that were specified above apply cross-age rather than within-age, although even here there are also pressures toward stability. Thus a working hypothesis is that children who have many friends and/or high peer status in one context will typically have equivalent experiences in other contemporaneous contexts. Children who have many friends and/or high peer status at one point in time may experience change with age, but here too there should also be consistency. Since the developmental implications of experiences that are wide ranging and durable are likely to be very different from those of experiences that are relatively contained, the issue of variation in informal peer group experiences is highly significant in the present context. As a result, the remainder of the chapter is devoted to discussing how the hypothesis fares against available research.

Context dependency

Considering that virtually all of the research discussed in this chapter has been conducted in classrooms, the key issue as regards contextual variation is whether classroom status and friendships predict status and friendships in other settings. Given the classroom focus, the dearth of directly relevant material scarcely needs stating. As noted in chapter 5, a small number of studies have considered status and friendships in non-classroom settings, for example Criss et al.'s (2009) research in summer camps. However, the number is indeed very small, and even fewer of the studies have linked status and friendship in out-of-class settings to status and friendship in classrooms. This is despite the fact that, for friendship at least, there is every reason to believe that out-of-school experiences are extensive. For instance, the research of Heim et al. (2004), which was mentioned in chapter 5, indicates that among a multiethnic sample aged 15 to 25 years, only the participants of Pakistani origin formed more than half of their friendships at school, college, or university. Among the White youngsters, friendships were as likely to have been forged in the neighborhood as they were in educational settings, and religious and ceremonial occasions were a significant source of friends for young people of Indian and Pakistani origin.

Some guidance about cross-context constancies over friendship can be obtained from a study reported by Kiesner, Poulin, and Nicotra (2003). Here, 577 Italian children aged 12 to 14 years were asked to identify the members of one group that they spent time with at school, and the members of one group that they spent time with after school. The results indicate divergence in membership across the two types of group. The average overlap in nominations was only 33%, although an average of 61% of the members of out-of-school groups attended the same schools. For 23% of the sample, there was no overlap in membership of the two groups, and only 7% reported full overlap. Of course, Kiesner et al.'s insistence that children report one group only for each setting may have exaggerated divergence. However, they also told their respondents that the groups must contain at least three people, and even though the exclusion of dyads can be challenged on theoretical grounds (see chapter 1), it probably operated as a force *against* divergence here by encouraging children to think about larger sets of peers. Nevertheless, while indicating divergent membership, Kiesner et al.'s results also suggest that children who have relatively large social networks within school have relatively large networks outside school. The average number of times that each child was nominated by other children as members of their groups was 4.0 for school groups and 2.4 for out-of-school groups. However, children who were nominated relatively frequently within school were also nominated relatively frequently out of school: there was a correlation of +.62 between the number of nominations received in the two settings.

Furthermore, both sets of nominations were strongly associated with within-school popularity assessed by standard techniques.

Much earlier, Kurdek and Lillie (1985) reported data, from 135 children aged 9 to 13 years, which also suggest cross-context consistency over group size, but introduce a further significant factor. Kurdek and Lillie asked each child in their sample to nominate three best friends from the children in their class and three children whom they disliked. The children were also asked to rate each classmate on a 5-point scale for how much they liked to work and play with them. The data were used to classify each child as popular, rejected, neglected, and average (no use being made of the "controversial" category). In addition, Kurdek and Lillie asked the children's parents (who were unaware of the status ratings) to record what their sons and daughters did during each hour between 3:00 p.m. and 9:00 p.m., and crucially for present purposes who they did this with. Logs were kept across each of five successive days, and on one day the children made logs too, revealing 94% agreement with their parents. Analysis of the parents' logs revealed that children who were classified as popular using classroom data had significantly more neighborhood friends ($M = 6.20$ friends) than children classified as rejected ($M = 4.38$) and average ($M = 4.25$). Given the known association between popularity and number of classroom friends (e.g., Gest et al., 2001, as well as Kiesner et al., 2003), this aspect of Kurdek and Lillie's data is further evidence for cross-context consistency over size of network. What is initially surprising is that the results also indicate neglected children having more neighborhood friends ($M = 6.64$ friends) than rejected and average children, while not differing statistically from popular children. However, neglected children had more neighborhood friends from younger age groups ($M = 2.82$ friends) than children from the other three status categories ($M = 1.25$–1.80 friends). One interpretation is that neglected children compensate for their exclusion from peer groups by forging cross-age relations.

Two studies cannot be regarded as sufficient to make a convincing case. Nevertheless, while indicating differences in *who* children become friends with in and out of school, both Kiesner et al. (2003) and Kurdek and Lillie (1985) suggest a degree of consistency across contexts regarding quantitative indicators like numbers of friends. Moreover, it is not simply that within-school friendships predict out-of-school relations, but also the reverse. Dunn (2004) reports that children who have relatively high numbers of friends during the preschool years make relatively high numbers of friends at primary school, even if they do not go to the same schools as their preschool friends. This was a consistent finding across data collected in England and the United States. Without doubt, quantitative indicators do no more than partial justice to capturing the essence of friendship, although as will have become clear from research reported throughout the chapter, numbers of friends have been relied upon in many studies in addition to the ones under consideration here. Assuming that the indicators do mean something, the work of Dunn, Kiesner et al. and Kurdek and Lillie provides a modicum of evidence for cross-context stability. It would be inappropriate to conclude with conviction that classroom friendship patterns predict friendship patterns in other settings, and in any event the predictive relations are only approximate, even for numbers of friends. Nevertheless, the possibility of association has not been ruled out, and in this sense our working hypothesis has been supported.

Change over time

With limited evidence for cross-context stabilities, the next issue is changes over time in experiences of status and friendship. The social world of children changes considerably over time. Within school, class composition alters, and out of school, children acquire new interests and hobbies. Such changes are undoubtedly relevant to peer group experiences. For example, Levinger and Levinger (1986) found that, among a sample of 11- and 12-year-olds, children's school friends typically came from their current classes, and not from the differently composed classes from one year earlier. Neckerman (1996) used social cognitive mapping to identify the informal groupings in 22 classes of 13-year-olds. The classes were spread across four schools, two of which reorganized classroom composition at the end of the year, and two of which maintained existing arrangements. None of the informal groups in the first two schools remained "stable" into the second year, stability being defined as preserving at least 50% of first-year membership. The majority of the groups in the other two schools were stable. Adler and Adler (1995, 2003) indicate that popular cliques are most open to new members at the start of the school year. Thus, alignments change and this is only to be expected. It is not the critical issue, for the key question is whether children's positions in terms of status, friendship, and centrality remain stable over time, despite shifts in their social milieu. For instance, do children who are rejected and lacking in friends during the early years of primary school typically continue to be rejected and friendless throughout their school career, even when their classmates change?

Both Cillessen and Mayeux (2004) and Gifford-Smith and Brownell (2003) signal a dearth of research on stabilities across time. Nevertheless, Lu Jiang and Cillessen (2005) were able to identify 77 studies that involved repeated assessments of the peers that children claimed to like and dislike. The work covered the preschool through to adolescent age group, and used nominations and ratings to make sequential assessments of liking, disliking, and related constructs. Considering that liking and disliking are relevant to both status and friendship, studies that assess them over a series of occasions ought to provide guidance about stability in the areas of interest. Thus, the conclusions that Lu Jiang and Cillessen drew from the studies would appear to be relevant. This recognized, the first point to note is that Lu Jiang and Cillessen divided the studies into two groups. When assessments were made less than three months apart, the work was deemed to address test–retest reliability. It was only when the gap was more than three months that the studies were regarded as concerned with stability over time. Focusing then on work in this second group, it is clear that, overall, stability was reasonably high—correlations between repeated assessments averaged +.50. Stability decreased as the gap between assessments increased, and curiously it was also related to the year when the research was published. Studies published in the early part of the period between 1980 and 2000 showed relatively high stability over positive assessments (e.g., liking), while stability over negative assessments characterized studies published during the later part of the period. Lu Jiang and Cillessen suggest that cultural changes in self-awareness and social anxiety may be relevant. Most importantly though, Lu Jiang and Cillessen found that stability in liking and disliking increased with age, while also being higher at all ages for girls than for boys.

Research that addresses status explicitly has focused on associations with age, although Sandstrom and Coie (1999) did examine gender differences and obtained results that concur with Lu Jiang and Cillessen (2005). Following 47 children who were aged about 11 years at the outset, Sandstrom and Coie found that girls were less likely to change rejected status over an 18-month period than boys, even when propensity to aggression was taken into account. As regards age effects, the picture of increasing stability with age is generally confirmed (e.g., Cowie et al., 1994; Ladd, 2005), although there appears to be variation depending on which status category is being examined. Hymel, Rubin, Rowden, and LeMare (1990) found that popularity was stable across a three-year period in a sample of 87 children, who were only about 7 years of age at the start of the study. Rejection also seems to be stable from a relatively young age, with Maszk, Eisenberg, and Guthrie (1999) obtaining a correlation of +.46 in a sample of 74 children between rejection at 5 years of age and rejection six months later. Moreover, the stability of rejected status seems to be even higher if rejection is based on aggression. For instance, Bierman and Wargo (1995) followed 81 children over two years, beginning when some children were as young as 6 years (although the starting age range was 6 to 12 years). Only 28% of rejected children who were also aggressive changed their status. Following 87 initially rejected boys over five years, Haselager et al. (2002) found relatively few status changes when high aggression was involved, especially if this was coupled with low sociability. There is very little research on the stability of average status, although Kuhne and Wiener (2000) indicate relatively little change in status among 24 normally developing children aged 9 to 12 years who were assessed as average at the start of the study and reassessed five months later. On the other hand, 10 of the 22 children in Kuhne and Wiener's sample who had learning difficulties changed status from average during the five-month period. In five cases, the children moved into the rejected category and in the other five cases they became neglected.

As regards controversial and neglected status, Rubin et al. (1998) indicate relatively low stability over time, a finding that may, in part, reflect the methodological difficulties with these categories that have been signaled already. There are problems with identifying controversial and neglected children (see chapter 5), and with obtaining a consistent impression of their behavioral characteristics (see earlier in the present chapter). On the other hand, methodology may not provide the full story. With the controversial category, its association with high sociability *and* high aggression may render it intrinsically non-stable. After all, if circumstances mean that sociability is transparent but aggression hidden, controversial children may move, perhaps temporarily, into the popular group. Too much aggression, and controversial children are in danger of becoming rejected. Certainly, Bierman and Wargo (1995) found status changes during their two-year study in more than 50% of the aggressive children who were not initially rejected (and therefore in many cases likely to have been controversial), compared with the much lower proportion of aggressive children who were initially rejected, as highlighted above.

With the neglected category, one significant factor may be its association with withdrawn behavior: as signaled in Table 6.1, neglected children tend to display at least moderate levels of social withdrawal. While sociability and aggression seem to be relevant to peer status throughout the school years (and probably earlier and later too), the importance of withdrawal increases through middle childhood. In Western children, withdrawal has little impact on status until about 10 years of age (Bukowski, Bowker, Zargarpour, & Hoza, 1995; Deater-Deckard, 2001; Rubin et al., 1998). This may be because, as mentioned already, young children scarcely notice when their peers are withdrawn. On the other hand, salience cannot explain why with a Chinese sample ($N = 612$) followed over two years, Chen et al. (1995) found that "shyness" (shown earlier in this chapter to be implicated in some forms of withdrawal) only became relevant to status around 12 years of age, that is, two years later than with Western groups. Chen et al. attribute the gap to the greater value placed upon shy behavior in Chinese culture than in the West, while also commenting upon the absence of cultural differences in the interpretation of sociability and aggression. Of course, the emergent significance of withdrawal (regardless of culture) does not only offer an explanation of why neglected status is unstable relative to other categories; it also accounts, in part at least, for the more general finding, that peer status as a whole becomes more stable with age.

A picture of increasing stability with age has also been painted from research into friendship (e.g., Degirmencioglu, Urberg, Tolson, & Protima, 1998; Epstein, 1985). Nevertheless, it would overstate matters to describe relations in the early years as entirely volatile, or to present relations in the later years as totally stable. For instance, when Estell et al. (2002) reassessed their initially 6-year-old sample 12 months later, the clusters that were described earlier emerged once more, and membership of each cluster was very similar to original membership (albeit not identical). On the other hand, basic demographics presented in chapter 5 imply change at later age levels: friendship groups were shown to become less consistently single sex as adulthood approaches. It will be recalled that one of the studies that demonstrates this trend (Connolly et al., 2000) indicates that mixed-sex groups often emerge from fusion of several single-sex groups. This study also shows that despite fusion and the consequent increase with age over group size, the size of group that each individual belongs to at 15 years of age predicts the size at 16 years, and the size of group at 16 years predicts the size at 17 years. Moreover, more than half the sample maintained their best friendships over one year, and half did this over two years. With a large sample of 12-, 14-, and 16-year-olds ($N > 1,000$), Degirmencioglu et al. (1998) found that girls were more likely to preserve their friendships than boys.

Also of interest is the work of Parker and Seal (1996), which shows that younger children in the age range 8 to 15 years changed friends more often than older children during the course of four-week summer camps. However, regardless of age, more friends were identified at the beginning of the camp ($M = 2.53$ friends) than in the middle ($M = 2.42$) or at the end ($M = 2.41$). Moreover, there were effects of gender, with boys' friendship networks becoming "denser" over time (i.e., the proportion of friends who were also friends with each other increased), and girls' networks becoming less dense. About 15% of the 216 children in Parker and Seal's sample remained friendless throughout the camp, and these children were not differentiated by age. Finally, in the specific context of juvenile gangs, membership may be relatively impermanent regardless of age. Baron and Tindall (1993) summarize a number of early studies, which suggest this, and Craig et al. (2002) implicitly endorse the point via their longitudinal study of 142 boys from low-income, high-crime neighborhoods. Data collected when the boys were 10, 11, 12, 13, and 14 years of age indicate an increase in gang membership with age (from 13% to 21% of the total sample reporting membership). However, it was not until the 13- to 14-year age level that gang membership showed any signs of stability. Prior to this, the boys drifted in and out of gangs.

Conclusions

The chapter started by asserting the universality of friendship, peer centrality, and peer status within the experience of children who live in societies that institutionalize peer groups. It also drew attention to obvious variations in the ways that individual children experience these constructs, and discussed how the variations come about. It used the latter discussion to frame an analysis of continuities and discontinuities in peer group experiences across time and place. As regards continuities over time, there is evidence for this happening across the school age range, although the situation becomes increasingly stable with age. With continuities across place, there is little directly relevant research, although the work that exists indicates a degree of stability.

There is, indeed, one reason for thinking that the stabilities may be even greater than the research implies. The studies discussed so far address face-to-face contact, but Internet communication (e.g., e-mail, blogs, chat rooms, and instant messaging) opens up additional possibilities. However, far from developing new relationships, children typically use the Internet to continue existing ones. Using diary records provided by 261 youngsters aged 12 to 15 years, Gross, Juvonen, and Gable (2002) estimate that 82% of instant messaging involves existing friends. New technology may therefore be boosting rather than diminishing continuities across place.

The continuities reported in the chapter were predicted and interpreted with reference to a model that depicts informal experiences of peer groups as resulting from the interplay between deep-rooted propensities toward sociability, aggression, and withdrawal on the one hand, and values, expectations, and practices on the other. Both the continuities and the model will prove to be of critical importance when in chapters 7 and 8 we move to what, in the final analysis, is one of the book's central questions: the implications of peer group experiences for children's development. As regards the continuities, they provide grounds for optimism that when researchers ask about the developmental implications of *classroom* status, centrality, and friendship (which, needless to say, is what they focus on), the results will not be irretrievably clouded by the (unknown) implications of out-of-class relations. In an ideal world, we should like to learn more about out-of-class relations so that they can be considered directly, but given their probable association with what happens in school, the current situation is not intractable. As for the model, we now know what to control when examining implications, so that associations with peer group experiences can be attributed to those experiences and not the factors upon which those experiences are based.

Chapter 7

Social and Personal Adjustment

Introduction

Chapter 5 attempted to characterize children's informal experiences of peer groups. Following well-established traditions, it differentiated between informal experiences within formal groups (overwhelmingly classrooms as far as current research is concerned), and experiences within groups that are themselves informal (overwhelmingly classroom subgroups as regards current research). Status emerged as a key construct for analyzing the first type of experience. Centrality and friendship were the key constructs to emerge in relation to the second type of experience. Chapter 6 focused on individual differences in children's experiences of these constructs. It found relatively little material relating to centrality, but a substantial quantity relating to status and friendship. Results identified differences in children's experiences, and showed that these differences are heavily dependent on social behavior. Children's propensities toward sociability, aggression, and withdrawal all proved relevant. Specifically, sociable children are relatively likely to be popular throughout the school years, and to have large numbers of friends. From around the middle school years (although this varies cross-culturally), withdrawn children are often neglected or, if they are also aggressive, rejected and lacking in friends. In many situations (and regardless of age), aggressive children are rejected, unless they are simultaneously relatively sociable, when they are likely to acquire controversial status. However, unless they are also withdrawn, aggressive children do not necessarily lack friends, and when they also have relatively high social skills, they often play central roles within friendship groups. In contexts where aggression is valued (or, at least, tolerated), aggressive children may turn out to be popular, particularly among boys.

In view of chapters 5 and 6, the key issue as regards developmental implications would seem to be the consequences of variations in status

and friendship (and of course should research have b
centrality). Unfortunately, as soon as this is accepted, pr\
formulating hypotheses become apparent. Favorable deve
outcomes might be expected for children who are popular, enga\
large numbers of friends, and central members of their informal net
However, are such outcomes to be expected of all such children, or
of those who achieve elevated positions by virtue of sociability? As noted,
aggressive children can, on occasion, be popular and central, and have
large numbers of friends. Conversely, poor outcomes might be anticipated
for children who are rejected, friendless, and peripheral within their networks, but does it make a difference whether their position is based upon
aggression, withdrawal, or a combination of these? What are the developmental consequences of being of controversial status and/or of being a
central group member by virtue of high sociability and high aggression?
What are the consequences of mismatch between status within formal
groups and subgroup experiences, for example being rejected by the class
as a whole yet having a central position within a sizeable network of
friends? Chapter 6 suggested that this scenario is not implausible, perhaps
particularly when boys are involved. Moreover, if formulating hypotheses about developmental outcomes is a challenge, so too is designing
research. It would seem inadvisable to look at status and friendship in
isolation from each other, or to ignore the precise combinations of sociability, aggression, and withdrawal in which they are grounded. Indeed,
unless sociability, aggression, and withdrawal are taken into consideration, it will be unclear whether peer group experiences are responsible
for observed outcomes, or the behavioral tendencies that led to these
experiences. Finally, it may be critical that sociability, aggression, and
withdrawal are all socially mediated constructs, whose meaning depends
on how behaviors are contextualized via values, expectations, and classroom practices.

The methodological challenge of studying the developmental consequences of informal peer group experiences is widely recognized, as is
the large-scale (and hence expensive) research that is required to address
the challenge. Nevertheless, relevant studies have been conducted, and
therefore the present chapter and its successor review the work and attempt
to draw conclusions. Research has addressed the implications of informal
peer group experiences for social, personal, and intellectual development,
and all three areas are covered across the two chapters. The present
chapter focuses on social and personal development, while chapter 8
considers the intellectual dimension. With regard to social and personal
development, the most general point to make is that research with school-
age children has emphasized developmental *problems* rather than positive

implications. In other words, the focus has been on antisocial rather than prosocial behavior, and psychopathology or maladjustment rather than psychological wellbeing. Interestingly, this is not the case with younger children: research into the consequences of peer group experiences during the preschool years has addressed sensitivity to the thoughts and feelings of others, and appreciation of morality (Dunn, 2004). However, with the school-age samples that the present volume is concerned with, the emphasis has been upon problems. Inevitably this emphasis constrains the story that can be told, for just as being disliked means something different from not being liked (as stressed in chapter 5), so being antisocial and maladjusted means something different from failing to be prosocial and psychically strong. Perhaps it is easier to obtain funds to study problems, but nevertheless it is to be hoped that the balance will be redressed at some point in the future.

Peer Groups and Antisocial Behavior

The social problems that feature in research include delinquency, criminality, smoking, alcohol abuse, bullying, and general disruptiveness, and of course the contribution of peer groups to these problems is also a recurring theme within the popular media. Stories abound of "good" children being led astray by disreputable friends. Indeed, similar lines are developed in works of fiction, perhaps most extremely in the novel *Lord of the Flies*. Yet the research to be reviewed below suggests a different story, while confirming the importance of informal peer group experiences. In the first place, peer status emerges as a significant influence on social development as well as friendship, meaning that informal positions within institutionalized groupings can also make an important contribution to antisocial behavior. In addition, the role of friendship is not typically to lead astray, but rather to exacerbate tendencies that already exist. The subtext of what follows is therefore the rejection of stereotypes, while associations are confirmed between informal peer group experiences and the very issues that the popular media are concerned with.

Rejection and antisocial behavior

A useful starting point for research into the developmental implications of peer group experiences is a review article published by Parker and Asher (1987). Parker and Asher synthesize and analyze the studies that were available in the mid-1980s which relate problematic peer experiences in childhood to unwelcome outcomes that have their onset no earlier than adolescence. As with the work discussed in chapters 5 and 6, most of the studies are restricted to peer experiences in classrooms. Furthermore, as Parker and Asher acknowledge, many have methodological limitations in addition to contextual ones. In the first place, a significant number used a "follow-back" methodology where respondents reflect upon peer relations earlier in their lives, with obvious problems of selective and/or faulty memory. A "follow-forward" methodology is to be preferred where measures are taken in childhood and their ability to predict later outcomes is ascertained subsequently. Second, many studies obtained information about peer relations and outcomes from the same informant, usually the children themselves or their classroom peers. As a result, the information is susceptible to the problem of "shared method variance" as discussed in chapter 6, that is, inflated correlations between scores due to their common source. Third, most of the research that was available to Parker and Asher was conducted before the need to assess both liking and disliking was recognized (see chapter 5). Thus peer experiences can only be characterized, rather nebulously, in terms of degrees of "acceptance." Mindful of the methodological shortcomings, Parker and Asher are circumspect about the conclusions they draw. Nevertheless, these conclusions have played a significant role in guiding subsequent research, and more often than not they have been confirmed rather than rejected by modern methods. Therefore, this section and the section that follows begin with Parker and Asher's review.

In the specific area of social development, Parker and Asher (1987) focused on delinquency and adult criminality, where they found literature that provides 54 distinct attempts to examine the association between peer relations and outcome. In the majority of cases, the research addresses the relations forged by boys aged between 8 and 10 years of age, but girls and older or younger children feature to some extent. Unfortunately, only 13 of the 54 investigations are concerned with acceptance, with the remainder focusing on the behaviors (primarily aggression, but also withdrawal) that chapter 6 showed to be related to acceptance (and its contemporary, status equivalents). Nine of the 13 studies demonstrate that low peer acceptance in childhood is associated with high levels of delinquent and criminal behavior from adolescence onwards. The remaining four studies are characterized by the absence of clear relationships, rather than, say, relations in the reverse direction. However, high levels of delinquency and criminality were as strongly associated with high aggression as they were with low peer acceptance, and thus by 1987 it was already apparent that there were potential confounds between the effects of peer group experiences and the effects of the characteristics that underpin those experiences. Since evidence for direct links between aggression and delinquency/criminality has continued to be published (e.g., Moffitt, 1993), a key concern of recent research has been estimating the strength of peer group effects, while controlling for aggression.

One of the earliest attempts to tease the effects of peer relations apart from the effects of aggression is the study reported in Ollendick, Weist, Borden, and Greene (1992). This study focused on children who were classified as rejected, popular, neglected, average, and controversial at about 10 years of age. Impressively, both nomination and rating methods (see chapter 5) were used in classification for additional reliability. At the same time, peer, teacher, and self-reports were employed to assess sociability, aggression, and withdrawal. Five years later, information about conduct problems, substance abuse, and court offenses was obtained for the 267 members of the original sample ($N = 297$) who could be contacted. Results indicate that all three types of social problem were more frequent with the children classified as rejected and controversial at 10 years of age than with the children placed in the other three categories. Rejected and controversial children were also identified as displaying relatively high levels of aggression and relatively low levels of withdrawal. (In other words, the rejected children were what chapter 6 termed rejected-aggressive, not rejected-withdrawn.) However, rejected and controversial status predicted subsequent conduct problems, substance abuse, and court offenses, even when behavioral characteristics were taken into account.

Rejection falls into Parker and Asher's broader concept of low peer acceptance, and therefore Ollendick et al.'s findings about rejected children concur with the general picture. However, the controversial category is associated with high peer acceptance, meaning that Ollendick et al.'s findings here are not consistent. It is surprising therefore that most subsequent research has looked exclusively at the rejection–problem relation, ignoring the corresponding relation involving controversial status. This said, it is encouraging that most studies of rejection have obtained confirmatory results. For instance, Miller-Johnson, Coie, Maumary-Gremaud, Lochman, and Terry (1999) found that rejected status and childhood aggression *independently* predicted subsequent delinquency in a sample of African American youngsters. Specifically, participants who were both aggressive and rejected during childhood engaged more often in the most serious forms of delinquency than participants who were only aggressive or only rejected. In a study detailed in chapter 6, Bierman and Wargo (1995) observed that children whom they classified as aggressive/rejected between 6 and 12 years of age were more likely than children whom they classified as aggressive/non-rejected to be rated as disruptive and antisocial by their teachers and peers, when assessments were made two years later. Similar findings were reported in Hymel et al. (1990), based on assessments made of 87 children when they were midway through their 8th and 11th years. Children who were unpopular with their peers at the time of the first assessment were rated by teachers as displaying more antisocial problems three years later, even when account was taken of first and second assessment aggression and first assessment popularity. Dodge et al. (2003) obtained equivalent results from a large sample of children whom they assessed annually for five years from the first years of schooling (see chapter 6 for details). Across the sample, aggression was found to predict subsequent rejection, but rejection itself predicted future disruptive behavior (including future aggression) with earlier aggression taken into account.

Nevertheless, despite the impressive consistency of the research summarized above, there are studies that do not find associations between rejection and social problems. A recent example is reported in Pedersen, Vitaro, Barker, and Borge (2007), based on data collected annually from a sample of French Canadian children ($N = 551$) whose average age was around 6 years at the start of the study and 13 years at the end. Ratings of "disruptiveness" obtained from mothers and teachers when the children were 6 and 7 years of age predicted self-reported delinquency six years later. Ratings of disruptiveness, which covered aggression, opposition, hyperactivity, lying, cheating, and stealing, also predicted peer rejection when the children were aged 8 to 9 years and 10 to 11 years. However, neither 8- to 9-year rejection nor 10- to 11-year rejection predicted subsequent delinquency. Pedersen et al. propose a number of reasons for their negative results, but one factor that stands out to me is the low frequency with which delinquency was reported across the sample as a whole. Response options on the scale that was used ranged from 1 (*never been involved in the behavior*) to 4 (*often been involved*). With a mean score of 1.48 (and a standard deviation of 0.08) a high proportion of the sample must have selected "never." Pedersen et al. use statistical techniques that correct to some extent for the skewed distribution, but the scope for statistical correction of genuinely non-differentiating data is limited. Later in the chapter, we shall examine other aspects of Pedersen et al.'s results, and find them helpful. However, in the specific context of rejection–delinquency relations, the results seem insufficient to challenge the message from other work that peer rejection is associated with social problems later in life.

Friendship and antisocial behavior

With a few exceptions, then, children classified as rejected in terms of peer status turn out to be relatively high risk for problematic social behavior when reassessed several years later. This is the case even when aggression is taken into consideration. However, children classified as rejected are also relatively likely to lack friends. Therefore even though peer rejection and lack of friends are not perfectly correlated (see chapter 5), relations might also be expected between problematic social behavior and small numbers of friends. Bagwell, Newcomb, and Bukowski (1998) detect such relations among a sample of 60 young adults (average age = 23 years). Self-reported "trouble with the law" was associated with being rejected by peers at around 11 years of age and with lacking in friends, with the strength of association proving roughly equivalent across the two factors. On the other hand, while the work of Gest et al. (2001) with 7- and 8-year-olds that was discussed in previous chapters indicates that rejection is related to antisocial behavior, it detects no parallel association for numbers of friends. Specifically, children who were frequently nominated as "liked least" (one component of rejection) were also reported as more frequently engaging in all seven of the disruptive behaviors that were assessed (e.g., loses temper easily, picks on others, shows off a lot, too bossy). There was virtually no relation between the frequency of these behaviors and the reported numbers of friends. Furthermore, Claes and Simard (1992) detected no differences between a delinquent sample and non-delinquent controls over reported numbers of friends and acquaintances, although the delinquents did report fewer close friends. Working with 100 German adolescents, who were followed for two years from midway through their 16th year, Bender and Lösel (1997) found no relation between antisocial tendencies at the end of the study and the number of "good friends" (or the possession of a single good friend) reported at the beginning.

In general then, friendlessness seems less consistently related to social problems than rejection, despite being related to rejection itself. One way of making sense of this is to suggest *two* forms of linkage between numbers of friends and antisocial behavior, but only one form of linkage involving rejection. Specifically, peer rejection is always a risk factor for subsequent problems, and on average rejected children have relatively few friends. However, some children who have reasonable numbers of friends (and are typically not rejected) are also at risk of social difficulties. Certainly, chapter 6 identified children who might fall into this group, namely children who, by 6 and 7 years of age, were forming Estell et al.'s (2002) aggressive clusters. As noted in chapter 6, some of these clusters comprise children who are interpersonally competent and aggressive, while the members of other clusters are aggressive and academically weak. Members of the second type of cluster were pinpointed by Estell et al. as being at particular risk of long-term problems, although this was not actually studied, and nor was the level of risk associated with membership of the first type of cluster.

Actually, independently of Estell et al.'s research, there are at least three reasons for anticipating links between membership of aggressive friendship groups and subsequent social problems, beyond the links already documented for rejection. First, as we saw earlier, Ollendick et al. (1992) found that controversial children are as likely as rejected children to experience conduct problems, substance abuse, and court offenses. Chapter 6 presented evidence that controversial children play central roles in aggressive friendships. Second, some antisocial behavior is known to occur in groups, a well-documented example being bullying. Characterized in chapter 6 as repeated aggression involving power asymmetries between perpetrators and victims, bullying seldom involves solitary perpetrators (Salmivalli, Kaukiainen, & Lagerspetz, 1998). Rather, it is a group phenomenon, with one or more children variously adopting the roles of bully, bully's assistant, and bully's reinforcer.

Third, as well as sometimes occurring in the company of friends, antisocial behavior is, in some circumstances, magnified in the presence of friends. Research into what, in social psychology, is termed "group polarization" (Myers & Lamm, 1976) indicates that when group members resemble each other over social characteristics, group interaction strengthens these characteristics. Once this is recognized, it becomes significant that aggression is one of the dimensions identified in chapter 5 along which friends tend to be similar. The implication is that, because the friends that aggressive children make are likely to be aggressive, aggressive children display even greater levels of aggression by virtue of having friends than would otherwise be the case. Bagwell and Coie's (2004) study provides support for this suggestion, through observations that were made when aggressive friends worked together on a puzzle, and their behavior was compared with non-aggressive friends who also worked jointly on the puzzle. The high levels of aggression between aggressive friends could only be partially explained through pre-existing tendencies. Even more telling support comes from a study by Coie et al. (1999), which involved African American children about 9 years of age. Based on the ratings of teachers and classroom peers, groups were formulated comprising two highly aggressive children and four classmates selected at random. Groups were recorded while they played with toys, and instances of aggression (both proactive and in response to the aggression of others) were coded. The aggressive children displayed about twice as much aggression toward each other as toward the non-aggressive children, and their displays of aggression went considerably beyond what would be predicted from their pre-existing tendencies.

Further evidence along the same lines comes from the work of Dishion and colleagues (e.g., Dishion, McCord, & Poulin, 1999), who found that antisocial youth taught each other delinquent acts, and reinforced their performance by laughter, encouragement, and so forth. Peer encouragement toward antisocial behavior is also a central theme in the research of Chen, Greenberger, Lester, Deng, and Guo (1998). Working with 591 teenagers from China, Taiwan, and the United States (including Chinese Americans), Chen et al. found that peer approval for antisocial behavior predicted self-reported misdemeanors in all cultures. However, the absolute levels of approval were highest in the United States (including for Chinese Americans), and the predictive relation was stronger. Finally, even though Bender and Lösel (1997) found no relation between numbers of friends and antisocial behavior in the longitudinal study summarized earlier, they did observe associations involving clique membership and clique size. All of the participants in Bender and Lösel's study were "high risk" due to difficult family backgrounds (e.g., parental conflict, divorce, poverty, drug/alcohol abuse, poor child-rearing). Nevertheless, while some participants displayed "deviant" tendencies at the start of the study, others appeared "resilient." Belonging to peer cliques (and, for girls, especially if the cliques were relatively large) resulted two years later in heightened antisocial behavior among the initially deviant participants, and reduced antisocial behavior among the initially resilient. All in all then, available research provides clear evidence for Hay et al.'s (2004) observation that "friendships amongst aggressive youth constitute an important, emotionally-charged arena for the further soci-alisation of aggression and other forms of criminal offending" (p. 98).

Mutual support or bad examples

The emphasis so far has been upon the support provided for antisocial behavior by friends who share antisocial tendencies, but as noted already media interest is typically in the promotion of antisocial behavior in children who are *not* that way inclined through exposure to their friends' "bad examples." Classic studies conducted by Sherif and colleagues (Sherif & Sherif, 1953; Sherif, Harvey, White, Hood, & Sherif, 1961; Sherif, White, & Harvey, 1955) could be interpreted as endorsing the media perspective. The studies involved 12-year-old boys attending summer camps in the United States. At each camp, the boys were divided into two groups of 11 or 12 children per group, division occurring in two studies after a short period without being divided and in a third study at the start of the camp. During the first phase after grouping, the two groups engaged in camp activities separately from each other, with friendships formed within and across the groups. During the second phase, the two groups were brought together to hold contests, for example tug-of-war, and complete a number of psychological tests disguised as games. Not only were there clear instances of within-group favoritism during this phase, for example judging own-group performance to be superior to other-group performance when both were in fact equivalent; there was also evidence of overt hostility and sometimes physical violence toward members of other groups. The tension was only defused when, during a third stage, group members were forced to cooperate toward a common goal. For instance, the researchers arranged for a truck bearing provisions to break down outside the camp, with the combined strength of both groups needed to move the truck so that it would start again.

Sherif and his colleagues placed great emphasis upon the "normality" of their samples of boys, and the absence of past histories of antisocial tendencies. Nevertheless, to the extent that the samples were representative of the 12-year-old population (as was also claimed), they would have contained individuals who were predisposed toward aggression, as well as individuals who were not predisposed. Therefore, insofar as all children were drawn into the second-phase violence (and there are hints that some children were not drawn in), this could mean that previously non-aggressive children followed the example of aggressive peers, thereby confirming media stereotypes of good children being led astray. However, even if non-aggressive children were coaxed into violence during the research, it needs to be remembered that Sherif and colleagues were working in contrived contexts, where relatively heterogeneous children "bonded" by virtue of camp activities and intergroup rivalries. As we have seen, homogeneity within friendships rather than heterogeneity is the norm in authentic settings, including over the key dimension of aggression. Therefore, when non-aggressive children interact with aggressive classmates in normal circumstances, the relationship will typically not get off the ground, or if it does progress, it will usually be short lived. From this perspective, the "group polarization" processes discussed

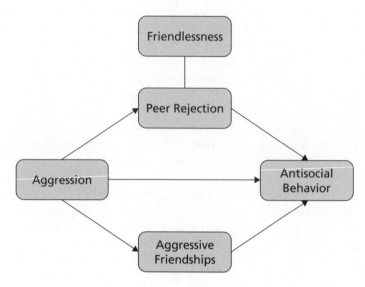

Figure 7.1   Peer groups and antisocial behavior.

above seem more relevant to children's actual friendships than the dynamics described by Sherif and colleagues and, for that matter, novels like *Lord of the Flies.*

In general then, two routes have been identified by which children's peer group experiences influence the probability of subsequent engagement in antisocial behavior. The routes are summarized in Figure 7.1, which highlights that one route involves peer rejection (which is associated with relatively small numbers of friends) and the other route involves friendships among aggressive children. In technical terms, both routes achieve "partial mediation" of a direct route from aggression to antisocial behavior. As we saw in chapter 6, aggression is a multifaceted concept, and its meaning is context dependent. This results in variations in the strength of the relation between aggression and peer rejection. However, this does not alter the basic pattern of influence, which I am suggesting is captured in Figure 7.1.

Peer Groups and Personal Adjustment

The high-profile nature of delinquency, criminality, bullying, and so on more or less guarantees that problematic social development will be heavily researched. In its most extreme form, problematic personal development encompasses mental illness and psychopathology, and although these issues too are addressed in movies, the press, and television reports, a modicum of social "embarrassment" surrounds them. This may be one reason why Deater-Deckard (2001) concludes that far less research has been conducted into the consequences of peer group experiences for problems of personal adjustment than into the consequences for antisocial behavior. Nevertheless, relevant research has been carried out, and it is reviewed below. In many respects, its message parallels what emerged in the previous section. In particular, peer status is robustly and, relatively speaking, straightforwardly associated with personal development, at least as regards the occurrence and absence of problems. Friendship patterns also make a contribution, but, as with antisocial behavior, in a complex fashion. However, in contrast to what emerged for antisocial behavior, the role of friendship in the sphere of personal adjustment appears to depend, in part, on the implications of status.

Status and internalizing difficulties

As with material discussed in the previous section, a landmark resource for research into the effects of peer group experiences on personal development is Parker and Asher's (1987) review. This is partly because of the thoroughness with which Parker and Asher surveyed preceding studies, but it is also because the focus of the review, which is adult psychopathology, shaped the direction of much subsequent research including the general emphasis upon developmental problems. Addressing adult psychopathology, Parker and Asher report 48 attempts to explore the association between peer group experiences and subsequent difficulties, again looking at behavioral style (aggression and withdrawal) as well as the "peer acceptance" variable that is more directly relevant here. Of the 21 analyses that address acceptance, 17 involved clinical or high-risk samples. Twelve were based on exclusively male samples, three were based on exclusively female samples, and six involved both sexes. Ten datasets were collected using a follow-back methodology, implying the difficulties from memory limitations that have been discussed already. Nevertheless, regardless of methodology, 16 of the 21 analyses provide evidence for an association between acceptance during childhood and adolescence and subsequent psychopathology. Specifically, individuals suffering from a range of disorders, which include neurosis, depression, psychosis, schizophrenia, and conduct disorder, were identified as experiencing relatively low levels of peer acceptance. Importantly, low acceptance was more consistently associated with psychopathology among the studies reviewed by Parker and Asher than were either aggression or withdrawal.

Subsequent investigations have by and large confirmed the conclusions that Parker and Asher drew in their 1987 paper, while addressing some of the methodological problems with the reviewed research. For instance, follow-forward rather than follow-back procedures have been employed in a significant number of recent studies. Moreover, although high-risk samples have continued to be included, the use of follow-forward approaches has resulted in reduced reliance upon clinical samples. Some studies have used samples that might be regarded as "representative of the population as a whole." Furthermore, with the shift away from clinical samples, the early emphasis upon psychopathology has broadened into a concern with "internalizing difficulties," while maintaining the "problem behavior" dimension. Internalizing difficulties include low self-esteem and high anxiety, as well as recognized clinical conditions. A good example of relevant research conducted post-Parker and Asher is the work of Hymel et al. (1990). As mentioned earlier, this work involved assessing 87 children on two occasions, first when the children were midway through their 8th year and again when they were about three years older. On both occasions, peers and teachers provided data from which measures of internalizing difficulties could be derived. Measures obtained on the first occasion strongly predicted measures obtained three years later, regardless of whether they were obtained from teachers or peers. In addition, measures of internalizing difficulties obtained on the second occasion were predicted by earlier assessments of peer popularity. Children who were relatively unpopular with their peers were more likely than children who were relatively popular to be assessed as having internalizing difficulties three years later.

Focusing on rejection per se rather than acceptance in general, DeRosier, Kupersmidt, and Patterson (1994) consider the implications within a sample of 622 children whom they assessed once per year across four consecutive years. Data collection began when the children were aged 7 to 9 years. Annual ratings from teachers provided information about internalizing problems. Rejected children were found to display more internalizing difficulties than non-rejected children, and the more stable the rejection (i.e., for one, two, or three years duration), the greater the problems. Working with a sample of 405 children who were assessed between the ages of 5 and 12 years, Kraatz Keiley, Bates, Dodge, and

Pettit (2000) examined the effects of rejection on internalizing problems, with race, socioeconomic level, and gender taken into account. They found that children categorized as rejected using classmate assessments displayed trajectories of mother-reported internalizing difficulties that began at higher levels than the trajectories for non-rejected children, and either remained stable or increased more rapidly over the assessment period. Internalizing symptoms in non-rejected children decreased over time. Finally, Coie, Lochman, Terry, and Hyman (1992) assessed internalizing symptoms among a subsample of a large African American cohort. Clinical interviews were held with 293 members of the cohort when they were aged 12 to 13 years, while 275 parents of cohort members described their children via the *Child Behavior Checklist* (Achenbach & Edelbrock, 1986). Results were related to aggressive tendencies and peer acceptance, as assessed from classmate ratings obtained three years earlier (and not known to either parents or children). The parents of children whose peer acceptance was low reported more internalizing symptoms in their children than the parents of children whose peer acceptance was high. Similar results were obtained from the children themselves, but only when peer-reported aggression was low. The incidence of internalizing symptoms was consistently high at 12 to 13 years of age, when the children had been identified as highly aggressive three years earlier.

Internalizing versus externalizing

In contemporary literature, the concept of internalizing difficulties is often contrasted with the notion of externalizing difficulties (Rubin & Coplan, 2004), with the latter typically used to cover some or all of the antisocial behaviors discussed in the previous section, for example delinquency, criminality, bullying, and disruptiveness. Since these behaviors are also associated with peer rejection, the implications are a very poor prognosis for children who fall into this status category, namely susceptibility to both internalizing and externalizing problems. Nevertheless, even if this is accepted, it does not necessarily mean that the same rejected children will experience both types of problem, and there are inconsistencies in the literature over this point. All of the studies summarized in the previous two paragraphs examined externalizing behaviors as well as internalizing, and without exception they confirm the associations between antisocial tendencies and rejection/low acceptance that were documented earlier. However, they vary considerably over the extent to which they find internalizing and externalizing problems to be correlated with each other, and therefore over the extent to which they indicate co-occurrence within individuals. For example, Coie et al. (1992) found correlations between their internalizing and externalizing measures that ranged from +.45 to +.79, with the higher correlations in the range obtained when boys were assessed rather than girls, and when parental reports were used rather than self-reports. DeRosier et al. (1994) obtained two measures of externalizing problems (one from classmates and one from teachers), and these were correlated +.17 and +.19 with teacher-assessed indices of internalizing difficulties. Although lower than the values obtained by Coie et al., these correlations remain statistically significant. However, Hymel et al. (1990) found a correlation of only +.02 between their measures of internalizing and externalizing difficulties, a value that, in its own right, would indicate no relationship.

The absence of perfect associations between internalizing and externalizing problems in the studies summarized above is scarcely surprising when, as we saw in the previous section, rejection is not the only peer group experience to be associated with antisocial behavior. Aggressive children sometimes become friends with other aggressive children, and by virtue of such friendships find their antisocial tendencies magnified. These children would not necessarily be categorized as rejected in terms of overall peer status. On the other hand, the fact that some studies find *no* relation between internalizing and externalizing problems suggests that even among rejected children, there are some who show only internalizing problems and some who show only externalizing problems. Recognizing this, many researchers have drawn upon the rejection subcategories discussed in chapter 6, in particular the distinction between rejected-withdrawn, rejected-aggressive, and rejected-aggressive-withdrawn. The broad hypothesis has been that internalizing difficulties are most likely when rejection is associated with withdrawal, while externalizing problems are most likely when the source of rejection includes aggression (Deater-Deckard, 2001). The implication is that only rejected-aggressive-withdrawn children typically experience both types of difficulty. Support for the hypothesis has been obtained in several studies, perhaps most notably in Hecht, Inderbitzen, and Bukowski's (1998) research with 1,687 children in the 10- to 17-year age range. Here, elevated depressive symptoms in rejected children were found to be associated with social withdrawal, while peer interaction difficulties in rejected children were found to be associated with high aggression.

Rejection and neglect

The fact that withdrawal seems to be implicated in the relation between peer rejection and internalizing difficulties raises questions about the personal adjustment of neglected children, for as noted in chapter 6, these children typically display moderate to high levels of social withdrawal. Based on a review of relevant literature, Gifford-Smith and Brownell (2003) assert that "neglected children are not at substantially heightened risk for negative developmental outcomes" (p. 246). Nevertheless, three studies, which are all easily missed since they do not emphasize neglect, suggest that matters may be less satisfactory. The first study is by Vandell and Hembree (1994) and examined the extent to which the peer status of 326 children aged 9 years (along with their friendship patterns) predicts their self-concepts and teacher plus parent ratings of their adjustment (along with their school performance). Thus, many relationships were analyzed in addition to the one between status and internalizing difficulties that is of present interest. Therefore the fact that neglected children were found to have relatively poor self-concepts easily escapes notice. The second study is the research of Sanson et al. (1998) with 10- to 11-year-old children that was described in chapter 5. Sanson et al.'s emphasis is upon discrepancies between ratings obtained from teachers, peers, and the children themselves. Yet despite the discrepancies, many sets of ratings point in broadly similar directions. One such set bears on how neglect and rejection relate to internalizing problems, and its overall message is relatively high levels of difficulty in neglected children as well as rejected.

The third study that, elliptically, addresses neglect is by Qualter and Munn (2002). Here, the study's relevance is eclipsed by the absence of standard status categories, the focus on loneliness rather than withdrawal, and a minor inconsistency over data interpretation. Nevertheless, the study *is* relevant. It involved 640 British children aged 4 to 8 years, who together with their teachers and classmates completed questionnaires covering many aspects of social and personal development. The children's social behavior was also observed. Associations within the data indicated that the children fell into four clusters, of which the largest (Cluster A, accounting for 59% of the sample) contained children who were generally accepted by their peers. Had standard categories been used, these children would almost certainly have been categorized as popular, controversial, or average. Two of the remaining clusters (both accounting for 9% of the sample) contained children who were liked by relatively few classmates and disliked by many, implying rejected status. The clusters were differentiated according to the levels of loneliness that the children reported, that is, low in Cluster B and high in Cluster C. Although loneliness is conceptually distinct from withdrawal, measures of the two constructs have emerged as strongly correlated across a wide range of studies (for a review see Rubin & Coplan, 2004), suggesting that Clusters B and C were also differentiated in terms of withdrawal. The children in Cluster B were identified from teacher ratings as demonstrating externalizing but not internalizing difficulties, suggesting that they may have been rejected-aggressive. The children in Cluster C were identified as demonstrating both forms of difficulty, indicating perhaps that they were rejected-aggressive-withdrawn. The final cluster (Cluster D, accounting for 23% of the sample) is the one that bears on neglect, for (using Qualter and Munn's data and not their partially inconsistent interpretation) its members were neither liked nor disliked by their peers, and therefore neglected in standard terms. Based on teachers' ratings, these children displayed internalizing but not externalizing problems.

Even though the evidence for internalizing difficulties in neglected children has to be treated with caution, the fact that evidence exists raises two questions. The first is whether status adds anything to withdrawal in predicting internalizing difficulties, when such difficulties may be common to both of the status categories that are associated with relatively high levels of withdrawal. This question is easily answered in the affirmative. Apart from Parker and Asher's (1987) original evidence indicating more consistent associations between low acceptance and psychopathology than between withdrawal and psychopathology, virtually all of the more recent studies summarized above explored the effects of status with levels of withdrawal taken into account. The second question is whether rejected-withdrawn status needs to be differentiated from neglected status in the specific context of predicting internalizing difficulties. This question is less easily answered, because much of the research considered so far addresses low acceptance in general, and this incorporates both rejection and neglect. Low acceptance was the focus of Parker and Asher's review, and also of Hymel et al. (1990) and Coie et al.'s (1992) follow-up studies. While other work (e.g., DeRosier et al., 1994; Kraatz Keiley et al., 2000) pinpoints rejected children specifically, this work does not also consider neglected children. Therefore, the scope of its findings remains unclear. It is only in the research of Hecht et al. (1998) that neglected children are both included and explicitly differentiated from rejected-withdrawn children (although Hecht et al. use a different label for the latter group). There were no significant differences between the two groups over depressive symptomatology.

More research is needed before we decide for certain that levels of internalizing difficulty are equivalent across the neglected and rejected-withdrawn groups. Nevertheless, even if we do eventually reach this conclusion, it does not necessarily follow that the status distinctions are irrelevant. For one thing, there may be differences between the status groups in the routes to difficulty. Certainly, research demonstrates differences in the ways that peers treat rejected and neglected children, specifically whether or not peers *victimize* these children, and there are several reasons for thinking that this is relevant to developing difficulties. In the first place, it is known that, of all the status categories, rejected children are most likely to be victimized by their peers (e.g., Boulton & Smith, 1994; Perry, Kusel, & Perry, 1988). This includes being bullied, as defined above. Moreover, being victimized is particularly characteristic of children who are rejected by virtue of withdrawal (Boivin, Hymel, & Hodges, 2001). Remembering the evidence presented in chapter 6 that withdrawal contributes strongly to the rejection of children with learning difficulties, this may explain why Nabuzoka and Smith (1993) found victimization reported for 33% of their sample with learning difficulties but only 8% of their mainstream sample.

However, peer victimization is not only associated with status; there is also extensive evidence of associations between peer victimization and internalizing difficulties. For instance, in a comprehensive review covering studies published between 1978 and 1997, Hawker and Boulton (2000) identify nine analyses showing associations between victimization and depression, 10 showing associations between victimization and anxiety, and 15 showing associations between victimization and low self-esteem. The analyses cover the full school age range (i.e., 6 to 18 years), and in most cases are based on large samples. Racist abuse is a specific form of victimization, and extending the research of Schmitt and Branscombe (2002), Heim et al. (2004) report strong relations between experiences of racism early in their study and high levels of anxiety and depression toward the end. It will be remembered from chapter 5 that Heim et al. conducted a four-year longitudinal study of adolescents and young adults, with a sample that included White participants and participants from a range of minority ethnic groups. Noret and Rivers (2007) report research into "cyber-bullying," that is, hurtful e-mail or text messages. Based on interviews with 11,227 British children aged 11 to 13 years, they indicate links between technology-mediated victimization and internalizing difficulties.

In any event, when peer victimization is associated with internalizing difficulties and rejected-withdrawn children are particularly likely to be victimized, it seems probable that victimization is part of the process through which rejected-withdrawn children develop difficulties. In other words, the development of internalizing difficulties in rejected-withdrawn children involves social processes in which classroom peers are actively (and viciously) involved. As their category label suggests, neglected children are more likely to be overlooked than singled out for victimization, suggesting that their pathway to internalizing difficulties is less social and (perhaps) more heavily dependent on introspection and negative self-appraisal. The social comparison processes that chapter 1 identified with Sullivan (1953) may be relevant. So returning to the key question of whether rejected children need to be differentiated from neglected children in the context of internalizing difficulties, it is possible that they should be because the *routes* to difficulties may differ between the two groups.

The protective status of friendship

So far, the emphasis has been upon peer status as a predictor of victimization and/or internalizing difficulties rather than friendship. On one level this seems justified, for the majority of studies have demonstrated a stronger role for status. For instance, Ladd, Kochenderfer, and Coleman (1997) followed 200 children for six months from midway through their 5th year, and found victimization to be more strongly associated with acceptance than with numbers of friends. This was despite the fact that the latter two variables were themselves closely related. In two studies with, respectively, 389 children followed from preschool to 8 or 9 years and 243 children followed from around 6 years to 9 years, Schwartz, Pettit, Dodge, Bates, and the Conduct Problems Prevention Research Group (2000) found stronger correlations between acceptance and later victimization (−.45 and −.40 from the two studies) than between numbers of friends and later victimization (−.25 and −.09). While Hanish, Ryan, Martin, and Fabes (2005) found that levels of victimization could be predicted from low acceptance *and* low numbers of friends in a sample of 4- to 7-year-olds ($N = 81$), assessments were made at one time point only. Therefore directions of causality and long-term implications are both unclear.

Yet, even if friendship plays a lesser role than status in determining susceptibility to victimization, Hodges, Boivin, Vitaro, and Bukowski

(1999) suggest that it can contribute in a different way, namely by ameliorating the consequences of victimization once this occurs. Using data from a one-year longitudinal study of 393 children aged between 10 and 11 years at the beginning, Hodges et al. found that even though internalizing (and externalizing) problems were strongly associated with victimization, the problems only increased over the duration of the study when victimized children lacked best friends. This may be why, in a study introduced in the previous section, Pedersen et al. (2007) found a direct relation between low numbers of friends at 10 to 11 years of age and depressive symptoms two years later. Symptoms were measured via an instrument known as the *Children's Depression Inventory* (Kovacs, 1992). On the other hand, the relation between peer rejection at 10 to 11 years and subsequent symptoms of depression was indirect, being mediated by numbers of friends. Also mentioned in the previous section was research by Bagwell et al. (1998), which related peer experience at 11 or 12 years of age to psychological adjustment in early adulthood. Like Petersen et al., Bagwell and colleagues found direct relations between being "chum-less" or "friend-ed" at 11 or 12 years and showing subsequent signs of depression. Again there were no direct relations involving peer status.

The suggestion that friendship ameliorates the problems caused by low status and/or victimization is consistent with what Hartup and Stevens (1997) identify as a pervasive tendency in the literature as a whole, namely an emphasis upon friendships as "protective factors or 'buffers' that mitigate the effects of stress and privation in everyday life" (pp. 359–360). The emphasis may stem from early (and dramatic) research with Holocaust children, which is described in Freud and Dann (1951). Here, preschool children who were imprisoned in concentration camps and whose parents had been gassed looked after each other and developed very strong bonds. Although hostile to adults in childhood, the children were found to be emotionally secure in adulthood, and capable of good interpersonal relationships. Freud and Dann regarded the early friendships as the primary explanation of why the children "survived" emotionally, despite extreme hardship. Moving to contemporary contexts, Dunn (2004) reviews a number of studies, including her own work with 10- to 16-year-olds, which suggest that children with friends cope better with parental separation and divorce. This is mainly because they talk their feelings through with their friends. Finally, in one of the few studies to examine friendship quality rather than mere numbers of friends, Gauze, Bukowski, Aquan-Assee, and Sippola (1996) indicate that quality more strongly predicts personal development when family relations are poor.

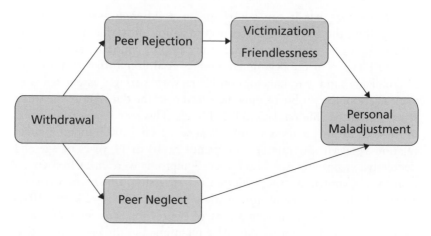

Figure 7.2 Peer groups and personal maladjustment.

Specifically, Gauze et al. followed a sample of 135 children for nine months from shortly before their 11th birthday, relating the manner in which nominated best friends were rated using the *Friendship Qualities Scale* (see chapter 5) to the children's own perceived competence and general self-worth. Relationships between scores on the Scale and perceived competence/self-worth were stronger when parental questionnaire responses suggested a troublesome family atmosphere than when family relations were reported as good.

Surveying the material presented in the section as a whole, it can be concluded that peer group experiences are relevant to the occurrence or avoidance of difficulties with personal adjustment. Moreover, experiences of status and friendship are both significant. However, while Figure 7.2 seems to be a reasonable summary of what available research shows, I should not be surprised to find some aspects (especially links in the middle of the diagram) requiring adjustment or supplementation as further data are obtained. Whatever the situation, Figure 7.2 is a model of difficulties, and by implication the avoidance of difficulties. It is not a model of psychological wellbeing, for the material presented in this section amply confirms the point raised in the introduction to the chapter. Research into personal adjustment focuses on problems. Yet, as noted in chapter 1, Sullivan (1953) wrote about peer group experiences as positive influences on self-worth. Many decades later, this perspective remains underexplored.

Summary and Conclusions

The chapter has surveyed literature that relates children's experiences of status and friendship to their social and personal development. As regards status, the literature provides compelling evidence for associations between peer rejection and both aspects of development. Specifically, children whose rejection is grounded in aggression are at heightened risk for problems of social adjustment. The probability of criminality, substance abuse, and conduct disorders (and so-called "externalizing" difficulties in general) is significantly increased when aggressive children are rejected by their peers. Children whose rejection is based on withdrawal are more likely than average to experience problematic personal development. The probability is increased of anxiety, depression, low self-esteem, and "internalizing" difficulties in general. As regards friendship, the literature shows that when aggressive children (often also of low academic ability) make friends with each other, they can push each other into more extreme forms of antisocial behavior. At the same time, friendship can protect children to some extent from the adverse consequences of peer victimization.

These conclusions, which are presented diagrammatically in Figures 7.1 and 7.2, seem reasonably compelling. They are grounded in a substantial body of research, which by and large provides a consistent message. Yet for all their persuasiveness, the conclusions signal a literature that is incomplete. The regrettable emphasis upon problematic development has been mentioned already. Considering that positive social and personal development is more than merely avoiding difficulties, work needs to be done here. In addition, the literature focuses on the relation between peer group experiences and social and personal development with aggression and withdrawal taken into account. What is lost is the fact that, as chapter 6 demonstrated, aggression and withdrawal are complex phenomena. Children differ in their propensities toward aggression and withdrawal, but their values and the values and practices of the formal settings that children move through influence how these characteristics are displayed and interpreted. This grounding of developmental consequences within an institutional framework is discussed in detail within chapter 9.

Chapter 8

School Performance Revisited

Introduction

In chapter 7, we saw how peer status and friendship influence the likelihood that children will experience long-term difficulties in the social and personal domains. Current evidence indicates a particularly poor prognosis for children who are rejected by their peers. Such children are at risk of developing antisocial tendencies if their rejection is grounded in aggression. At their most extreme, these tendencies include delinquency and criminality. When rejection stems from withdrawal (perhaps, but not necessarily, in tandem with aggression), there is a relatively high probability of difficulties at the personal level. At its most extreme, this includes recognized clinical disorders like depression. Chapter 7 presented evidence that neglected children may also experience difficulties with personal development, but suggested that the routes may differ from the ones that rejected children follow. Specifically, rejected children may be more at risk than neglected children of experiencing overt victimization. On the other hand, chapter 7 proposed that, no matter which route is followed, the probability of personal difficulties in rejected and neglected children is diminished when children have networks of friends. Thus, with personal adjustment, friendship seems to operate as a buffer against difficulties. Friendship is also relevant to social development, but as an occasional promoter of difficulties rather than as a buffer against these. In particular, chapter 7 showed that when aggressive children make friends with other aggressive children, they have a tendency to edge each other into antisocial behavior, even when none of these children is technically rejected.

Some of the processes that lead experiences of status and friendship to become associated with social and personal difficulties take place in schools. Children are ignored, ostracized, and victimized in classrooms and playgrounds, as well as in other contexts. Thus, these processes are occurring while children are engaged in the formal business of teaching and learning, which inevitably raises questions about their implications for educational outcomes. Is children's learning compromised when their peer status is low and/or when patterns of friendship prove problematic? If so, does this signify a relationship between peer influences on school performance and peer influences on social and personal adjustment? In chapter 7, we saw that despite their mutual linkage with rejection, social and personal difficulties (i.e., externalizing and internalizing problems) were not closely associated with each other. Some studies obtained modest positive correlations, while others obtained correlations that are close to zero. Therefore, it is entirely possible that status and friendship are associated with school performance in a fashion that mirrors what has been observed already, yet school performance is unrelated to social and personal adjustment. The present chapter addresses the issue by examining how and why problematic experiences of status and friendship relate to school dropout and other indices of academic failure, and what this signifies for the relationship between problems in the academic, social, and personal domains.

In starting with educational problems, the chapter is not only selecting the aspects of school performance that relate most obviously to the themes of chapter 7; it is also reflecting the traditional emphasis of relevant research. As with social and personal adjustment, the research focus has habitually been on school failure rather than school success. Paradoxically though, results obtained while examining failure suggest that peer group experiences are relevant not merely to whether children succumb to or avoid difficulties, but also to how much they positively achieve. Thus, as the chapter progresses, the perspective broadens to encompass achievement as well as difficulties. As this happens, it also becomes increasingly clear that the evidence does not point to peer group influences in isolation. Rather it highlights peer group influences as contextualized through the organization and activity practices that were discussed in chapters 2 and 3. Thus, the chapter concludes by coming full circle. In many cases, schools wish to marginalize the peer group realities of classrooms, and they adopt practices that seem on the surface to achieve this. These practices may even ensure that peers have little direct influence on educational outcomes. Nevertheless, because peer group realities are in fact real, they cannot simply be pushed aside. They resurface through the indirect relations that children have with their peers, sometimes in a benign fashion that supports the educational agenda, but sometimes in a fashion that from an educational perspective is troubling.

The key question is therefore whether the balance between benign and troubling consequences could be adjusted in a favorable direction through an alternative perspective upon the peer group nature of classrooms. This question is addressed in chapter 9.

Peer Groups and Educational Failure

Reviewing "a century of progress" in relevant research, Ladd (2005) comments that "not until the 1990s did researchers systematically explore the hypothesis that children's and adolescents' classroom peer relationships affect their school adjustment" (p. 244). However, Ladd himself reports research on the issue dating back to the 1950s, for instance Buswell's (1953) evidence that children who are accepted by their classmates are more successful academically than children who are rejected. Moreover, school adjustment was a major theme in the review article of Parker and Asher (1987) that played such a focal role in chapter 7, with 39 relevant datasets identified and analyzed. Thus, there was no shortage of research on school adjustment prior to the 1990s, implying that when Ladd made his comment, he was alluding not to a lack of data but rather to an absence of systematic procedures. Certainly, much of the work that Parker and Asher survey is open to criticisms that were mentioned in chapter 7, such as the use of outdated status categories, and follow-back rather than follow-forward designs. Most of the work conducted subsequently has addressed these difficulties. However, much of this work has also taken Parker and Asher's article as its starting point, which may be why failure in the educational system was, as noted, the initial focus. Paralleling their concern with criminality in the social sphere and psychopathology in the personal sphere, Parker and Asher were interested in adolescent dropout rates in relation to schooling. Even when dropout rates have been supplemented or replaced with alternative indices in later research, this negative orientation has often been perpetuated. Thus, as a prelude to a discussion of school performance in general, the present section begins by examining what is now known about dropout and other indices of failure.

Status and performance

It will be recalled from chapter 7 that the database for Parker and Asher's (1987) review was studies that explore the developmental consequences of aggression, withdrawal, and acceptance. From the present perspective, aggression and withdrawal are characteristics that influence how status and friendship are experienced, while acceptance is a broader precursor of status itself. Thus, when the concern is with the consequences of concepts like status, the key studies are the ones that examine acceptance. Ideally, the effects of aggression and withdrawal will have been factored out in these studies, but as we have seen this level of control was unusual in the mid-1980s. Within the 39 datasets that Parker and Asher identified on the theme of school dropout, 19 address acceptance. Sixteen of these datasets indicate significant *negative* relations between acceptance and dropout, such that the probability of dropout increases as peer acceptance decreases.

Some of the studies outlined in chapter 7 as follow-ups to Parker and Asher's work on social and personal development examined dropout (or the presumably related concept of absenteeism). Broadly speaking, their results concur with what Parker and Asher suggest. For example, with the 267 children whom they assessed at 10 and 15 years of age, Ollendick et al. (1992) examined how peer status predicts school dropout along with academic performance. The children classified as rejected at 10 years were more likely than the children classified as popular, controversial, average, and neglected to have dropped out five years later. Teachers assessed the rejected children and the controversial children to be performing academically below the popular, average, and neglected children. With the large sample ($N > 600$) that they followed for three years from the ages of 7 to 9 years, DeRosier et al. (1994) found that peer rejection predicted both absenteeism and academic performance. Children who were initially high on absenteeism and then experienced rejection showed higher levels of subsequent absenteeism than children who were initially high on absenteeism and not subject to rejection. Rejection was also negatively associated with academic performance, but since performance levels remained relatively stable across the study, the implication is that poor performance predicted rejection as well as being predicted by rejection.

Further studies of relevance that were also cited in chapter 7 in relation to social and/or personal development focus on school performance alone rather than performance in conjunction with dropout/absenteeism. An example here is the work of Coie et al. (1992), which used peer ratings to categorize the status of a large sample of children when they were 9 to 10 years of age. Habitual levels of aggression were also assessed. Three years later, teachers rated around 700 members of the original sample on an adjustment scale, which covered academic achievement, conduct, maturity, and peer social skills. It is unfortunate that social skills were included, for they are known to *contribute* to peer status (see chapter 6) and therefore their validity in measuring *consequences* of status is uncertain. Nevertheless, social skill scores only contributed weakly to the overall ratings of adjustment, while academic achievement contributed strongly. In any event, children classified as rejected obtained significantly lower scores on the adjustment scale than other children, and they were also more likely to have to repeat a grade. Being male and/or highly aggressive was also associated with poor adjustment, but the effects of rejection were independent of these two influences. Another study that has been discussed on several occasions already is the work of Bagwell et al. (1998) on the relation between peer group experiences in middle childhood and adult adjustment. Bagwell et al. found that peer rejection in childhood was strongly and negatively predictive of subsequent academic success and career aspirations.

Further research confirms and consolidates the general picture. For instance, in a study with more than 1,000 New Zealand children, Woodward and Fergusson (2000) found that relational problems at 9 years of age were associated with poor performance in public examinations at 16 and 18 years and (for those children who had left school) high unemployment at 18 years. This was with family social background, child IQ, and parent–child relations taken into account. Working with 399 children aged around 5½ years, Buhs and Ladd (2001) found that peer rejection, as assessed during the autumn through peer nomination, was associated with poor scores on school readiness tests, when these were administered during the following spring. All in all then, there is every reason to suppose that peer rejection has the negative implications for school performance that it has already been shown to possess for social and personal development. As far as I can tell, it does not matter whether the basis of rejection is aggression, withdrawal, or the two factors combined. Moreover, as can be seen from the six studies outlined here, a wide range of performance measures have been used in the research. These include academic attainment, career aspirations, and attitudes to study, as well as the dropout rates that Parker and Asher pioneered.

Status and friendship

While research relating to status essentially underlines the troubling implications of peer rejection, research relating to friendship indicates that the consequences for school performance may be slightly different from those detected with social and personal development. Specifically, lack of friends seems to be directly (and negatively) related to school performance in a fashion that was not observed in the social and personal domains. An illustration is Ladd's (1990) work with 125 children as they moved through their first year of formal schooling. Ladd found that when the children did not have preschool friends in their school class and/or did not quickly make new friends, they obtained relatively low attainment test scores later in the year and/or displayed more negative attitudes to school. Likewise, Wentzel, Barry, and Caldwell (2004) followed a sample of 242 children for two years from about 12 years of age. They asked the children to nominate their friends, and focused on reciprocal nominations. Children without reciprocated friendships at the start of the study obtained lower scores on an academic attainment test when this was administered two years later (and with test scores at the start of the study taken into account). In research with an Indonesian sample aged 8 to 11 years (detailed in chapter 6), French et al. (2003) found that children without friends achieved lower academic grades than their counterparts with friends. Importantly, this linkage was sustained when social preference scores were taken into account. Since social preference scores are used to categorize children as rejected, this indicates that the effects of friendship may be independent of the effects of status. It could even mean that the apparent effects of status are actually effects of friendship.

At present, there is very little research that takes results like French et al.'s as its starting point, and attempts to tease out the relative contributions of friendship and status. A pioneering exception is, however, the work of Vandell and Hembree (1994) that was referred to in chapter 7. Vandell and Hembree established friendship patterns and peer status within a sample of 9-year-olds, and unsurprisingly found the two constructs to be highly correlated. Nevertheless, friendship and status could still be shown to operate as independent predictors of academic adjustment (as measured by IQ, achievement tests, grades, and ratings for work habits). Children without friends and/or of low peer status performed relatively poorly. Similar results are reported in Ladd et al. (1997), although their data suggest that friendship is actually a stronger predictor of academic progress than status. On the other hand, status was the only unique predictor of school satisfaction over a one-year period.

Longitudinal research described in Wentzel and Caldwell (1997) looks not only at status and friendship (which was construed as exclusively dyadic), but also at membership of larger groups within which dyadic friendships are embedded. Two studies are reported, both beginning when the participants were 12 years of age. One study involved 213 children who were followed for two years, and the other involved 404 children who were followed for three years. In both studies, the focus was on the degree to which friendships, peer acceptance, and group membership at the start of the study predicted academic achievement at the end. With academic achievement at the start taken into account, group membership proved to be the most consistent predictor. Low levels of group membership were associated with low academic achievement. The other two variables were found to have effects independently of group membership and of each other, but the strength of the effects varied across studies and (within study) with participant gender. At first sight, the differences between dyadic friendships and larger groups seem to challenge the policy adopted throughout the present book of not differentiating between dyads and other peer groups. However, there is an alternative possibility, namely that membership of large groups is a proxy for having relatively large numbers of friends. In other words, the "dyadic" and "large group" variables were actually tapping a single dimension equivalent to numbers of friends. Whatever the case, Wentzel and Caldwell's results confirm the main point, that friendship and related constructs predict academic performance independently of status.

Final endorsement of the point can be obtained from the work of Véronneau, Vitaro, Brendgen, and Tremblay (2007). Here, 437 French Canadian children were assessed annually between the ages of 7 and 13 years. Measures were taken of: (a) peer status, assessed via the difference between the number of like-most and like-least nominations from peers; (b) number of reciprocated friends, assessed via mutual nominations as a best friend; and (c) academic achievement, assessed via teacher ratings from 1 (*failure*) to 5 (*excellent*). The results show that peer status and reciprocated friendship independently predicted subsequent academic achievement. For instance, status and friendship when the children were around 8 years of age predicted school performance one year later. The higher the children's status and the more friends they possessed, the better they performed. Interestingly, there were also signs of the converse relationship: academic achievement around 7 years of age and again at around 9 years predicted status and friendship at around, respectively, 8 and 10 years. Children who performed well achieved higher status and made more friends. This aspect of Véronneau et al.'s results will be considered below. For now, the key point is the continuing evidence that friendship is as relevant as status to subsequent academic outcomes. In other words, lacking friends compounds the effects of peer rejection as regards school performance, just as peer rejection compounds the effects of lacking friends. This is despite the close intercorrelation between the two factors.

Diverse Consequences of Friendship

So far, the emphasis has been upon lacking friends. Once we shift focus to possessing friends, the situation becomes more complicated. Building upon chapter 5's evidence that members of friendship groups resemble each other over behavioral and intellectual characteristics, chapter 6 highlighted considerable variation between groups over the characteristics that they typically display. Some friendships comprise members who are highly sociable, above average scholastically, and inclined to relatively low levels of aggression. In other friendship groups, the levels of aggression are relatively high, and school performance is typically below average. Chapter 7 outlined how group polarization theory predicts that membership of the latter type of group will magnify aggressive tendencies beyond what would be anticipated from individual predispositions. Evidence was presented to support the prediction: when aggressive children hang around with other aggressive children, they become more susceptible to long-term difficulties in social behavior. However, if group polarization processes apply with aggression, they ought also to apply with academic achievement. In other words, it can be predicted that children whose academic performance is relatively strong will gain academically from association with similarly performing friends. Children whose academic performance is relatively weak will be handicapped further by virtue of their friendships. The present section begins with research that tests these predictions. It then moves, with reference to this research, to a more comprehensive picture of how status and friendship contribute to academic achievement, and ultimately to a sense of how development in the academic sphere relates to social and personal growth.

Friends and academic polarization

One piece of work used in chapter 5 to establish within-friendship similarities over academic performance was the research of Altermatt and Pomerantz (2003). This work was conducted with 929 children in the 9- to 11-year age range. It will be recalled that data were collected on three occasions six months apart, and on each occasion performance levels within pairs of friends were positively correlated. What was not mentioned in chapter 5 is that Altermatt and Pomerantz also detected strong *predictive* relations across time when school performance was similar. Moreover, this was not just with their measures of performance, but also with their indices of scholastic motivation. In other words, the progress made over time was greater in initially high-achieving dyads than in initially low-achieving dyads, implying increasing differentiation. Interestingly, the more stable the friendship, the stronger the predictive relationship.

Such results can be interpreted as reflecting the normal situation, since more often than not friends are in fact similar as regards school performance. However, Altermatt and Pomerantz detected a small number of dissimilar friendships, and in a subsequent article (Altermatt & Pomerantz, 2005) reported on their developmental profiles. They found that the relatively low-achieving children in these asymmetric groups progressed most academically, but their sense of personal worth suffered. In other words, at the end of the study, low-achieving children with high-achieving friends displayed poorer self-esteem, had a lower sense of personal competence, and explained events in a more self-deprecating manner than they did at the start. Reading these results, I cannot help wondering whether these dissimilar friendships overlapped with popular cliques as described in chapter 5. Certainly, members of popular cliques have been shown to differ in academic prowess, and as chapter 6 explained, there is evidence for within-clique derision that would threaten the self-esteem of those on the receiving end. Whatever the case, it is important not to infer too much here, since dissimilarity between friends is atypical. The crucial finding in the present context is Altermatt and Pomerantz's evidence for polarizing effects over performance and motivation when friends are similar.

Focusing on motivation specifically, Kindermann (1993) obtained parallel results in a study with 109 children who were aged around 10 to 11 years. Motivation was assessed via teacher nomination of "engagement" versus "disaffection." Friendship groupings were identified by asking the children who "hangs about together," and compiling social cognitive maps (see chapter 5). Motivation levels within friendship groupings were positively correlated throughout the eight months of the study. This was despite the fact that group membership changed by as much as 50% during that period. Most importantly, motivation levels across friendship groupings at the start of the study strongly predicted individual motivation levels at its conclusion. The children who belonged to motivated groups became even more motivated over time, and the children whose groups were initially demotivated increasingly lost interest.

Subsequently, Sage and Kindermann (1999) have made proposals about the mechanisms through which these effects are achieved. Classroom observations were made of 28 children to determine the incidence of on- versus off-task behavior and partner approval versus disapproval of this behavior. Highly motivated children were most likely to receive peer approval for on-task behavior from other members of their friendship group. Poorly motivated children were most likely to receive peer disapproval after off-task behavior from non-members of their groups. Assuming that group members matter more to children than non-members, the implication is that highly motivated children receive encouragement to study from valued peers, while poorly motivated children do not receive criticism for failure to study from such peers. Criticism comes from outsiders whose opinions are, presumably, of little consequence. This said, Sage and Kindermann's results require replication, for other interpretations are possible, and in any event the study uses a very small sample.

One implication from Sage and Kindermann's observations around on-task behavior is that highly motivated children are more likely than other children to discuss schoolwork with their friends—in which case, it is relatively easy to see why Altermatt and Pomerantz (2003) found that performance and motivation went hand in hand, with both polarizing over time as a function of friendship. In particular, there is growing evidence that when children discuss academic material with their friends, their interaction is more productive than when they discuss this material with other children. Newcomb and Bagwell (1995) drew attention to some of this evidence in the review article discussed in chapter 6. It stems primarily from research in the Piagetian tradition, as summarized in chapter 4. Indeed, it typically deploys the concept of "transactive dialogue" as outlined in that chapter. One example is Azmitia and Montgomery's (1993) work with 11-year-olds ($N = 72$) solving science problems (e.g., which of leaf lotion, type of soil, amount of water, etc. cause a plant to die when some factors co-vary with outcome and some do not co-vary). Here, children who worked on the task with a friend produced more transactive dialogue than children who worked with a classroom acquaintance, and learned more from the experience (as revealed in change from individual pre-tests prior to the task to individual post-tests after their completion). Also relevant is Miell and MacDonald's (2000) study where 40 children aged 11 to 12 years engaged in musical composition. Here both dialogic sequences and collaborative sequences of music were more transactive between friends than between acquaintances. Transactive interaction predicted the superior compositions that pairs of friends were found to produce.

On the face of it, results reported in Kutnick and Kington (2005) seem more qualified. These results are based on observations of 18 pairs of same-sex friends, who were aged 5, 8, or 10 years, solving science problems. Comparisons were made with the performance of 18 pairs of same-sex acquaintances of equivalent age. For girls, the pairs of friends were more successful than the pairs of acquaintances, but for boys the reverse applied. On the other hand, Kutnick and Kington's sample was younger than Azmitia and Montgomery's and Miell and MacDonald's. Therefore it is possible that at the age levels that Kutnick and Kington worked with transactive dialogue was not routinely available in problem solving. It was more accessible to girls than boys given their proverbially superior linguistic skills, and within girls it was more accessible to friends than non-friends. Certainly, Hartup et al. (1993) found that, with a sample of 9- to 10-year olds playing a board game, girls operating with friends produced significantly more assertions with rationales than girls with non-friends, boys with friends, or boys with non-friends. The concept of "assertions with rationales" is conceptually related to transactive dialogue. In any event, with the possible exception of young boys, friendship does appear to draw out academically productive dialogue. Thus, returning to the main point, if we assume that academically motivated children are more likely than their demotivated counterparts to discuss schoolwork with their friends, we can perhaps also assume that these discussions will prove beneficial. The relevant discussions may take place during lessons, or they may take place afterwards (face to face, over the phone, or via e-mail). Nevertheless, they could provide the mechanism, which links the motivational polarization that Kindermann (1993) and Altermatt and Pomerantz (2003) both describe with the performance polarization that is Altermatt and Pomerantz's primary focus.

Actually, evidence already exists that children do vary in the extent to which they discuss schoolwork with friends, and that the children who engage in such discussions are academically able. On the first point, Galton, Gray, and Ruddock (2003, pp. 79–80) find some children making interview comments like "When I'm stuck, my best friend helps me and when he's stuck I help him" and "If you work with a friend you are getting more ideas and comfort while you're doing it." They find other children saying things like "If you don't know many people in your class I think you will get on more because there will be nothing else to do. If you are with your friends, you may have a little laugh and you won't get much done" and "Victor is one of my friends but he sometimes gets on my nerves. When we're working, he puts me off colouring." As regards evidence that children who make the first kind of comment are relatively able, Azmitia and Cooper's (2001) work with 11- and 12-year-olds in California demonstrates: (a) variation across children over whether they regard friends as learning resources or obstacles; (b) associations between regarding friends as resources and soliciting help from friends with schoolwork; and (c) associations between regarding friends as resources and being scholastically able (as indicated through grades in mathematics and English). In other words, scholastically able children were more likely than other children to discuss schoolwork with friends, and therefore obtain the benefits that such discussions imply.

All in all then, research focusing on the friendship groups that children belong to indicates that the consequences of peer group experiences for intellectual development are much broader than those suggested in the chapter's opening section. It is probably true that peer rejection and lack of friends increase the probability of academic failure, with the two factors most likely operating independently and additively as indicated in Figure 8.1, despite their mutual association. However, it seems equally probable that the possession of friends can influence outcomes, with membership of homogeneously low-achieving groups acting as an additional risk factor. Thus, a second pathway is indicated in Figure 8.1, epitomized perhaps through a further comment from one of Galton et al.'s (2003) interviewees: "If you fall into a bad group of friends then . . . I know one group; their kind of mission is not to do well, to mess around, to get told off" (p. 87). Figure 8.1 illustrates the problematic side of school performance, partly because this was the initial research focus, and partly to facilitate comparisons with Figures 7.1 and 7.2 in the previous chapter, which represent problems in the social and personal

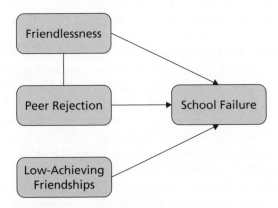

Figure 8.1 Peer groups and school failure.

domains. Nevertheless, the emphasis of the immediately preceding paragraphs has been upon school success as much as failure. In particular,
friendship has emerged as a positive influence on performance when groups
are homogeneously above average, most likely because of the academically relevant discussions that group members hold. This introduction
of a positive perspective does not, as yet, have parallels in the social and
personal domains. In the academic domain, the (welcome) breadth
could be due in part to the supplementation of the original dropout/
absenteeism measures with performance measures. After all, the opposite of dropout is the relatively neutral concept of continuation, and the
opposite of absenteeism is the equally neutral concept of attendance.
However, the opposite of low achievement is high achievement, implying
a bipolar continuum with a neutral point in the middle.

Toward an integrated perspective

Once comparisons are made between Figure 8.1 and the two figures in
the previous chapter, it becomes possible to formulate hypotheses about
the relation between school performance and social and personal development. Specifically, it would be very surprising if there were no overlap,
when peer rejection has emerged as a risk factor across all three aspects
of development. Indeed, the risk as regards school failure seems to apply
regardless of whether rejection is grounded in aggression, withdrawal,
or both. Thus, even though the forms of rejection implicated in social
and personal development appear to vary, both ought to be linkable
with school performance. On the other hand, it would also be surprising
if the overlap were substantial, given the subtle differences in the roles
played by friendship across the three domains. Friendlessness is implicated negatively in social, personal, and intellectual development, but in
a different fashion in each domain. Low-achieving friendships are often
also aggressive (see chapter 6) and therefore at risk of social difficulties
as well as academic. However, the overlap is not exact. Overall then,
the pointers are toward positive but imperfect associations between school
performance and social and personal development, and this is precisely
what available research suggests: difficulties in the academic sphere are
related to, but not co-extensive with, problems elsewhere.

For instance, the correlations that Coie et al. (1992) obtained between
teacher-completed adjustment scores (which, as noted above, relate primarily to academic adjustment) and parental assessments of internalizing
and externalizing behaviors (reported in chapter 7) were all statistically

significant and indicative of poor adjustment being associated with social and personal difficulties. Correlations between adjustment scores and child assessments of internalizing and externalizing difficulties pointed in the same direction, but were not always statistically significant. Addressing academic performance and self-concept only (i.e., not social or antisocial behavior), Vandell and Hembree (1994) obtained correlations between the two domains that ranged between +.09 and +.57, depending on the measures used. In other words, all correlations were positive but their magnitude varied. Buhs and Ladd (2001) included two measures of what they term "emotional attitudinal adjustment," and these measures could be construed as addressing the personal dimension of development (although there is a "scholastic" flavor to some items, which makes them less than ideal in the present context). Low scores on the two academic achievement scales were associated with high scores for emotional attitudinal problems (correlations −.13 to −.28, all statistically significant).

Assuming that scholastic performance is, broadly speaking, associated with other aspects of development, a further issue relates to *how* they are associated, and specifically how peer group experiences are implicated. For instance, are school failure, social difficulties, and personal difficulties all *independent* consequences of rejection and/or problematic friendship patterns, or are they interconnected? Independence is certainly indicated in the results reported by Buhs and Ladd (2001), for here academic achievement and emotional attitudinal adjustment do not appear to be directly associated—rather their association looks to be an indirect consequence of their mutual relation with rejection. Similarly, while Wentzel et al. (2004) found interrelations between personal difficulties (described as "distress") and poor school performance when their sample was 12 years of age, personal difficulties did not appear to be implicated in performance changes between 12 and 14 years. Nevertheless, it needs to be remembered that Buhs and Ladd's sample were very young, and therefore the patterns of association in this study (at least) may not have been stable. Moreover, the analytic procedures used in the studies may not have discriminated between independent consequences of problematic experiences and complex chains of direct and indirect relationships.

One scenario in which complex chains would be flagged places school failure as a *cause* of rejection and problematic friendships in addition to being a *consequence*, given that rejection and problematic friendships are known to underpin social and personal problems. After all, in these circumstances, a chain of dependencies would exist that moved from school failure through rejection and friendship problems (and back again) to difficulties at the social and personal level. Strangely, two studies that have been discussed already indicate that this chain may be precisely what happens. One study is the work of DeRosier et al. (1994), which, as noted, suggests that rejection may be an effect of poor academic performance as well as one of its causes. The other study is the one reported in Véronneau et al. (2007), which demonstrated that academic achievement around 7 and 9 years of age predicts status and friendship one year later, while also being predicted by status and friendship. Even more recently, Chen, Liu, Chang, and He (2008) have reported results relating to academic similarities within friendship groups, which provide further support. Specifically, Chen et al. show how academic similarities at one point in time predict social adjustment and social acceptance at a later point, but not vice versa. When social acceptance is closely related to peer status (including rejection) and academic achievement is influenced by status, the cause–consequence relationship becomes transparent.

In detail, Chen et al.'s work was conducted in Shanghai, China, and involved 265 children who were assessed initially when they were aged around $9\frac{1}{2}$ years or $12\frac{1}{2}$ years, and again two years later. Academic achievement in Chinese, English, and mathematics was recorded, and friendship groups were ascertained using social cognitive maps. A total of 117 groups were identified, typically involving around four or five members. Once more, group members were relatively similar as regards academic achievement. At the same time, Chen et al. indexed "social competence" through teacher and peer ratings of sociability/leadership and peer-nominated liking. They determined "social problems" from teacher and peer ratings of aggression/disruptiveness and peer-nominated disliking. Thus, the social competence and social problems measures encompassed liking and disliking, which are the criteria against which peer status is traditionally assessed. They also encompassed sociability/ leadership and aggression/disruptiveness, which are the criteria upon which status and friendship are traditionally thought to depend (see chapter 6). What Chen et al. found is that, with the groups whose academic achievement was relatively high at the start of the study, the most highly achieving members gained more two years later in terms of social competence than the less highly achieving members. In other words, the brightest children in bright groups made the most social progress. Chen et al. believe that the self-esteem of such children is boosted through seeing themselves contribute disproportionately to their groups' academic goals. On the other hand, when academic achievement across the group was initially relatively low, the least able members of those groups were most likely to develop social problems over the next two years. In other words, the least able members of poorly performing groups suffered most.

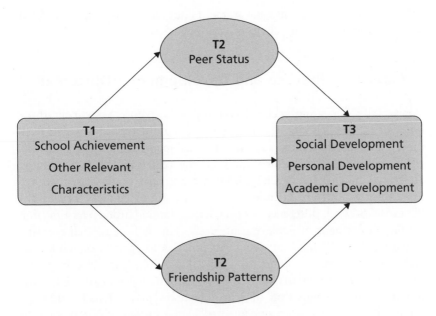

Figure 8.2   Peer groups and children's development.

The general message from Chen et al.'s work is that a child's scholastic ability, mediated by the academically similar children that they
normally hang out with, influences how they are positioned in relation
to characteristics that are directly relevant to status. As we know, peer
status is, at the same time, an influence on scholastic performance. Taken
with the related message from DeRosier et al. (1994) and Véronneau et
al. (2007), the implication is relationships along the lines illustrated in
Figure 8.2. Figure 8.2 is a highly schematic presentation of influences
across two time periods, namely between Time 1 (T1) and Time 2 (T2),
and between Time 2 and Time 3 (T3). It also acknowledges a direct line
between T1 and T3, but this is less important in the present context.
Peer status and friendship patterns at T2 are subject to influences from
school achievement levels at T1, along with a host of other relevant
characteristics (including sociability, aggression, and withdrawal as discussed in chapter 6). Peer status and friendship patterns at T2 affect school
achievement levels at T3, together with social and personal adjustment.
The manner in which influence is achieved varies between the academic,
social, and personal domains as already represented in Figures 7.1, 7.2,
and 8.1. Since school achievement at T3 becomes school achievement

at T1 across a subsequent time frame, Figure 8.2 should be interpreted as a constantly recycling chain of contingencies.

Classroom Practice and Developmental Outcomes

Viewed as a repeating cycle of contingencies, Figure 8.2 carries three noteworthy implications. First, disparities should typically widen over time. This is because membership of friendship groups is associated with polarization processes, which apply (at the very least) to aggression as illustrated in chapter 7 and school achievement as discussed above. Friendship groups are included at T2 in the figure, under "Friendship Patterns." Second, differences in peer status should harden over time due to the involvement of achievement levels. This is because achievement disparities (at T3) should widen under polarization pressures, while also acting as influences on status (at a subsequent T1). Chapter 6 provided evidence that peer status does in fact harden, without at that stage offering a full explanation of why this takes place. Finally, through summarizing the relations documented in the present chapter between peer group experiences and school achievement, Figure 8.2 highlights what must be regarded as a major paradox of contemporary educational practice. Despite the best efforts of schools to marginalize the peer group realities of classrooms (as detailed in chapters 2 and 3), these realities exert a significant influence on what teachers are attempting to achieve. This paradox provides the starting place for the present, concluding section, for the section discusses the relation between marginalization and developmental outcomes. To what extent does marginalization *influence* the manner in which peer group experiences have their impact, and to what extent are the two factors separate?

A degree of interconnection has already been signaled in the associations made between the modes of classroom interaction that were described in chapter 3 and the crucially important constructs of status and friendship. Chapter 3 showed how the performance mode is predominant in classrooms, and interpreted this as a strategy for downplaying peer group diversity in what are widely regarded as the interests of teaching. Chapter 3 also documented stable individual differences in the roles that children play within the performance mode, and as chapter 4 explained, all relevant social psychological theories would expect these differences to influence the personality characteristics attributed to the children. Chapter 6 then demonstrated that attributed characteristics, specifically sociability, aggression, and withdrawal, make a critical contribution to differential experiences of status and friendship. It also pointed out that the performance mode suppresses opportunities for sociability while necessitating varying degrees of withdrawal and influencing how aggression is interpreted. Thus, the performance mode, which is a consequence of attempts to minimize the peer dimension of classrooms, influences the behavioral characteristics that children attribute to peers. These characteristics play a crucial role in creating differential experiences of status and friendship.

There is, moreover, a second reason for implicating classroom customs in developmental outcomes. This relates to the homogenizing of ability within teaching groups, which chapter 2 presented as a further strategy for minimizing peer group realities. As chapter 2 explained, children are regrouped into ability-based classes for certain subjects. Moreover, when teachers divide their classes into smaller subgroups, they frequently make the division on the basis of ability. Thus, as discussed in chapter 5, the pool from which children naturally select their friends is constrained along ability grounds. No doubt this is one important reason for the ability homogeneity that occurs within friendship groups, and therefore for the low-ability friendships that are also highly aggressive. Homogeneity is a precondition for the polarizing effects that have been discussed already. As noted, the mechanisms by which members of relatively high-ability groups support each other's academic success may include beneficial, transactive dialogues about schoolwork. So the polarizing potential of friendship groups, with all this implies for children's social and intellectual development, can be traced directly to the use of homogeneous-ability teaching groups. The use of such groups can be traced in turn to an attitude toward classroom organization that regards peer groups as marginal.

I do not wish to overstate the connections that I am currently making. Children's propensities toward sociability, aggression, and withdrawal are not wholly (or even mainly) "constructed" in classrooms. As noted in chapter 6, they are deep rooted, and probably have biological origins (Rothbart & Bates, 1998). Nevertheless, because the connections are defensible, they need to be considered when drawing implications for practice. Certainly, practical implications are required. While research traditions have been criticized on several occasions already for emphasizing problematic aspects of development, the fact that problems have been exposed means that intervention is needed. Bearing the connections in mind, chapter 9 focuses on the practical dimension.

Chapter 9

Implications for Practice and Future Research

Summary and Introduction

This book has been concerned with children's experiences of peer groups, and the implications of those experiences for their social, personal, and intellectual development. It has focused on school-age children in societies where schooling is mandatory for all children in the relevant age group. In principle, children from any such society have been of interest, although in practice most of the relevant research has been conducted in the so-called "English-speaking world," that is, countries where English is the majority first language. Nevertheless, studies have been reported that were carried out in China, Denmark, France, Germany, Greece, India, Indonesia, Israel, Italy, Japan, Kenya, Liberia, Mexico, the Netherlands, New Guinea, Nigeria, the Philippines, Russia, South Africa, and Switzerland. Using this rich array of material, a detailed picture has been painted of the peer groups that children experience when they are actually based in schools, and therefore the message about developmental implications is largely drawn from what happens in school. This is not because alternative out-of-school peer groups have been regarded as irrelevant. On the contrary, it has been recognized from the outset that many school-age children engage in formal out-of-school activities, like sports associations, youth movements, and extracurricular classes. Moreover, many of these children meet peers in their homes and neighborhoods, and these meetings are potential sources of informal relationships. Unfortunately, there is very little relevant research at present on out-of-school peer groups, and for that reason only the book has been obliged to focus on schools.

Within the school context, the picture of peer groups has been multilayered. First and foremost, there is the classroom, which, as far as possible, is organized to consist of peers. In relatively affluent countries, the current practice is to arrange classrooms so that 20+ children of roughly similar age are brought together for instruction. However, while classes are peer groups, there is seldom any recognition of this fact within the educational activities that actually take place. When teaching is directed at the whole class, contributions from children normally come in the form of the responses that selected individuals make to teachers' initiations. The remainder of the class operates as the audience for the chosen child's performance, including the feedback that he (sometimes, she) receives on the adequacy of their contribution. In some classrooms, this whole-class activity takes place while children are seated in smaller subgroups, and occasionally these subgroups are given tasks that they are expected to work on separately from the rest of the class. Sometimes, subgroups are reconfigured for purposes of these tasks, and when this happens the new arrangements are typically homogeneous with respect to ability. Frequently, the tasks assigned to subgroups turn out to involve independent study, with teachers intervening from time to time using discourse forms that precisely mirror the whole-class arrangements. On rare occasions, the tasks require joint activity among children, and the style of interaction shifts from the predominant "performance mode" to an alternative "cooperative mode."

In general then, the message has been of peers being marginalized from classroom teaching and learning. Nevertheless, even with this message accepted, it would be a mistake to infer that children are insensitive to their peers within classroom contexts. On the contrary, children make social judgments about these peers, partly on the basis of what they witness during lessons. These judgments provide the foundations for informal experiences of peers within the formal structure of schooling, specifically for the status that children acquire across the whole class and the friendships that they form with a subset of classmates. Status differentials are normally characterized in terms of the distinctions between being popular, controversial, rejected, neglected, or average, with all distinctions based on patterns of liking and disliking. Friendships are typically formed among children who like each other and who are similar across a range of demographic, cognitive, and behavioral characteristics. However, within some friendships there are asymmetries of power, and admiration plays as great a role as liking. Within such friendships too, there is variation in demographic, cognitive, and behavioral characteristics, as well as similarity. The attitudes that underpin informal peer group experiences are heavily dependent on how children are regarded by their peers in terms of sociability, aggression and withdrawal. In other words, there is a (perceived) personality dimension to informal experiences. Nevertheless, while personality is important, the organizational and activity structures of classrooms also play a critical role. They affect how children are differentiated in terms of sociability, aggression, and withdrawal. They influence how these characteristics are valued, and therefore how they translate into status and friendship. The formal subgroups that children are assigned to for educational purposes bear upon the nature of their informal arrangements, for instance ability homogeneity within teaching subgroups contributes to ability homogeneity within friendships.

So classrooms are constellations of formal and informal associations between peers, some of these associations operating at the whole-class level and some at the subgroup level. Experiences of peers at the formal level have been shown to have little direct impact on children's development, not even upon the educational outcomes that are central at this level. Working cooperatively with peers (i.e., adopting the cooperative mode) is generally beneficial for academic achievement, but cooperative activity is rare in classrooms. It currently has the status of untapped potential. On the other hand, experiences at the informal level have proved to be of the greatest significance, including for school performance. Peer status affects the likelihood of a wide range of long-term difficulties, covering the social, personal, and intellectual domains. In particular, the prognosis for children who are rejected by their peers (i.e., liked by few, and disliked by many) is very poor. The prognosis is also poor for children who, by virtue of their high levels of aggression and/or low levels of scholastic ability, make friends with children of similarly high aggression and/or low ability. At the same time, children who have high-achieving friends are helped scholastically by virtue of their friendships.

Thus, there can be no doubt that peer group experiences in classrooms matter for children's development, and in some cases the consequences are disturbing. The key question for practice is what can be done about this, and the bulk of the present chapter is devoted to discussing answers. The chapter begins with the traditional approach, which is to attempt remedial work with children who are having difficulties (or regarded as at risk of having difficulties). Remedial strategies have undoubtedly become more successful over the years, but equally they have also become more elaborate. As a consequence, resourcing is an issue except in the most specialized circumstances. When peer group experiences are dependent on institutionalized structures and practices as well as individual propensities, it might be worth considering an alternative approach that focuses less on individual children and more on classrooms. The chapter discusses this possibility, offering qualified endorsement. At the same time, gaps in the literature are highlighted and consolidated, and the chapter ends with suggestions for future research and theoretical development. The restriction of peer group research to classroom contexts is revisited, as is the broad sociocultural perspective that has been adopted throughout.

Remedial Work with Individuals

Unsurprisingly, children who experience peer rejection have been the focus of remedial activities. Intervention programs have been designed and evaluated, which aspire to support such children in overcoming their difficulties. Tracing how these programs have evolved historically, Bierman (2005) notes that they are rooted in discussions that were held in the late 1930s and early 1940s. It was not, however, until the 1960s that remedial intervention was attempted on a sizeable scale, meaning that at the time of writing there is around 50 years of experience to draw upon. There have been significant changes in approach during the relevant period, and these changes are summarized below. Despite the changes, the emphasis is invariably upon the behavioral characteristics that underpin problematic experiences, primarily the low sociability, high aggression, and/or high withdrawal that are associated with peer rejection. Remedial work is attempted with young children who are at risk of difficulties because they display the behavioral characteristics in school contexts, or with older children who are already experiencing difficulties in such contexts by virtue of these characteristics.

Skills training for at-risk children

Focusing on individual children with problems, remediation programs have typically been delivered by counselors, therapists, and school psychologists. Parental support (and sometimes involvement) is regarded as critical, and no doubt parents who are concerned about their children emulate the techniques in their homes. However, when delivered by counselors, therapists, and psychologists, the programs take place in schools, usually in out-of-class settings.

Techniques have reflected the orthodoxies of psychological theorizing that were current at the time. For instance, as noted in Bierman (2005), the initial intervention programs, that is, the ones that were used in the 1960s, deployed behaviorist techniques. Children prone to withdrawal were positively reinforced for engaging with peers, and negatively reinforced for holding back. Children with aggressive tendencies were positively reinforced for non-aggressive responses to peer provocation, and negatively reinforced for aggressive responses. The approach proved reasonably effective at boosting rates of interaction among withdrawn children, but higher rates were not necessarily associated with superior quality. For instance, some initially withdrawn children became more aggressive as levels of interaction increased (presumably because they were "rejected-aggressive-withdrawn" according to the terms used in chapter 6). Furthermore, acquired behavioral patterns were often relatively inflexible, proving hard to generalize beyond the specific context of reinforcement. Finally, there are few reports of behavioral improvement translating into enhanced standing with peers, for instance losing rejected status, let alone of positive developmental outcomes in other spheres.

The failure of behaviorist approaches to promote flexibility was one reason why, from the mid-1970s, there has been increasing emphasis upon what is referred to as "social skills training." The approach involves identifying deficits, coaching in more effective strategies via guided practice and feedback, analyzing how new strategies might be used in preference to old ones in a range of situations, and receiving opportunities to apply strategies in practice. One example is described in Christoff et al. (1985). It involved six extremely shy adolescents aged 12 to 14 years, who were all attending the same school. During the first phase, the participants engaged in "problem-solving skills training," where, working together under therapist guidance, they were invited to reflect upon a series of scenarios. For instance, they were asked to imagine being given the opportunity to collaborate on a science project with another member of their class, and being told that someone else in the class had compatible interests and that they would end up working with this person. The task was to sketch the events leading up to the joint activity. The second phase of the project covered conversational skills, for example initiating conversation, listening to others, talking about oneself, and making requests to others. The participants practiced these skills with each other. Christoff et al. report improvements across the duration of the project in the levels of problem solving and conversation that the six participants achieved when working together. On the other hand, observations that were made in the school cafeteria revealed no improvement over time in the skill with which the participants interacted with other pupils.

The Christoff et al. study is small scale, and also suffers from the lack of a control group. However, its techniques are typical of what is now a widely used approach, for as Nangle, Erdley, Carpenter, and Newman

(2002) point out in a review article, social skills training "has become an established frontline treatment approach" (p. 170). Nangle et al.'s review focuses on studies that evaluate the approach's effectiveness, and includes 48 investigations with school-age samples. The full school age range is covered. The skills trained in the studies encompass participation, cooperation, communication, and conflict negotiation, with social problem solving used to provide meaning and support generalization. Nangle et al. report comprehensive evidence of behavioral improvement, in terms of both increased sociability and decreased aggression. However, looking through their database, I found fewer signs of improvement in peer status or patterns of friendship, or of enhanced developmental outcomes. Bierman (2005) too has detected a mixed message, concluding that "these studies demonstrated promising but mixed findings in regard to sociometric impact. . . . behavioral changes were more consistent . . ." (p. 169). Bierman also points out that over time social skills programs have become more sustained, and include more extensive opportunities for practice with peers, both of which have contributed to improved effectiveness. She cites two meta-analytic reviews, which document positive effects on behavior that are at least moderate in scale. Nevertheless, Bierman remains concerned about the extent to which trained skills generalize, the risk of dissipation over time, and the lack of impact on authentic peer group experiences.

Skills training in context

Faced with results like those summarized above, many commentators have come to regard social skills training as a partial but incomplete solution, to be supplemented with other forms of support. Thus recent interventions have often been multifaceted, including social skills training as one component among many. Without doubt, the most ambitious example is the *Fast Track* program, which was implemented in the United States beginning in 1991 (see, e.g., Conduct Problems Prevention Research Group, 2004). *Fast Track* is a long-term program, involving children from 56 schools spread across four U.S. states. The schools were identified as high risk for social problems, and the 891 participants were selected because screening at 5 years had revealed them to be within the top 10% in terms of risk when assessed against other pupils from these (generally high-risk) schools. Screening covered the behavioral characteristics of relevance to peer group experiences. Intervention began when the participants were 6 years of age, and included: (a) a teacher-administered social skills program known as PATHS (for Promoting Alternative Thinking Strategies), which lasted for two to three hours per week; (b) two-hourly family counseling sessions, which covered issues like appropriate parental reactions to child misdemeanors; and (c) (upon request) academic tutoring, home visits, and peer support. From adolescence, these initiatives were supplemented with group discussions, which were held away from parents and other authority figures, and covered topics like identity, goals, and decision-making. Sex education and advice about substance abuse were provided.

Evaluations of *Fast Track* have detected positive implications for social, personal, and intellectual development, with all (or virtually all) of its components contributing to the outcomes. Since social skills training (via PATHS) was one of the contributory components, this means that, in contrast to much of the research that was summarized above, *Fast Track* has demonstrated an effect of skills training that is not restricted to the skills themselves. It is unclear what it was about the program that allowed this to happen, including whether improved peer group experiences were directly or indirectly involved. We do not know, for instance, whether the proportion of rejected children decreased as a result of *Fast Track*, and if this happened whether this was a contributory factor to the successful outcomes. It is entirely possible that *Fast Track* suppressed peer influences rather than worked through these. Whatever the case, *Fast Track* is both impressive and disheartening. It is impressive because it shows how much can be achieved with an extremely unpromising sample of children, given a coordinated approach. It is disheartening because the cost of the program must have been enormous, and well beyond what is available for general implementation. Moreover, when all of the components seem to have contributed to *Fast Track*'s success, solving the resource issue through selecting some components rather than all does not seem to be an option. Indeed, the interwoven nature of the components is confirmed through points already made about social skills training. In isolation, such training can be relied upon to improve behavior, without necessarily impacting upon anything else. Contextualized with other provision as happened with *Fast Track*, the benefits of social skills training appear somewhat broader.

Yet while all of *Fast Track*'s components may be necessary with the program as designed, it is possibly significant that the program was planned to *supplement* normal school provision. Although delivered by teachers, PATHS was added to what the teachers ordinarily did. Likewise, the family counseling, home visits, academic tuition, peer support systems, and group discussions were all presented as supplements. As far as I can tell, no attempt was made to change the core activities of teaching and learning. Thus, like all of its less ambitious predecessors, *Fast Track* was fighting against the institutional structures and practices that contribute to the problems in the first place. There is, for instance, no reason to think that *Fast Track* schools made less use than other schools of grouping by ability, or of the performance mode of interaction that minimizes opportunities for sociability and maximizes opportunities for withdrawal. Suppose then that institutional structures and practices were modified, so that the negative consequences of informal peer group experiences were no longer underwritten. It would be naïve to imagine that all children would find themselves accepted by peers and/or making friends, but perhaps the problem cases would be fewer in number or lower in severity. Perhaps then, it would no longer be necessary to go to quite the lengths that *Fast Track* indicates when attempting remediation.

Qualified Endorsement of the Cooperative Approach

It is tempting to jump from the conclusions drawn in the previous paragraph to a recommendation that more extensive use be made in classrooms of the cooperative mode of interaction. The cooperative mode undoubtedly provides greater opportunities for sociability than its performance counterpart, while also restricting opportunities for withdrawal. It minimizes the forms of teacher feedback that chapter 6 shows to magnify aggression. Furthermore, it is associated with patterns of interaction that are known to support curriculum mastery. Evaluations of cooperative learning programs, which have been depicted throughout the book as specific instances of the cooperative mode, have produced encouraging results. Indeed, Roseth, Johnson, and Johnson (2008) have recently published a meta-analytic review that covers both the educational and social benefits of cooperative learning. Focusing on research concerned with adolescents aged 12 to 15 years, Roseth et al. include 148 studies in their review, and although 73% of the studies were conducted in the United States, data from at least 10 other countries are included. The results show that cooperative learning has positive effects on academic achievement, peer status, and patterns of friendship, and the effects are highly interconnected. The cooperative mode does, in other words, seem to be a very good bet, and in that sense it can probably be recommended. Nevertheless, endorsing an approach is a far cry from specifying an educational program, and it seems to me that several issues remain before the latter can be achieved. These issues are discussed below.

Maximizing the "promotiveness" of promotive interaction

Cooperative learning is far and away the best-developed, most widely used, and most comprehensively evaluated manifestation of the cooperative mode as used in classrooms. Therefore, anyone wishing to shift teaching practices in a cooperative direction will be tempted to adopt an existing cooperative learning program, in effect off the shelf. The results should be positive, yet evidence presented in chapter 4 suggests that they may not be as good as they could be. As we have seen, a central component of cooperative learning programs is promotive interaction within classroom subgroups. However, promotive interaction comes in two forms— a symmetric form that revolves around the exchange of opinions, and an asymmetric form that centers on the provision of assistance. Both forms are potentially helpful, but while all children can, in principle, benefit from the symmetric form, the benefits from the asymmetric form are typically restricted. The implication is that to maximize "promotiveness," subgroup interaction needs to be constrained to a greater degree than is usual within cooperative learning, so that the balance shifts toward the exchange of views. Indeed, deployment of the symmetric form should also provide all children with opportunities to display the behaviors associated with sociability, while the asymmetric form will most likely result in selectivity. Given everything that has emerged about the positive implications of sociability, the significance of doing this will be obvious.

A prerequisite for shifting the balance toward an exchange of views is heterogeneity within classroom subgroups, for only in these circumstances will there be a range of perspectives to be shared. Homogeneity of ability does not necessarily preclude a mixture of views, but as signaled in chapter 3, heterogeneity of ability virtually guarantees this. Therefore, for reasons that are rather different from those discussed in earlier chapters, I believe that mixed-ability subgroups should become the norm. A crucial factor in drawing differences out, once they can be presumed to exist, is, in my opinion, task design. I am thinking here about my own research on conceptual growth in science, where, as explained in chapter 4, the tasks that the children were given seemed to play a crucial role in shaping their interaction. In particular, opinion exchange in small groups was promoted, as far as I can tell, through tasks that required children to: (a) predict outcomes privately, for example record on cards whether a series of objects would float or sink, or whether warm water would cool quickly or slowly from contrasting containers; (b) share private predictions across the group and talk about these until everyone agrees about what will happen; and (c) test predictions empirically, for example by immersing objects or measuring temperature, and talk about why things turned out as they did until everyone agrees. I believe that tasks with this structure could be used in many domains in addition to science, and I think this would be helpful.

Nevertheless, while advocating that attention be paid to task design, I doubt whether task manipulations are sufficient to achieve present goals. Paralleling the problems encountered with remediation programs that were discussed in the previous section, there seems a danger that, coaxed into productive forms of interaction through task design without necessarily being aware that this is happening, children will not generalize beyond the specific context. Remediation programs began to improve when social skills training was incorporated, which required children to address target behaviors directly and explicitly. Perhaps something similar is required here. In other words, perhaps children need to be taught how to exchange opinions in the service of education. Research summarized in Mercer and Littleton (2007) not only provides an affirmative answer but also indicates how training should proceed. The research was referred to briefly in chapter 4, as evidence that opinion exchange can promote reasoning ability and curriculum mastery in authentic classrooms. What chapter 4 did not mention is that the positive results were obtained through an intervention program called *Thinking Together*, which includes "ground rules" for stimulating productive interaction. Researchers worked with teachers and children to devise rules that would encourage "exploratory talk," which as chapter 4 explained is Mercer and Littleton's term for a form of talk that includes the exchange of opinions and the analysis of differences. Thus, the rules devised within a class of 9-year-olds were: (a) share ideas; (b) give reasons; (c) question ideas; (d) consider; (e) agree; (f) involve everybody; and (g) everybody accepts responsibility. The rules devised among 10-year-olds were: (a) we share ideas and listen to each other; (b) we talk one at a time; (c) we respect each other; (d) we give reasons to explain our ideas; (e) if we disagree, we ask "why?"; and (f) we try to agree in the end. Negotiated ground rules were reproduced in posters, which were displayed in classrooms to provide frames of reference for cooperative activity. The success of *Thinking Together* in promoting precisely the forms of interaction that we are concerned with here, as well as boosting educational performance, suggests that it might be taken further.

The problem of aggression

So far, the message is that established cooperative learning programs should provide the starting place for practice, but these programs should be modified to constrain interaction toward the discussion of contrasting opinions. This can probably best be achieved through a combination of task design and conversational ground rules, both contextualized in mixed-ability settings. However, even this may not be sufficient, once we think back to why the cooperative mode is currently being advocated. As well as being consistent with intellectual growth, the cooperative mode increases opportunities for sociability while reducing the likelihood of withdrawal. Sociability is positively associated with the peer group experiences that support children's development, while withdrawal is negatively associated. However, no mention has so far been made of aggression, yet as we have seen it is just as significant in the context of peer group experiences as sociability and withdrawal. Unfortunately, research that evaluates cooperative learning seldom has anything to say about aggression. Research concerned with aggression per se is not particularly encouraging.

As regards cooperative learning, one of the few attempts to address aggression is reported in Cowie et al. (1994), specifically in the context of the authors' own project on bullying. The project ran for two years, and involved children aged 7 to 12 years. During the first year, six classes spread across three schools participated in a cooperative learning program, and three classes spread across two of the schools provided "normal curriculum" controls. One school withdrew at the end of the first year, so during the second year, there were four cooperative learning classes spread across two schools, and one control class. All schools were located in inner city districts of a large industrial city in the north of England. Like so many of the cooperative learning programs described in previous chapters, Cowie et al.'s project involved a preparatory phase where children were trained in relevant skills, followed by a series of classroom tasks to be completed in small groups. As far as I can tell, the project was entirely faithful to the key principles of formal cooperative learning. Cowie et al. used a wide range of qualitative and quantitative measures to assess the project's effectiveness, but most relevant here are the measures of bullying and victimization. At the start and end of the year, children were asked to group photographs of classmates, first into those who bully and those who do not bully, and second into those who get "picked on or bullied for no reason" and those who do not get picked on or bullied. "Bullies" were defined as children selected as bullies by at least 50%

of their classmates, and "victims" were defined as children selected as "picked on or bullied" by at least 50% of their classmates. Evaluated in comparison with control classes, the cooperative learning program had no discernible impact on bullying, and little impact on victimization. Specifically, all comparisons produced statistically non-significant results, apart from those relating to the number of victims identified in the second year of the project. Here the number increased from the start of the year to the end in all classes, but the increase was less steep for the children who had participated in the cooperative learning program.

The message from research that focuses on aggression per se is, if anything, more discouraging. Although the discussion of contrasting opinions may be optimal from the academic point of view, it is bound to involve disagreement and opposition as well as sociocognitive conflict, transactive dialogue, and exploratory talk. There is considerable evidence that opposition and disagreement boost the probability that children with aggressive tendencies will display aggressive behavior. The evidence includes research like Arsenio and Lover (1997), Calkins, Gill, Johnson, and Smith (1999), Caspi, Henry, McGee, Moffitt, and Silva (1995), and Eisenberg et al. (1997), but it is undoubtedly supplemented by results that Donna McWilliam and I obtained from work that was mentioned in earlier chapters (Howe & McWilliam, 2006). We found that, averaged across our full sample of 5- to 8-year-olds, 13% of utterances where one child opposed another were accompanied with aggression, while aggression only occurred with 1% of non-oppositional utterances. Moreover, once the children were considered individually, it became apparent that the average trends were masking considerable variation. Some children characteristically responded to opposition with reasoned argument and reconciliation. An example appears in Sequence 9.1 below. Other children characteristically responded aggressively as in Sequence 9.2. Prior to the study, these latter children had been identified as temperamentally inclined toward aggression, and as lacking in the self-control needed to deal with this.

Sequence 9.1

FIONA: [*Puts a toy pig inside a hula-hoop*] You're the farmer. You're the one who clears up the grass. I'm the one who works him.
SARAH: But he wants out, he wants out. [*Lifts the pig*]
FIONA: No you can't touch him. You can't touch him because you're the one who cleans up all the grass, not the one who looks after him.
SARAH: I look after him. [*Cuddles the pig*]
FIONA: No, I look after him.

SARAH: No, I look after him. I don't want to clear up.

FIONA: Well you be the farmer for a little while, and then you can give him some grass to eat.

SARAH: We can play house, and piggy can get some food. [*Returns the pig to the hula-hoop*]

Sequence 9.2

SCOTT: [*Skips with the hula-hoop*] I can't even do it yet. Watch.

GARY: [*Tries to grab the hula-hoop*] Come on.

SCOTT: Watch, watch. Just watch. [*Pulls the hoop back*]

GARY: I can do it. Let me have a go. [*Grabs the hula-hoop again*]

SCOTT: Don't move. Just watch.

GARY: I don't want to watch. Nor does he. [*Picks the pig up*]

SCOTT: Put him down on the ground. [*Shoves Gary aside*]

GARY: Ow. Ow. [*Snatches the hula-hoop*]

Morton Deutsch, the acknowledged forefather of cooperative learning (see chapter 3), distinguished between constructive and destructive conflict (e.g., Deutsch, 1973). It would be ironic indeed if the educational approach that his work precipitated were to be undermined through boosted levels of destructive behavior. The best way to pre-empt this within the framework being developed here is probably through explicit treatment during the formulation, presentation, and implementation of ground rules. I can imagine Mercer and Littleton's (2007) examples expanded into, for example, "If we disagree, we don't hit, shove, or make fun of each other. We give reasons." I can also imagine implementation guided via the re-mediation programs that were discussed in the previous section. After all, modern skills-based programs have achieved success in reducing aggression (Nangle et al., 2002). So qualifying the conclusions drawn a few paragraphs earlier, the way forward seems to rest upon the discussion of contrasting opinions in conjunction with steps to minimize aggression.

Teacher involvement

Of course, one strategy for minimizing aggression would be to involve teachers in direct supervision of children's discussions. Cooperative learning programs typically envisage an indirect role for teachers, that is, one that is limited to designing tasks which classroom subgroups complete without their immediate participation. Taking cooperative learning as its starting point, the material discussed so far in this section has also presupposed subgroups that operate without direct involvement from teachers. However, when chapter 3 introduced the concept of a cooperative mode (as opposed to cooperative learning per se), it acknowledged the possibility of subgroups and even full classes operating cooperatively together with teachers. Therefore, there is nothing in the cooperative concept that in principle precludes direct input from teachers, including the monitoring of aggression. It is simply that this is not how things have evolved in practice. Moreover, at this point in time, it is impossible to comment with conviction about whether matters should be different. As we saw in chapter 4, the rare instances of pupil cooperation orchestrated by teachers have not been adequately evaluated. What can be discussed is whether the backroom role that is currently envisaged for teachers is problematic, such that the viability of an alternative strategy is worth exploring.

The most obvious potential problem stems from the fact that teachers cannot sustain an indirect role throughout the school day. No matter how successfully they plan tasks for children to complete in unmonitored subgroups, these tasks alone will not deliver the curriculum. Children working apart from their teachers will not, for instance, discover calculus, Newtonian physics, or the mechanisms of inheritance. Even if subgroup activity paves the way, children still require direct instruction from teachers. However, as we saw in earlier chapters, teachers can inadvertently undermine rather than consolidate the positive consequences of cooperative activity. Thus, a major issue is whether there is a set of strategies that teachers can adopt that allows consolidation to occur. Until recently, next to nothing was known about the issue, but four newly completed studies (reviewed in Webb, 2009) offer guidance. In particular, the studies indicate a "softly-softly" role for teachers, coaxing subgroups to explain their reasoning and via gentle probing moving them gradually toward superior analyses. My own limited sorties into the field suggest that this coaxing is most effective if groups reach consensus about the problems that they are working on. In two studies with 9- to 12-year-old children (Howe & Tolmie, 2003; Howe, Tolmie, Duchak-Tanner, & Rattray, 2000), what was called "expert guidance" was much more beneficial when directed at consensual positions than when supporting groups who had not achieved consensus. It did not matter whether the consensual positions showed good or poor understanding of the topic being studied, namely the factors relevant to shadow size (Howe et al., 2000) or rate of cooling (Howe & Tolmie, 2003). Equally, it did not matter whether progress was going to take place immediately, or whether post-group reprocessing was required, as detailed in chapter 4.

All in all then, an approach to teaching is recommended that: (a) starts with existing cooperative learning programs; (b) modifies these programs through judicious design of tasks and of ground rules for subgroup activity, so that they optimize non-aggressive exchanges of opinion, and the achievement of consensus; (c) delivers the programs in mixed-ability settings; (d) refrains from direct teacher intervention when subgroups are in session; and (e) uses guidance rather than instruction to bridge the gaps between what subgroups achieve and target curricula. Such an approach requires a relatively non-pressurized curriculum, and given its organizational demands presupposes reasonably small classes. Thus, there is a policy dimension to implementation as well as a practical one. Nevertheless, the requirements do not strike me as impossibly utopian, at least when viewed from the perspective of affluent countries in the English-speaking world.

On the other hand, we saw in chapter 2 that class sizes in developing countries can be more than three times the norm for affluent societies. Moreover, many countries, both developing and affluent, do not use the two-tier, whole-class plus subgroup structure onto which cooperative learning (and its current derivative) neatly rests. Yet the case for the cooperative mode of interaction must be assumed to apply with these countries in just the way that it applies with the United States, the United Kingdom, and so on. There is very little that is culturally specific about the behavioral characteristics that underpin experiences of status and friendship, nor about the classroom features which mediate these characteristics. Going back to chapter 1, there can also be nothing specific about the mechanisms that translate experiences into developmental outcomes. Therefore, the safest assumption is that the relationships described in chapters 7 and 8 apply with all children who participate in schooling, regardless of culture. Certainly, the small amount of research conducted in non-English-speaking countries supports this assumption. Thus, insofar as the cooperative mode is a partial antidote to problematic peer group experiences, it is required in contexts that do not have the luxury of smallish classes and/or do not favor subgroup activity. To support needs in such contexts, I believe that it is worth developing current analyses of cooperation orchestrated by teachers, referring to the whole-class as well as subgroup level. A start has been made (see Alexander, 2006; Cazden, 2001), but there is a long way to go.

Future Research and Theoretical Development

The issue of whether the cooperative mode can be extended beyond the five (subgroup-focused) steps listed above is clearly a significant issue for future research. Of equal importance, though, is evaluation of programs based on the five steps, should such programs be implemented. We can be confident that the programs will prove productive, but how productive and by what routes? Will any benefits be restricted to direct consequences of the modified practices? Or will changed opportunities for sociability, aggression, and withdrawal create changed patterns of status and friendship with indirect consequences for academic achievement? Moreover, will these changed patterns of status and friendship have beneficial consequences for social and personal development, such that remedial intervention is not quite the challenge that it currently seems? The practical significance of studying these issues is transparent, but I should like to conclude the book by highlighting their theoretical importance, given the sociocultural perspective that has been adopted throughout.

Developing the sociocultural perspective

Chapter 1 defined a sociocultural perspective as one that recognizes the broader cultural and historical contexts in which peer groups are embedded. It explained that the perspective imposes constraints upon how developmental influences should be theorized, and awareness of these constraints has proved useful elsewhere in the book. For instance, it helped in making sense of the contrasting learning mechanisms that were discussed in chapter 4. When justifying the sociocultural perspective, chapter 1 emphasized cross-cultural variability in access to peer groups, and the association of this variability historically with the provision of schooling. Across the chapters, a degree of cultural relativity has been detected in the way that peer groups are structured, even when schooling can be presumed. Some of this relativity was revisited above, for example class size variation and differences over whole-class teaching versus whole-class plus subgroup.

On the other hand, a great deal of cross-cultural commonality has also been detected, including over ability-based segregation and the performance mode of classroom interaction. Both factors have been implicated in the relation between peer group experiences and developmental outcomes, and this of course is theoretically significant. It means that sociocultural factors are interacting with other characteristics (e.g., sociability, aggression, withdrawal, ability) to shape the course of children's development, and this needs to be taken into account when building theoretical models. However, because the factors are, in effect, cross-cultural constants, it is impossible to introduce them into models in anything but a vague and general fashion. It is impossible, in other words, to say how strongly the factors are implicated, and how they relate to other factors. Variability is required to do this, and educational reform as sketched above should provide opportunities, so long as it is appropriately evaluated. In particular, clarification should in principle be obtainable through comparing whatever relationships are detected in the future under mixed-ability arrangements and the cooperative mode with the relationships charted throughout this book for the single-ability/performance mode status quo. Via such comparisons, we should be in a position to progress beyond a broad sociocultural perspective to detailed analysis of how children's predispositions interrelate with institutional structures to determine development. This would be a major step toward a full-fledged sociocultural theory.

While educational reform would provide opportunities, it may not be the only context for moving the field forward. As noted, existing research does not permit more than a cursory glimpse at peer groups in out-of-school settings. In some respects, the glimpse, consolidated in chapter 6, suggests that out-of-school experiences can be predicted from what happens in classrooms, but equally there are occasional signs of divergence. For instance, chapter 5 cited the research of Decker and Curry (2000), which indicates looser leadership structures in adolescent gangs. This implies that the significance of the concept of centrality (see chapter 5) may differ between classroom and out-of-class contexts. Of course, centrality warrants additional research even within school settings. Nevertheless, this is one example of how research conducted beyond the confines of schooling might generate some of the variability that, as explained in the previous paragraph, is critical for theoretical development. Such research would not compromise the relationships that this book has described. The very fact that peer group experiences in schools predict long-term outcomes demonstrates robustness against the influence of peer group experiences in other settings. What research in these other settings would achieve is clarification of how relationships are to be interpreted, and the point made here is that from a theoretical perspective this would be important.

No matter whether it addresses cooperation in classrooms or out-of-school relations, future research should follow the practice adopted throughout this book of regarding peer groups as associations involving *two* or more persons. As detailed in chapter 1, Harris (e.g., 1995, 1998) argues that the concept of a group should be reserved for triads upwards, on the grounds that group pressures are exclusively normative and norms do not operate at the dyadic level. Normative influences have been highlighted here too. For instance, they were called upon in chapter 6 to explain some aspects of the aggression–status relation. However, non-normative influences have also proved significant. The contrasting learning mechanisms discussed in chapter 4 are, for example, exclusively informational. Moreover, the cases supporting a dyad versus larger group distinction have proved few and far between. Chapter 3 indicated that gender differences during computer-based group work vary depending on whether dyads or larger groups are involved, but this instance was exceptional. Typically, group size made no difference to reported results, and where differences were observed they were more often relative rather than absolute. For instance, popular cliques were differentiated from other friendship groups in chapter 5 partly in terms of being the *largest* classroom group, and the whole-class versus subgroup distinction is also dependent on relativities. All in all then, there are no grounds whatsoever for excluding dyads from the concept of groups, and the recommendation is that future research includes them.

Conclusion

It is clear that much work remains to be done, and therefore the book does not, and could not, paint a definitive picture of children's peer group experiences and the developmental consequences of these experiences. Nevertheless, it has hopefully provided a reasonably comprehensive summary of what research currently shows. This is not because the literature relating to each of the chapter topics has been presented in full. That would have been impossible when the topics have themselves generated book-length reviews. These reviews have been cited, so that readers know where to look for detailed analysis.

Rather, the book's claims to comprehensiveness stem from the links that have been made between educational and psychological research. To date, such links have been the exception not the rule, yet they are crucial. Quite apart from the relationships charted in previous chapters, the present chapter has revisited two quintessentially educational concerns—class size reduction and mixed-ability teaching—and taken a stand that is based not simply on classic research (as outlined in chapter 2) but also on the requirements of the cooperative mode. The cooperative mode is advocated as a practice that should reduce the adverse (and educationally relevant) consequences of informal experiences of peers as analyzed by psychologists. On the other hand, the present chapter has also underlined the fact that these informal experiences are shaped via institutional structures such as schools, and theoretical models should take this into account. Psychological analyses sometimes read as if this point has been forgotten, with causal chains restricted to links between individual characteristics (sociability and so on) through peer group experiences to developmental outcomes. Analyses would be enriched through recognition of the sociocultural dimensions as studied, for schools, by educationalists. Chapter 1 signaled that an interdisciplinary perspective was being adopted. The hope is that this perspective is now regarded as warranted.

References

Achenbach, T. M., & Edelbrock, C. S. (1986). *Manual for the Child Behavior Checklist*. Burlington: University of Vermont.

Adler, P. A., & Adler, P. (1995). Dynamics of inclusion and exclusion in preadolescent cliques. *School Psychology Quarterly, 58*, 145–162.

Adler, P. A., & Adler, P. (2003). *Peer power: Preadolescent culture and identity*. New Brunswick, NJ: Rutgers University Press.

Alexander, R. J. (2001). *Culture and pedagogy: International comparisons in primary education*. Oxford: Blackwell.

Alexander, R. J. (2006). *Towards dialogic teaching: Rethinking classroom talk*. Cambridge: Dialogos.

Altermatt, E. R., Jovanovic, J., & Perry, M. (1998). Bias or responsivity? Sex or achievement-level effects on teacher classroom questioning practices. *Journal of Educational Psychology, 90*, 516–527.

Altermatt, E. R., & Pomerantz, E. M. (2003). The development of competence-related and motivational beliefs: An investigation of similarity and influence among friends. *Journal of Educational Psychology, 95*, 111–123.

Altermatt, E. R., & Pomerantz, E. M. (2005). The implications of having high-achieving versus low-achieving friends: A longitudinal analysis. *Social Development, 14*, 61–81.

Ames, G. J., & Murray, F. B. (1982). When two wrongs make a right: Promoting cognitive change by social conflict. *Developmental Psychology, 18*, 894–897.

Anderson, A., Tolmie, A., McAteer, E., & Demissie, A. (1993). Software style and interaction around the microcomputer. *Computers and Education, 20*, 235–250.

Archer, J., & Lloyd, B. (1985). *Sex and gender*. Cambridge: Cambridge University Press.

Argyle, M. (1988). *Bodily communication* (2nd ed.). London: Routledge.

Aronson, E. (1978). *The jigsaw classroom*. Beverley Hills, CA: Sage Publications.

Arsenio, W. F., & Lover, A. (1997). Emotions, conflicts and aggression during preschoolers' freeplay. *British Journal of Developmental Psychology, 15*, 531–542.

Asher, S. R. (1983). Social competence and peer status: Recent advances and future directions. *Child Development, 54*, 1427–1434.

Asher, S. R., & Dodge, K. A. (1986). Identifying children who are rejected by their peers. *Developmental Psychology, 22*, 444–449.

Asher, S. R., Singleton, L. C., Tinsley, B. R., & Hymel, S. (1979). A reliable sociometric measure for preschool children. *Developmental Psychology, 15*, 443–444.

Atkins, M. S., Stoff, D. M., Osborne, M. L., & Brown, K. (1993). Distinguishing instrumental and hostile aggression: Does it make a difference? *Journal of Abnormal Child Psychology, 21*, 355–365.

Azmitia, M., & Cooper, C. R. (2001). Good or bad? Peer influences on Latino and European American adolescents' pathways through school. *Journal of Education for Students Placed at Risk, 6*, 45–71.

Azmitia, M., & Montgomery, R. (1993). Friendship, transactive dialogues, and the development of scientific reasoning. *Social Development, 2*, 202–221.

Bagwell, C. L. (2004). Friendships, peer networks and antisocial behavior. In J. B. Kupersmidt & K. A. Dodge (Eds.), *Children's peer relations: From development to intervention* (pp. 37–57). Washington, DC: American Psychological Association.

Bagwell, C. L., & Coie, J. D. (2004). The best friendships of aggressive boys: Relationship quality, conflict management, and rule-breaking behavior. *Journal of Experimental Child Psychology, 88*, 5–24.

Bagwell, C. L., Coie, J. D., Terry, R. A., & Lochman, J. E. (2000). Peer clique participation and social status in preadolescence. *Merrill-Palmer Quarterly, 46*, 280–305.

Bagwell, C. L., Newcomb, A. F., & Bukowski, W. M. (1998). Preadolescent friendship and peer rejection as predictors of adult adjustment. *Child Development, 69*, 140–153.

Baines, E., Blatchford, P., & Kutnick, P. (2003). Changes in grouping practices over primary and secondary school. *International Journal of Educational Research, 39*, 9–34.

Baines, E., & Howe, C. (in press). Discourse topic management and discussion skills in middle childhood: The effects of age and task. *First Language*.

Bargh, J. A., & Schul, Y. (1980). On the cognitive benefits of teaching. *Journal of Educational Psychology, 72*, 605–609.

Barnes, D. (1973). *Language in the classroom.* Milton Keynes: Open University Press.

Barnes, D., & Todd, F. (1977). *Communication and learning in small groups.* London: Routledge and Kegan Paul.

Baron, S. W., & Tindall, D. B. (1993). Network structure and delinquent attitudes within a juvenile gang. *Social Networks, 15*, 255–273.

Bearison, D. J., Magzamen, S., & Filardo, E. K. (1986). Socio-cognitive conflict and cognitive growth in young children. *Merrill-Palmer Quarterly, 32*, 51–72.

Bender, D., & Lösel, F. (1997). Protective and risk effects of peer relations and social support on antisocial behaviour in adolescents from multi-problem milieus. *Journal of Adolescence*, 20, 661–678.

Bender, W. N. (1985). Differences between learning disabled and non-learning disabled children in temperament and behavior. *Learning Disability Quarterly*, 8, 11–18.

Bennett, S. N., Desforges, C. W., Cockburn, A., & Wilkinson, B. (1984). *The quality of pupil learning*. Hove, Sussex: Lawrence Erlbaum Associates.

Berkowitz, M. W., Gibbs, J. C., & Broughton, J. M. (1980). The relation of moral judgment stage disparity to developmental effects of peer dialogues. *Merrill-Palmer Quarterly*, 26, 341–357.

Berndt, T. J., & Perry, T. B. (1986). Children's perceptions of friendships as supportive relationships. *Developmental Psychology*, 22, 640–648.

Bierman, K. L. (2005). *Peer rejection: Developmental processes and intervention strategies*. New York: The Guilford Press.

Bierman, K. L., & Wargo, J. B. (1995). Predicting the longitudinal course associated with aggressive-rejected, aggressive (non-rejected) and rejected (nonaggressive) status. *Development and Psychopathology*, 7, 669–682.

Bigelow, B. J. (1977). Children's friendship expectations: A cognitive developmental study. *Child Development*, 48, 246–253.

Bigelow, B. J., & LaGaipa, J. J. (1975). Children's written descriptions of friendship: A multidimensional analysis. *Developmental Psychology*, 11, 857–858.

Billig, M. (1996). *Arguing and thinking: A rhetorical approach to social psychology*. Cambridge: Cambridge University Press.

Blatchford, P. (2003). *The class size debate: Is small better?* Maidenhead: Open University Press.

Blatchford, P., Baines, E., Kutnick, P., & Martin, C. (2001). Classroom contexts: Connections between class size and within class grouping. *British Journal of Educational Psychology*, 71, 283–302.

Blatchford, P., Baines, E., & Pellegrini, A. (2003). The social context of school playground games: Sex and ethnic differences, and changes over time after entry to junior school. *British Journal of Developmental Psychology*, 21, 481–505.

Blatchford, P., Baines, E., Rubie-Davies, C., Bassett, P., & Chowne, A. (2006). The effect of a new approach to group work on pupil–pupil and teacher–pupil interactions. *Journal of Educational Psychology*, 98, 750–765.

Blatchford, P., Bassett, P., & Brown, P. (2008). *Do low attaining and younger students benefit most from small classes? Results from a systematic observation study of class size effects on pupil classroom engagement and teacher pupil interaction*. Paper presented at the American Educational Research Association Annual Meeting, New York.

Blatchford, P., Kutnick, P., Baines, E., & Galton, M. (2003). Toward a social pedagogy of classroom group work. *International Journal of Educational Research*, 39, 153–172.

Blaye, A. (1990). Peer interaction in solving a binary matrix problem: Possible mechanisms causing individual progress. *Learning and Instruction*, 2, 45–56.

Boaler, J., Wiliam, D., & Brown, M. (2000). Students' experiences of ability grouping—disaffection, polarisation and the construction of failure. *British Educational Research Journal*, 26, 631–648.

Boivin, M., Hymel, S., & Hodges, E. V. E. (2001). Toward a process view of peer rejection. In J. Juvonen & S. Graham (Eds.), *Peer harassment in schools: The plight of the vulnerable child* (pp. 265–289). New York: The Guilford Press.

Bond, C. F., & Titus, L. J. (1983). Social facilitation: A meta-analysis of 241 studies. *Psychological Bulletin*, 94, 265–292.

Bonney, M. (1943). Personality traits of socially successful and socially unsuccessful children. *Journal of Educational Psychology*, 34, 449–472.

Boulton, M. J., & Smith, P. K. (1994). Bully/victim problems in middle-school children: Stability, self-perceived competence, peer perceptions and peer acceptance. *British Journal of Developmental Psychology*, 12, 315–329.

Bousted, M. W. (1989). Who talks? The position of girls in mixed sex classrooms. *English in Education*, 23, 41–51.

Boydell, D. (1975). Pupil behaviour in junior classrooms. *British Journal of Educational Psychology*, 45, 122–129.

Boyle, D. E., Marshall, N. L., & Robeson, W. W. (2003). Gender at play: Fourth grade girls and boys on the playground. *American Behavioral Scientist*, 46, 1326–1345.

Bradac, J. J. (1990). Language attitudes and impression formation. In H. Giles & W. P. Robinson (Eds.), *Handbook of language and social psychology* (pp. 387–412). Chichester: John Wiley & Sons.

Brown, P., & Levinson, S. (1978). Universals in language use: Politeness phenomena. In E. N. Goody (Ed.), *Questions and politeness* (pp. 56–289). Cambridge: Cambridge University Press.

Brown, R. (1988). *Group processes: Dynamics within and between groups*. Oxford: Blackwell.

Buhs, E. S., & Ladd, G. W. (2001). Peer rejection as an antecedent of young children's school adjustment: An examination of mediating processes. *Developmental Psychology*, 37, 550–560.

Bukowski, W., Bowker, A., Zargarpour, S., & Hoza, B. (1995). *An analysis of the structure of social isolates*. Paper presented at the Biennial Meeting of the Society for Research in Child Development, Indianapolis.

Bukowski, W. M., Hoza, B., & Boivin, M. (1994). Measuring friendship quality during pre- and early adolescence: The development and psychometric properties of the Friendship Qualities Scale. *Journal of Social and Personal Relationships*, 11, 471–484.

Burns, C., & Myhill, D. (2004). Interactive or inactive? A consideration of the nature of interaction in whole class teaching. *Cambridge Journal of Education*, 34, 35–49.

Buswell, M. (1953). The relationship between the social structure of the classroom and the academic success of the pupils. *Journal of Experimental Education, 22,* 37–53.

Buunk, B. P. (2001). Affiliation, attraction and close relationships. In M. Hewstone & W. Stroebe (Eds.), *Introduction to social psychology: A European perspective* (3rd ed.) (pp. 371–400). Oxford: Blackwell.

Cairns, R. B., Cairns, B. D., Neckerman, H. J., Gest, S. D., & Gariépy, J-L. (1988). Social networks and aggressive behavior: Peer support or peer rejection. *Developmental Psychology, 24,* 815–823.

Calkins, S. D., Gill, K. L., Johnson, M. C., & Smith, C. L. (1999). Emotional reactivity and emotional regulation strategies as predictors of social behavior with peers during toddlerhood. *Social Development, 8,* 310–334.

Card, N. A., Stucky, B. D., Sawalani, G. M., & Little, T. D. (2008). Direct and indirect aggression during childhood and adolescence: A meta-analytic review of gender differences, intercorrelations, and relations to maladjustment. *Child Development, 79,* 1185–1229.

Caspi, A., Henry, B., McGee, R. O., Moffitt, T. E., & Silva, P. A. (1995). Temperamental origins of child and adolescent behavior problems: From age three to age fifteen. *Child Development, 66,* 55–68.

Cazden, C. B. (2001). *Classroom discourse: The language of teaching and learning* (2nd ed.). Portsmouth, NH: Heinemann.

Chen, C., Greenberger, E., Lester, J., Deng, Q., & Guo, M-S. (1998). A cross-cultural study of family and peer correlates of adolescent misconduct. *Developmental Psychology, 34,* 770–781.

Chen, X., Liu, H., Chang, L., & He, Y. (2008). Effects of peer group on the development of social functioning and academic achievement. *Child Development, 79,* 235–257.

Chen, X., Rubin, K. H., & Li, Z-Y. (1995). Social functioning and adjustment in Chinese children: A longitudinal study. *Developmental Psychology, 31,* 531–539.

Chi, M. T. H., De Leeuw, N., Chiu, M-H., & LaVancher, C. (1994). Eliciting self-explanations improves understanding. *Cognitive Science, 18,* 439–477.

Christie, D., Tolmie, A., Thurston, A., Howe, C., & Topping, K. (2009). Supporting group work in Scottish primary classrooms: Improving the quality of collaborative dialogue. *Cambridge Journal of Education, 39,* 141–156.

Christoff, K. A., Scott, W. O. N., Kelley, M. L., Schlundt, D., Baer, G., & Kelly, J. A. (1985). Social skills and social problem-solving training for shy young adolescents. *Behaviour Therapy, 16,* 468–477.

Cillessen, A. H. N., & Mayeux, L. (2004). Sociometric status and peer group behaviors: Previous findings and current directions. In J. B. Kupersmidt & K. A. Dodge (Eds.), *Children's peer relations: From development to intervention* (pp. 3–20). Washington, DC: American Psychological Association.

Cillessen, A. H. N., van IJzendoorn, H. W., van Lieshout, F. M., & Hartup, W. W. (1992). Heterogeneity among peer-rejected boys: Subtypes and stabilities. *Child Development, 63,* 893–905.

Claes, M., & Simard, R. (1992). Friendship characteristics of delinquent adolescents. *International Journal of Adolescence and Youth, 3,* 287–301.

Cohen, E. G. (1994). Restructuring the classroom: Conditions for productive small groups. *Review of Educational Research, 64,* 1–35.

Coie, J. D., Cillessen, A. H. N., Dodge, K. A., Hubbard, J. A., Schwartz, D., Lemerise, E., et al. (1999). It takes two to fight: A test of relational factors and a method for assessing aggressive dyads. *Developmental Psychology, 35,* 1179–1188.

Coie, J. D., & Dodge, K. A. (1988). Multiple sources of data on social behavior and social status in the school: A cross-age comparison. *Child Development, 59,* 815–829.

Coie, J. D., Dodge, K. A., & Coppotelli, H. (1982). Dimensions and types of social status: A cross-age perspective. *Developmental Psychology, 18,* 557–570.

Coie, J. D., Lochman, J. E., Terry, R., & Hyman, C. (1992). Predicting early adolescent disorder from childhood aggression and peer rejection. *Journal of Consulting and Clinical Psychology, 60,* 783–792.

Conduct Problems Prevention Research Group. (2004). The Fast Track experiment: Translating the developmental model into a prevention design. In J. B. Kupersmidt & K. A. Dodge (Eds.), *Children's peer relations: From development to intervention* (pp. 181–208). Washington, DC: American Psychological Association.

Connolly, J., Furman, W., & Konarski, R. (2000). The role of peers in the emergence of heterosexual romantic relationships in adolescence. *Child Development, 71,* 1395–1408.

Conwell, C., Griffin, S., & Algozzine, B. (1993). Gender and racial differences in unstructured learning groups in science. *International Journal of Science Education, 15,* 107–115.

Cooper, H., Valentine, J. C., Nye, B., & Lindsay, J. J. (1999). Relationships between five after-school activities and academic achievement. *Journal of Educational Psychology, 91,* 369–378.

Coulthard, M. (1977). *An introduction to discourse analysis.* London: Longman Group Ltd.

Cowie, H., Smith, P., Boulton, M., & Laver, R. (1994). *Co-operation in the multi-ethnic classroom: The impact of co-operative group work on social relationships in middle schools.* London: David Fulton.

Craig, W. M., Vitaro, F., Gagnon, C., & Tremblay, R. E. (2002). The road to gang membership: Characteristics of male gang and nongang members from ages 10 to 14. *Social Development, 11,* 53–68.

Crick, N. R., & Dodge, K. A. (1996). Social information-processing mechanisms in reactive and proactive aggression. *Child Development, 67,* 993–1002.

Crick, N. R., & Grotpeter, J. K. (1995). Relational aggression, gender, and social-psychological adjustment. *Child Development, 66,* 710–722.

Criss, M. M., Shaw, D. S., Moilanen, K. L., Hitchings, J. E., & Ingoldsby, E. M. (2009). Family, neighborhood, and peer characteristics as predictors of child adjustment: A longitudinal analysis of additive and mediation models. *Social Development, 18,* 511–535.

Damon, W., & Killen, M. (1982). Peer interaction and the process of change in children's moral reasoning. *Merrill-Palmer Quarterly, 28,* 347–367.

Damon, W., & Phelps, E. (1988). Strategic uses of peer learning in children's education. In T. J. Berndt & G. W. Ladd (Eds.), *Peer relations in child development* (pp. 135–157). New York: John Wiley & Sons.

Damon, W., & Phelps, E. (1989). Critical distinctions among three approaches to peer education. *International Journal of Educational Research, 5,* 9–19.

Dart, B., & Clarke, J. (1988). Sexism in schools: A new look. *Educational Review, 40,* 41–49.

Deater-Deckard, K. (2001). Annotation: Recent research examining the role of peer relationships in the development of psychopathology. *Journal of Child Psychology and Psychiatry, 42,* 565–579.

Decker, S. H., & Curry, G. D. (2000). Addressing key features of gang membership: Measuring the involvement of young members. *Journal of Criminal Justice, 28,* 473–482.

Degirmencioglu, S. M., Urberg, K. A., Tolson, J. M., & Protima, R. (1998). Adolescent friendship networks: Continuity and change over the school year. *Merrill-Palmer Quarterly, 44,* 313–337.

Deptula, D. P., & Cohen, R. (2004). Aggressive, rejected, and delinquent children and adolescents: A comparison of their friendships. *Aggression and Violent Behavior, 9,* 75–104.

DeRosier, M. E., Kupersmidt, J. B., & Patterson, C. J. (1994). Children's academic and behavioral adjustment as a function of the chronicity and proximity of peer rejection. *Child Development, 65,* 1799–1813.

Deutsch, M. (1949). A theory of cooperation and competition. *Human Relations, 2,* 129–152.

Deutsch, M. (1973). *The resolution of conflict: Constructive and destructive processes.* New Haven, CT: Yale University Press.

Dewey, J. (1916). *Democracy and education.* New York: The Macmillan Company.

Dishion, T. J., McCord, J., & Poulin, F. (1999). When interventions harm: Peer groups and problem behavior. *American Psychologist, 54,* 755–764.

Dodge, K. A., Lansford, J. E., Burks, V. S., Bates, J. E., Pettit, G. S., Fontaine, R., et al. (2003). Peer rejection and social information-processing factors in the development of aggressive behavior problems in children. *Child Development, 74,* 374–393.

Doise, W., & Mackie, D. (1981). On the social nature of cognition. In J. P. Forgas (Ed.), *Social cognition: Perspectives on everyday understanding* (pp. 53–83). London: Academic Press.

Doise, W., & Mugny, G. (1979). Individual and collective conflicts of centrations in cognitive development. *European Journal of Psychology, 9,* 105–108.

Doise, W., & Mugny, G. (1984). *The social development of the intellect.* Oxford: Pergamon.

Doise, W., Mugny, G., & Perret-Clermont, A-N. (1975). Social interaction and the development of cognitive operations. *European Journal of Social Psychology, 5,* 367–383.

Douvan, E., & Adelson, J. (1966). *The adolescent experience.* New York: John Wiley & Sons.

Duffy, J., Warren, K., & Walsh, M. (2001). Classroom interactions: Gender of teacher, gender of student, and classroom subject. *Sex Roles, 45,* 579–593.

Dunn, J. (2004). *Children's friendships: The beginnings of intimacy.* Oxford: Blackwell.

Eder, D. (1995). *School talk: Gender and adolescent culture.* New Brunswick, NJ: Rutgers University Press.

Edwards, C. P. (1992). Cross-cultural perspectives on family–peer relations. In R. D. Parke & G. W. Ladd (Eds.), *Family–peer relationships: Modes of linkage* (pp. 285–316). Hove, Sussex: Lawrence Erlbaum Associates.

Edwards, D., & Mercer, N. (1987). *Common knowledge: The development of understanding in the classroom.* London: Methuen/Routledge.

Eisenberg, N., Fabes, R. A., Shepard, S. A., Murphy, B. C., Guthrie, I. K., Jones, S., et al. (1997). Contemporaneous and longitudinal prediction of children's social functioning from regulation and emotionality. *Child Development, 68,* 642–664.

Eisenberg, N., Pidada, S., & Liew, J. (2001). The relations of regulation and negative emotionality to Indonesian children's social functioning. *Child Development, 72,* 1747–1763.

Ellis, S., & Rogoff, B. (1982). The strategies and efficacy of child versus adult teachers. *Child Development, 53,* 730–735.

Epstein, J. L. (1985). The selection of friends: Changes across the grades and in different school environments. In T. J. Berndt & G. W. Ladd (Eds.), *Peer relations in child development* (pp. 158–187). New York: John Wiley & Sons.

Erwin, P. G. (1985). Similarity of attitudes and constructs in children's friendships. *Journal of Experimental Child Psychology, 40,* 470–485.

Estell, D. B., Cairns, R. B., Farmer, T. W., & Cairns, B. D. (2002). Aggression in inner-city early elementary classrooms: Individual and peer-group configurations. *Merrill-Palmer Quarterly, 48,* 52–76.

Feltham, R. F., Doyle, A. B., Schwartzman, A. E., Serbin, L. A., & Ledingham, J. E. (1985). Friendship in normal and socially deviant children. *Journal of Early Adolescence, 5,* 371–382.

Finn, J. D., & Achilles, C. M. (1999). Tennessee's class size study: Findings, implications, misconceptions. *Educational Evaluation and Policy Analysis, 21,* 97–109.

Fish, M. C., & Feldman, S. C. (1987). Teacher and student verbal behavior in microcomputer classes: An observational study. *Journal of Classroom Interaction, 23,* 15–21.

Flanders, N. A. (1970). *Analyzing teacher behavior*. Reading, MA: Addison-Wesley.

Frederickson, N. L., & Furnham, A. F. (1998). Sociometric-status-group classification of mainstreamed children who have moderate learning difficulties: An investigation of personal and environmental factors. *Journal of Educational Psychology, 90*, 772–783.

Fredricks, J. A., & Eccles, J. S. (2006). Is extracurricular participation associated with beneficial outcomes? Concurrent and longitudinal relations. *Developmental Psychology, 42*, 698–713.

French, D. C., Jansen, E. A., Riansari, M., & Setiono, K. (2003). Friendships of Indonesian children: Adjustment of children who differ in friendship presence and similarity between mutual friends. *Social Development, 12*, 605–621.

French, J., & French, P. (1984). Gender imbalances in the classroom: An interactional account. *Educational Research, 26*, 127–136.

Freud, A., & Dann, S. (1951). An experiment in group upbringing. In *Psychoanalytic Study of the Child: Vol. VI* (pp. 123–168). New York: International Universities Press.

Furman, W., & Bierman, K. L. (1983). Developmental changes in young children's conceptions of friendship. *Child Development, 54*, 549–556.

Furman, W., & Buhrmester, D. (1985). Children's perceptions of the personal relationships in their social networks. *Developmental Psychology, 21*, 1016–1024.

Galton, M. (1999). Commentary: Interpreting classroom practice around the globe. In R. Alexander, P. Broadfoot, & D. Phillips (Eds.), *Learning from comparing: New directions in comparative educational research* (pp. 181–187). Oxford: Symposium Books.

Galton, M., Gray, J., & Ruddock, J. (2003). *Transfer and transitions in the middle years of schooling (7–14): Continuities and discontinuities in learning* (Research Report No. 443). London: Department for Education and Skills.

Galton, M., Hargreaves, L., Comber, C., Wall, D., & Pell, A. (1999). *Inside the primary classroom: 20 years on*. London: Routledge.

Galton, M., Hargreaves, L., & Pell, A. (2009). Group work and whole-class teaching with 11- to 14-year-olds compared. *Cambridge Journal of Education, 39*, 119–140.

Galton, M., & Patrick, H. (1990). *Curriculum provision in small primary schools*. London: Routledge.

Galton, M., Simon, B., & Croll, P. (1980). *Inside the primary classroom (the ORACLE project)*. London: Routledge and Kegan Paul.

Gauze, C., Bukowski, W. M., Aquan-Assee, J., & Sippola, L. K. (1996). Interactions between family environment and friendship and associations with self-perceived well-being during early adolescence. *Child Development, 67*, 2201–2216.

Gest, S. D., Graham-Bermann, S. A., & Hartup, W. W. (2001). Peer experience: Common and unique features of number of friendships, social network centrality, and sociometric status. *Social Development, 10*, 23–40.

Gifford-Smith, M. E., & Brownell, C. A. (2003). Childhood peer relationships: Social acceptance, friendships, and peer networks. *Journal of School Psychology, 41,* 235–284.

Goldstein, H., & Blatchford, P. (1998). Class size and educational achievement: A review of methodology with particular reference to study design. *British Educational Research Journal, 24,* 255–268.

Good, T., Cooper, H., & Blakely, S. (1980). Classroom interaction as a function of teacher expectations, student sex and time of year. *Journal of Educational Psychology, 72,* 378–385.

Good, T., Sikes, N., & Brophy, J. (1973). Effects of teacher sex and student sex on classroom interaction. *Journal of Educational Psychology, 65,* 74–87.

Goodlad, S., & Hirst, B. (1989). *Peer tutoring: A guide to learning by teaching.* New York: Nichols.

Greener, S. H. (2000). Peer assessment of children's prosocial behaviour. *Journal of Moral Education, 29,* 47–60.

Gresham, F. M. (1982). Misguided mainstreaming: The case for social skills training with handicapped children. *Exceptional Children, 48,* 422–431.

Gronlund, N. E. (1959). *Sociometry in the classroom.* New York: Harper and Brothers.

Gross, E., Juvonen, J., & Gable, S. (2002). Online communication and well-being in early adolescence: The social function of instant messages. *Journal of Social Issues, 58,* 75–90.

Guralnick, M. J. (1990). Peer interactions and the development of handicapped children's social and communicative competence. In H. C. Foot, M. J. Morgan, & R. H. Shute (Eds.), *Children helping children* (pp. 275–305). New York: John Wiley & Sons.

Guralnick, M. J., & Paul-Brown, D. (1984). Communicative adjustments during behavior-request episodes among children at different developmental levels. *Child Development, 55,* 911–919.

Haag, P. (1998). Single-sex education in Grades K-12: What does the research tell us? In American Association of University Women Educational Foundation (Ed.), *Separated by sex: A critical look at single-sex education for girls* (pp. 13–34). Washington, DC: AAUWEF.

Hallinan, M. T., & Sorensen, A. B. (1985). Ability grouping and student friendships. *American Educational Research Journal, 22,* 485–499.

Hamm, J. V. (2000). Do birds of a feather flock together? The variable bases for African American, Asian American, and European American adolescents' selection of similar friends. *Developmental Psychology, 36,* 209–219.

Hanish, L. D., Ryan, P., Martin, C. L., & Fabes, R. A. (2005). The social context of young children's peer victimization. *Social Development, 14,* 2–19.

Hardman, F. (2008). Teachers' use of feedback in whole-class and group-based talk. In N. Mercer & S. Hodgkinson (Eds.), *Exploring talk in schools* (pp. 131–150). London: Sage Publications.

Harlen, W., & Malcolm, H. (1997). *Setting and streaming: A research review.* Edinburgh: Scottish Council for Research in Education.

Harris, J. R. (1995). Where is the child's environment? A group socialization theory of development. *Psychological Review, 102,* 458–489.

Harris, J. R. (1998). *The nurture assumption: Why children turn out the way they do.* London: Bloomsbury.

Harris, J. R. (2000). Socialization, personality development and the child's environments: Comments on Vandell. *Developmental Psychology, 36,* 711–723.

Harrist, A. W., Zaia, A. F., Bates, J. E., Dodge, K. A., & Pettit, G. S. (1997). Subtypes of social withdrawal in early childhood: Sociometric status and social-cognitive differences across four years. *Child Development, 68,* 278–294.

Hart, C. H., Yang, C., Nelson, L. J., Robinson, C. C., Olsen, J. A., Nelson, D. A., et al. (2000). Peer acceptance in early childhood and subtypes of socially withdrawn behaviour in China, Russia, and the United States. *International Journal of Behavioral Development, 24,* 73–81.

Hartup, W. W. (1978). Children and their friends. In H. McGurk (Ed.), *Issues in childhood development* (pp. 130–170). London: Methuen.

Hartup, W. W. (1983). Peer relations. In P. H. Mussen (Ed.), *Handbook of child psychology* (pp. 103–196). New York: John Wiley & Sons.

Hartup, W. W., French, D. C., Laursen, B., Johnston, M. K., & Ogawa, J. R. (1993). Conflict and friendship relations in middle childhood: Behavior in a closed-field situation. *Child Development, 64,* 445–454.

Hartup, W. W., & Stevens, N. (1997). Friendships and adaptation in the life course. *Psychological Bulletin, 121,* 355–370.

Harvey, T. J. (1985). Science in single-sex and mixed teaching groups. *Educational Research, 27,* 179–182.

Haselager, G. J. T., Cillessen, A. H. N., van Lieshout, C. F. M., Riksen-Walraven, J. M. A., & Hartup, W. W. (2002). Heterogeneity among peer-rejected boys across middle childhood: Developmental pathways of social behavior. *Developmental Psychology, 38,* 446–456.

Haselager, G. J. T., Hartup, W. W., van Lieshout, C. F. M., & Riksen-Walraven, J. M. A. (1998). Similarities between friends and nonfriends in middle childhood. *Child Development, 69,* 1198–1208.

Hawker, D. S. J., & Boulton, M. J. (2000). Twenty years' research on peer victimization and psychosocial maladjustment: A meta-analytic review of cross-sectional studies. *Journal of Child Psychology and Psychiatry, 41,* 441–455.

Hay, D. F., Payne, A., & Chadwick, A. (2004). Peer relations in childhood. *Journal of Child Psychology and Psychiatry, 45,* 84–108.

Hecht, D. B., Inderbitzen, H. M., & Bukowski, A. L. (1998). The relationship between peer status and depressive symptoms in children and adolescence. *Journal of Abnormal Child Psychology, 26,* 153–160.

Heim, D., Howe, C., O'Connor, R., Cassidy, C., Warden, D., & Cunningham, L. (2004). *A longitudinal investigation of the experiences of racism and discrimination by young people in Glasgow*. Final Report to Glasgow Anti-Racist Alliance.

Herdt, G. H. (1987). *The Sambia: Ritual and gender in New Guinea*. New York: Holt, Rinehart, & Winston.

Hertz-Lazarowitz, R. (1992). Understanding interactive behaviors: Looking at six mirrors of the classroom. In R. Hertz-Lazarowitz & N. Miller (Eds.), *Interaction in cooperative groups: The theoretical anatomy of group learning* (pp. 71–101). Cambridge: Cambridge University Press.

Hindy, C. G. (1980). Children's friendship concepts and the perceived cohesiveness of same-sex friendship dyads. *Psychological Reports, 47*, 191–203.

Hodges, E. V. E., Boivin, M., Vitaro, F., & Bukowski, W. M. (1999). The power of friendship: Protection against an escalating cycle of peer victimization. *Developmental Psychology, 35*, 94–101.

Hogg, M. A., & Vaughan, G. M. (2002). *Social psychology* (3rd ed.). Harlow: Pearson Educational Ltd.

Howe, C. J. (1989). Visual primacy in social attitude judgement: A qualification. *British Journal of Social Psychology, 28*, 263–272.

Howe, C. J. (1997). *Gender and classroom interaction: A research review*. Edinburgh: Scottish Council for Research in Education.

Howe, C. (2009). Collaborative group work in middle childhood: Joint construction, unresolved contradiction and the growth of knowledge. *Human Development, 52*, 215–239.

Howe, C., & McWilliam, D. (2001). Peer argument in educational settings: Variations due to socioeconomic status, gender and activity context. *Journal of Language and Social Psychology, 20*, 61–80.

Howe, C. J., & McWilliam, D. (2006). Opposition in social interaction amongst children: Why intellectual benefits do not mean social costs. *Social Development, 15*, 205–231.

Howe, C., McWilliam, D., & Cross, G. (2005). Chance favours only the prepared mind: Incubation and the delayed effects of peer collaboration. *British Journal of Psychology, 96*, 67–93.

Howe, C., Rodgers, C., & Tolmie, A. (1990). Physics in the primary school: Peer interaction and the understanding of floating and sinking. *European Journal of Psychology of Education, V*, 459–475.

Howe, C. J., & Tolmie, A. (2003). Group work in primary school science: Discussion, consensus and guidance from experts. *International Journal of Educational Research, 39*, 51–72.

Howe, C., Tolmie, A., Duchak-Tanner, V., & Rattray, C. (2000). Hypothesis testing in science: Group consensus and the acquisition of conceptual and procedural knowledge. *Learning and Instruction, 10*, 361–391.

Howe, C., Tolmie, A., Greer, K., & Mackenzie, M. (1995a). Peer collaboration and conceptual growth in physics: Task influences on children's understanding of heating and cooling. *Cognition and Instruction, 13*, 483–503.

Howe, C., Tolmie, A., & Mackenzie, M. (1995b). Computer support for the collaborative learning of physics concepts. In C. O'Malley (Ed.), *Computer-supported collaborative learning* (pp. 51–68). Berlin: Springer-Verlag.

Howe, C., Tolmie, A., & Rodgers, C. (1992). The acquisition of conceptual knowledge in science by primary school children: Group interaction and the understanding of motion down an incline. *British Journal of Developmental Psychology, 10*, 113–130.

Howe, C., Tolmie, A., Thurston, A., Topping, K., Christie, D., Livingston, K., et al. (2007). Group work in elementary science: Towards organisational principles for supporting pupil learning. *Learning and Instruction, 17*, 549–563.

Hymel, S., Bowker, A., & Woody, E. (1993). Aggressive versus withdrawn unpopular children: Variations in peer and self-perceptions in multiple domains. *Child Development, 64*, 879–896.

Hymel, S., Rubin, K. H., Rowden, L., & LeMare, L. (1990). Children's peer relationships: Longitudinal prediction of internalizing and externalizing problems from middle to late childhood. *Child Development, 61*, 2004–2021.

Hymel, S., Vaillancourt, T., McDougall, P., & Renshaw, P. D. (2002). Peer acceptance and peer rejection. In P. K. Smith & C. H. Hart (Eds.), *Blackwell handbook of childhood social development* (pp. 265–284). Oxford: Blackwell.

Ireson, J., Hallam, S., & Hurley, C. (2005). What are the effects of ability grouping on GCSE attainment? *British Educational Research Journal, 31*, 443–458.

Jackson, A., Fletcher, B. C., & Messer, D. J. (1986). A survey of micro-computer use and provision in primary schools. *Journal of Computer Assisted Learning, 2*, 45–55.

Jackson, C. (2002). Can single-sex classes in co-educational schools enhance the learning experiences of girls and/or boys? An exploration of pupils' perceptions. *British Educational Research Journal, 28*, 37–48.

Jackson, M. F., Barth, J. M., Powell, N., & Lochman, J. E. (2006). Classroom contextual effects of race on children's peer nominations. *Child Development, 77*, 1325–1337.

Johnson, D. W. (2003). Social interdependence: Interrelationships among theory, research, and practice. *American Psychologist, 58*, 934–945.

Johnson, D. W., & Johnson, F. P. (2000). *Joining together: Group theory and group skills* (7th ed.). Boston, MA: Allyn & Bacon.

Johnson, D. W., & Johnson, R. T. (1992). Positive interdependence: Key to effective cooperation. In R. Hertz-Lazarowitz & N. Miller (Eds.), *Interaction in cooperative groups: The theoretical anatomy of group learning* (pp. 174–199). Cambridge: Cambridge University Press.

Johnson, D. W., & Johnson, R. T. (1999). *Learning together and alone: Cooperative, competitive, and individualistic learning* (5th ed.). Boston, MA: Allyn & Bacon.

Johnson, D. W., Johnson, R. T., & Holubec, E. J. (1994). *New circles of learning: Cooperation in the classroom and school*. Alexandria, VA: Association for Supervision and Curriculum Development.

Jones, G., & Wheatley, J. (1989). Gender influences in classroom displays and student–teacher behaviour. *Science Education, 73*, 535–545.

Jones, M., & Gerig, T. (1994). Silent sixth-grade students: Characteristics, achievement, and teacher expectations. *The Elementary School Journal, 95*, 169–182.

Jones, M. G., Brader-Araje, L., Wilson Carboni, L., Carter, G., Rua, M. J., Banilower, E., et al. (2000). Tool time: Gender and students' use of tools, control, and authority. *Journal of Research in Science Teaching, 37*, 760–783.

Keenan, E. O. (1974). Conversational competence in children. *Journal of Child Language, 1*, 163–183.

Keenan, E. O., & Klein, E. (1975). Coherency in children's discourse. *Journal of Psycholinguistic Research, 4*, 365–380.

Kemp, C., & Carter, M. (2002). The social skills and social status of mainstreamed students with intellectual disabilities. *Educational Psychology, 22*, 391–411.

Kenrick, D. T., & Funder, D. C. (1991). The person–situation debate: Do personality traits really exist? In V. Derlaga, B. A. Winstead, & W. H. Jones (Eds.), *Personality: Contemporary theory and research* (pp. 149–174). Chicago, IL: Nelson-Hall.

Kessels, U., & Hannover, B. (2008). When being a girl matters less: Accessibility of gender-related self-knowledge in single-sex and coeducational classes and its impact on students' physics-related self-concept of ability. *British Journal of Educational Psychology, 78*, 273–289.

Kiesner, J., Poulin, F., & Nicotra, E. (2003). Peer relations across contexts: Individual-network homophily and network inclusion in and after-school. *Child Development, 74*, 1328–1343.

Kindermann, T. A. (1993). Natural peer groups as contexts for individual development: The case of children's motivation in school. *Developmental Psychology, 29*, 970–977.

Kistner, J., Metzler, A., Gatlin, D., & Risi, S. (1993). Classroom racial proportions and children's peer relations: Race and gender effects. *Journal of Educational Psychology, 85*, 446–452.

Koch, H. L. (1933). Popularity among preschool children: Some related factors and a technique for its measurement. *Child Development, 4*, 164–175.

Konner, M. (1975). Relations among infants and juveniles in comparative perspective. In M. Lewis & L. A. Rosenblum (Eds.), *Friendship and peer relations* (pp. 99–129). New York: John Wiley & Sons.

Kovacs, M. (1992). *The Children's Depression Inventory*. Santa Barbara, CA: Pearson Education.

Kraatz Keiley, M., Bates, J. E., Dodge, K. A., & Pettit, G. S. (2000). A cross-domain growth analysis: Externalizing and internalizing behaviours during 8 years of childhood. *Journal of Abnormal Child Psychology, 28*, 161–179.

Kruger, A. C. (1992). The effect of peer and adult–child transactive discussions on moral reasoning. *Merrill-Palmer Quarterly, 38*, 191–211.

Kuhne, M., & Wiener, J. (2000). Stability of social status of children with and without learning disabilities. *Learning Disability Quarterly, 23,* 64–75.

Kurdek, L. A., & Lillie, R. (1985). The relation between classroom social status and classmate likability, compromising skill, temperament, and neighborhood social interactions. *Journal of Applied Developmental Psychology, 6,* 31–41.

Kutnick, P., Blatchford, P., Clark, H., MacIntyre, H., & Baines, E. (2005a). Teachers' understandings of the relationship between within-class (pupil) grouping and learning in secondary schools. *Educational Research, 47,* 1–24.

Kutnick, P., & Kington, A. (2005). Children's friendships and learning in school: Cognitive enhancement through social interaction. *British Journal of Educational Psychology, 75,* 521–538.

Kutnick, P., Ota, C., & Berdondini, L. (2008). Improving the effects of group working in classrooms with young school-aged children: Facilitating attainment, interaction and classroom activity. *Learning and Instruction, 18,* 83–95.

Kutnick, P., Sebba, J., Blatchford, P., Galton, M., & Thorp, J. with MacIntyre, H., & Berdondini, L. (2005b). *The effects of pupil grouping: Literature review.* Brighton: The University of Brighton.

Labov, W. (1972). Rules for ritual insults. In D. Sudnow (Ed.), *Studies in social interaction* (pp. 120–169). New York: The Free Press.

Ladd, G. W. (1990). Having friends, keeping friends, making friends, and being liked by peers in the classroom: Predictors of children's early school adjustment? *Child Development, 61,* 1081–1100.

Ladd, G. W. (2005). *Children's peer relations and social competence.* New Haven, CT: Yale University Press.

Ladd, G. W., & Burgess, K. B. (1999). Charting the relationship trajectories of aggressive, withdrawn and aggressive/withdrawn children during early grade school. *Child Development, 70,* 910–929.

Ladd, G. W., Kochenderfer, B. J., & Coleman, C. C. (1997). Classroom peer acceptance, friendship and victimization: Distance relational systems that contribute uniquely to children's school adjustment. *Child Development, 68,* 1181–1197.

LaGreca, A. M., & Stone, W. L. (1990). Learning disability status and achievement: Confounding variables in the study of children's social status, self-esteem and behavioral functioning. *Journal of Learning Disabilities, 23,* 483–490.

Lancelotta, G. X., & Vaughn, S. (1989). Relation between types of aggression and sociometric status: Peer and teacher perceptions. *Journal of Educational Psychology, 81,* 86–90.

Lease, A. M., Kennedy, C. A., & Axelrod, J. L. (2002). Children's social constructions of popularity. *Social Development, 11,* 87–109.

Lee, M. (1993). Gender, group composition, and peer interaction in computer-based cooperative learning. *Journal of Educational Computing Research, 9,* 549–577.

Leman, P. L., & Duveen, G. (1999). Representations of authority and children's moral reasoning. *European Journal of Social Psychology, 29,* 557–575.

Levinger, G., & Levinger, A. C. (1986). The temporal course of close relationships: Some thoughts about the development of children's ties. In W. W. Hartup & Z. Rubin (Eds.), *Relationships and development* (pp. 111–133). London: Lawrence Erlbaum Associates.

Linchevski, L., & Kutscher, B. (1998). Tell me with whom you're learning and I'll tell you how much you've learned: Mixed-ability versus same-ability grouping in mathematics. *Journal for Research in Mathematics Education, 29*, 533–553.

Lipman, M., & Sharp, A. M. (1978). *Growing up with philosophy*. Philadelphia, PA: Temple University Press.

Lippitt, R. (1941). Popularity among preschool children. *Child Development, 12*, 305–332.

Little, S. A., & Garber, J. (1995). Aggression, depression and stressful life events predicting peer rejection. *Development and Psychopathology, 7*, 845–856.

Lou, Y., Abrami, P. C., Spence, J. C., Poulsen, C., Chambers, B., & d'Apollonia, S. (1996). Within-class grouping: A meta-analysis. *Review of Educational Research, 66*, 423–458.

Lu Jiang, X., & Cillessen, A. H. N. (2005). Stability of continuous measures of sociometric status: A meta-analysis. *Developmental Review, 25*, 1–25.

Maassen, G., van der Linden, J. L., Goossens, F. A., & Bokhorst, J. (2000). A ratings-based approach to two-dimensional sociometric status determination. *New Directions in Child and Adolescent Development, 88*, 55–73.

Maassen, G. H., & Verschueren, K. (2005). A two-dimensional ratings-based procedure for sociometric status determination as an alternative to the Asher and Dodge system. *Merrill-Palmer Quarterly, 51*, 192–212.

Maccoby, E. E., & Jacklin, C. N. (1974). *The psychology of sex differences*. Stanford, CA: Stanford University Press.

Maccoby, E. E., & Martin, J. A. (1983). Socialization in the context of the family: Parent–child interaction. In P. H. Mussen & E. M. Hetherington (Eds.), *Handbook of child psychology: Vol. 4. Socialization, personality, and social development*. New York: John Wiley & Sons.

MacQuarrie, S., Howe, C., & Boyle, J. M. E. (2008). *Group work and classroom interaction within science and English lessons*. Paper presented at the Scottish Educational Research Association Annual Conference, Perth, Scotland.

Marsh, H. W. (1992). Extracurricular activities: Beneficial extension of the traditional curriculum or subversion of academic goals? *Journal of Educational Psychology, 84*, 553–562.

Martinez, M. A. (1987). Dialogues among children and between children and their mothers. *Child Development, 58*, 1035–1043.

Masten, A. S., Morison, P., & Pellegrini, D. S. (1985). A revised class play method of peer assessment. *Developmental Psychology, 21*, 523–533.

Maszk, P., Eisenberg, N., & Guthrie, I. K. (1999). Relations of children's social status to their emotionality and regulation: A short-term longitudinal study. *Merrill-Palmer Quarterly, 45*, 468–492.

McAteer, E., Anderson, T., Orr, M., Demissie, A., & Woherem, E. (1991). Computer-assisted learning and groupwork: The design of an evaluation. *Computers and Education*, 17, 41–47.

McAteer, E., & Demissie, A. (1991). *Writing competence across the curriculum*. Report to Scottish Office Education Department.

McAuliffe, M. D., Hubbard, J. A., & Romano, L. J. (2009). *The role of teacher cognition and teacher behavior in children's peer relations*. Paper presented at the Biennial Meeting of the Society for Research in Child Development, Denver.

McCaslin, M., Tuck, D., Wiard, A., Brown, B., Lapage, J., & Pyle, J. (1994). Gender composition and small-group learning in fourth grade mathematics. *Elementary School Journal*, 94, 467–482.

McGuire, K. D., & Weisz, J. R. (1982). Social cognition and behavior correlates of preadolescent chumship. *Child Development*, 53, 1478–1484.

McTear, M. F. (1985). *Children's conversation*. Oxford: Blackwell.

Mercer, N. (2007). *Interactive whiteboards as pedagogic tools in primary schools* (Full Research Report: ESRC End of Award Report RES-000-22-1269). Swindon: Economic and Social Research Council.

Mercer, N., & Littleton, K. (2007). *Dialogue and the development of children's thinking: A sociocultural approach*. London: Routledge.

Miell, D., & Littleton, K. (2004). *Collaborative creativity*. London: Free Association Books.

Miell, D., & MacDonald, R. (2000). Children's creative collaborations: The importance of friendship when working together on a musical composition. *Social Development*, 9, 348–369.

Miller-Johnson, S., Coie, J. D., Maumary-Gremaud, A., Lochman, J., & Terry, R. (1999). Relationship between childhood peer rejection and aggression and adolescent delinquency severity and type among African American youth. *Journal of Emotional and Behavioral Disorders*, 7, 137–146.

Mischel, W. (1968). *Personality and assessment*. New York: John Wiley & Sons.

Moffitt, T. E. (1993). Adolescence-limited and life-course-persistent antisocial behavior: A developmental taxonomy. *Psychological Review*, 100, 674–701.

Monroe, W. F. (1898). Social consciousness in children. *Psychological Review*, 5, 68–70.

Moreno, F. (1942). Sociometric status of children in a nursery school group. *Sociometry*, 5, 395–411.

Moreno, J. L. (1934). *Who shall survive? A new approach to the problem of human interrelations*. Washington, DC: Nervous and Mental Disease Publishing Co.

Morgan, V., & Dunn, S. (1988). Chameleons in the classroom: Visible and invisible children in nursery and infant classrooms. *Educational Review*, 40, 3–12.

Mueller, E., & Tingley, E. (1989). *Cross-cultural perspectives on early peer relationships*. Paper presented at a meeting on socioemotional relationships in day care and nursery schools. Arezzo, Italy.

Mugny, G., & Doise, W. (1978). Socio-cognitive conflict and structure of individual and collective performances. *European Journal of Social Psychology*, 8, 181–192.

Myers, D. G., & Lamm, H. (1976). The group polarization phenomenon. *Psychological Bulletin*, 83, 602–627.

Nabuzoka, D., & Smith, P. K. (1993). Sociometric status and social behaviour of children with and without learning difficulties. *Journal of Child Psychology and Psychiatry and Applied Disciplines*, 34, 1435–1448.

Nangle, D. W., Erdley, C. A., Carpenter, E. M., & Newman, J. E. (2002). Social skills training as a treatment for aggressive children and adolescents: A developmental-clinical integration. *Aggression and Violent Behavior*, 7, 169–199.

Neckerman, H. J. (1996). The stability of social groups in childhood and adolescence: The role of the classroom social environment. *Social Development*, 5, 131–145.

Newcomb, A. F., & Bagwell, C. L. (1995). Children's friendship relations: A meta-analytic review. *Psychological Bulletin*, 117, 306–347.

Newcomb, A. F., Bukowski, W. M., & Pattee, L. (1993). Children's peer relations: A meta-analytic review of popular, rejected, neglected, controversial, and average sociometric status. *Psychological Bulletin*, 113, 99–128.

Noret, N., & Rivers, I. (2007). *The prevalence and correlates of cyberbullying in adolescence: Results of a five-year cohort study*. Edinburgh: Queen Margaret University.

Northway, M. L. (1944). Outsiders: A study of the personality patterns of children least acceptable to their age-mates. *Sociometry*, 7, 10–25.

Nussbaum, J., & Novick, S. (1981). Brainstorming in the classroom to invent a model: A case study. *School Science Review*, 62, 771–778.

Nystrand, M., Wu, L., Gamorgan, A., Zeiser, S., & Long, D. (2003). Questions in time: Investigating the structure and dynamics of unfolding classroom discourse. *Discourse Processes*, 35, 135–198.

O'Donnell, A., & Dansereau, D. F. (1992). Scripted cooperation in student dyads: A method for analyzing and enhancing academic learning and performance. In R. Hertz-Lazarowitz & N. Miller (Eds.), *Interaction in cooperative groups: The theoretical anatomy of group learning* (pp. 120–141). Cambridge: Cambridge University Press.

Ollendick, T. H., Weist, M. D., Borden, M. C., & Greene, R. W. (1992). Sociometric status and academic, behavioral, and psychological adjustment: A five-year longitudinal study. *Journal of Consulting and Clinical Psychology*, 60, 80–87.

Olweus, D. (1993). *Bullying at school: What we know and what we can do*. Oxford: Blackwell.

Organisation for Economic Cooperation and Development. (2008). *Education at a glance 2008*. Paris: Author.

Osborn, M. (2001). Constants and contexts in pupil experience of learning and schooling: Comparing learners in England, France and Demark. *Comparative Education*, 37, 267–278.

Osborn, M., Broadfoot, P., McNess, E., Raven, R., Planel, C., & Triggs, P., with Cousin, O., & Winther-Jensen, T. (2003). *A world of difference? Comparing learners across Europe.* Open University Press: McGraw-Hill Education.

Ottenberg, S. (1988). Oedipus, gender and social solidarity: A case study of male childhood and initiation. *Ethos, 16,* 326–352.

Palincsar, A. S., & Brown, A. L. (1984). Reciprocal teaching of comprehension-fostering and comprehension-monitoring activities. *Cognition and Instruction, 1,* 223–238.

Parker, J. G., & Asher, S. R. (1987). Peer relations and later personal adjustment: Are low-accepted children at risk? *Psychological Bulletin, 102,* 357–389.

Parker, J. G., & Seal, J. (1996). Forming, losing, renewing, and replacing friendships: Applying temporal parameters to the assessment of children's friendship experiences. *Child Development, 67,* 2248–2268.

Pate-Bain, H., Achilles, C. M., Boyd-Zaharias, J., & McKenna, B. (1992). Class size does make a difference. *Phi Delta Kappan, 74,* 253–256.

Pedder, D. (2006). Are small classes better? Understanding relationships between class size, classroom processes and pupils' learning. *Oxford Review of Education, 32,* 213–234.

Pedersen, S., Vitaro, F., Barker, E. D., & Borge, A. I. H. (2007). The timing of middle-childhood peer rejection and friendship: Linking early behavior to early-adolescent adjustment. *Child Development, 78,* 1037–1051.

Pekarik, E. G., Prinz, R. J., Liebert, D. E., Weintraub, S., & Neale, J. M. (1976). The Pupil Evaluation Inventory: A sociometric technique for assessing children's social behavior. *Journal of Abnormal Child Psychology, 14,* 83–97.

Pellegrini, A. D. (1982). The construction of cohesive text by pre-schoolers in two-play contexts. *Discourse Processes, 5,* 101–108.

Pellegrini, A. D., Blatchford, P., Kato, K., & Baines, E. (2004). A short-term longitudinal study of children's playground games in primary school: Implications for adjustment to school and social adjustment in the USA and the UK. *Social Development, 13,* 107–123.

Pender, J. (2003). *An examination of temperament, stereotypes and communicative skills as influences on the sociometric status of young children with learning difficulties.* Unpublished master's thesis, University of Strathclyde, Glasgow.

Perry, D. G., Kusel, S. J., & Perry, L. C. (1988). Victims of peer aggression. *Developmental Psychology, 24,* 807–814.

Petersen, P., Johnson, D., & Johnson, R. (1991). Effects of co-operative learning on perceived status of male and female pupils. *Journal of Social Psychology, 131,* 717–735.

Pettit, G. S., Clawson, M., Dodge, K. A., & Bates, J. E. (1996). Stability and change in children's peer-rejected status: The role of child behavior, parent–child relations, and family ecology. *Merrill-Palmer Quarterly, 43,* 515–538.

Piaget, J. (1926). *The language and thought of the child.* London: Routledge and Kegan Paul.

Piaget, J. (1932). *The moral judgment of the child.* London: Routledge and Kegan Paul.

Piaget, J. (1985). *The equilibration of cognitive structures*. Chicago, IL: University of Chicago Press.

Pontecorvo, C., Paoletti, G., & Orsolini, M. (1989). Use of the computer and social interaction in a language curriculum. *Golem, 5*, 12–14.

Pontefract, C., & Hardman, F. (2005). The discourse of classroom interaction in Kenyan primary schools. *Comparative Education, 41*, 87–106.

Posner, J. K., & Vandell, D. L. (1999). After-school activities and the development of low-income urban children: A longitudinal study. *Developmental Psychology, 35*, 868–879.

Psaltis, C., & Duveen, G. (2007). Conservation and conversation types: Forms of recognition and cognitive development. *British Journal of Developmental Psychology, 25*, 79–102.

Qualter, P., & Munn, P. (2002). The separateness of social and emotional loneliness in childhood. *Journal of Child Psychology and Psychiatry, 43*, 233–244.

Radziszewska, B., & Rogoff, B. (1991). Children's guided participation in planning imaginary errands with skilled adult or peer partners. *Developmental Psychology, 27*, 381–389.

Rampton, B. (2006). *Language in late modernity: Interaction in an urban school*. Cambridge: Cambridge University Press.

Rampton, B., & Harris, R. (in press). Change in urban classroom culture and interaction. To appear in K. Littleton & C. Howe (Eds.), *Educational dialogues: Understanding and promoting productive interaction*. London: Routledge.

Ray, G. E., Cohen, R., Secrist, M. E., & Duncan, M. K. (1997). Relating aggressive and victimization behaviors to children's sociometric status and friendships. *Journal of Social and Personal Relationships, 14*, 95–108.

Roberts, B. W., & Caspi, A. (2001). Personality development and the person–situation debate: It's déja vu all over again. *Psychological Enquiry, 12*, 104–108.

Roberts, C. M., & Smith, P. R. (1999). Attitudes and behaviour of children towards peers with disabilities. *International Journal of Disability, Development and Education, 46*, 35–50.

Rodkin, P. C., Farmer, T. W., Pearl, R., & Van Acker, R. (2000). Heterogeneity of popular boys: Antisocial and prosocial configurations. *Developmental Psychology, 36*, 14–24.

Rogoff, B. (2003). *The cultural nature of human development*. Oxford: Oxford University Press.

Roseth, C. J., Johnson, D. W., & Johnson, R. T. (2008). Promoting early adolescents' achievement and peer relationships: The effects of cooperative, competitive, and individualistic goal structures. *Psychological Bulletin, 134*, 223–246.

Rothbart, M. K., & Bates, J. E. (1998). Temperament. In N. Eisenberg (Ed.), *Handbook of child psychology: Vol. 3. Social, emotional, and personality development* (pp. 105–175). New York: John Wiley & Sons.

Roy, A. W. N., & Howe, C. J. (1990). Effects of cognitive conflict, socio-cognitive conflict and imitation on children's socio-legal thinking. *European Journal of Social Psychology, 20,* 241–252.

Rubin, K. H., Bukowski, W., & Parker, J. G. (1998). Peer interactions, relationships, and groups. In N. Eisenberg (Ed.), *Handbook of child psychology: Vol. 3. Social, emotional, and personality development* (pp. 619–700). New York: John Wiley & Sons.

Rubin, K. H., & Coplan, R. J. (2004). Paying attention to and not neglecting social withdrawal and social isolation. *Merrill-Palmer Quarterly, 50,* 506–534.

Sadker, M., & Sadker, D. (1985, March). Sexism in the schoolroom of the '80s. *Psychology Today,* 54–57.

Sage, N. A., & Kindermann, T. A. (1999). Peer networks, behavior contingencies, and children's engagement in the classroom. *Merrill-Palmer Quarterly, 45,* 143–171.

Salmivalli, C., Kaukiainen, A., & Lagerspetz, K. (1998). Aggression in the social relations of school-aged girls and boys. In P. T. Slee & K. Rigby (Eds.), *Children's peer relations* (pp. 60–75). London: Routledge.

Sandstrom, M. J., & Coie, J. D. (1999). A developmental perspective on peer rejection: Mechanisms of stability and change. *Child Development, 70,* 955–966.

Sanson, A., Finch, S., Matjacic, E., & Kennedy, G. (1998). Who says? Associations among peer relations and behaviour problems as a function of source of information, sex of child and analytic strategy. In P. T. Slee & K. Rigby (Eds.), *Children's peer relations* (pp. 183–204). London: Routledge.

Savin-Williams, R. C. (1979). Dominance hierarchies in groups of early adolescents. *Child Development, 50,* 923–935.

Scanlon, E. (2000). How gender influences learners working collaboratively with science simulations. *Learning and Instruction, 10,* 463–481.

Schmitt, M. T., & Branscombe, N. R. (2002). The meaning and consequences of perceived discrimination in disadvantaged and privileged social groups. In W. Stroebe & M. Hewstone (Eds.), *European Review of Social Psychology: Vol. 12* (pp. 167–199). Chichester: John Wiley & Sons.

Schwartz, D., Pettit, G. S., Dodge, K. A., Bates, J. E., & the Conduct Problems Prevention Research Group. (2000). Friendship as a moderating factor in the pathway between early harsh home environment and later victimization in the peer group. *Developmental Psychology, 36,* 646–662.

Schwarz, B. B., Neuman, Y., & Biezuner, S. (2000). Two wrongs may make a right. . . . If they argue together! *Cognition and Instruction, 18,* 461–494.

Selman, R. L., & Jaquette, D. (1977). Stability and oscillation in interpersonal awareness: A clinical-developmental analysis. In C. B. Keasey (Ed.), *The Nebraska Symposium on Motivation: Vol. 25* (pp. 261–304). Lincoln: University of Nebraska Press.

Shachar, H., & Sharan, S. (1994). Talking, relating, and achieving: Effects of cooperative learning and whole-class instruction. *Cognition and Instruction, 12,* 313–353.

Shah, S., & Conchar, C. (2009). Why single-sex schools? Discourses of culture/faith and achievement. *Cambridge Journal of Education, 39*, 191–204.

Shantz, C. U. (1987). Conflicts between children. *Child Development, 58*, 283–305.

Sharan, Y., & Sharan, S. (1992). *Expanding cooperative learning through group investigation*. New York: Teachers College Press.

Sherif, M., Harvey, O. J., White, B. J., Hood, W. E., & Sherif, C. W. (1961). *Intergroup conflict and cooperation: The Robbers Cave experiment*. Norman: University of Oklahoma Book Exchange.

Sherif, M., & Sherif, C. W. (1953). *Groups in harmony and tension: An integration of studies in intergroup behavior*. New York: Harper & Row.

Sherif, M., White, B. J., & Harvey, O. J. (1955). Status in experimentally produced groups. *American Journal of Sociology, 60*, 370–379.

Shrum, W., Cheek, N. H., & Hunter, S. MacD. (1988). Friendship in school: Gender and racial homophily. *Sociology of Education, 61*, 227–239.

Siann, G., & McLeod, H. (1986). Computers and children of primary school age: Issues and questions. *British Journal of Education Technology, 2*, 133–144.

Simpson, A. W., & Erickson, M. T. (1983). Teachers' verbal and nonverbal communication patterns as a function of teacher race, student gender, and student race. *American Educational Research Journal, 20*, 183–198.

Sinclair, J. McH., & Coulthard, M. (1975). *Towards an analysis of discourse: The English used by pupils and teachers*. Oxford: Oxford University Press.

Slavin, R. E. (1987). Ability grouping and student achievement in elementary schools: A best-evidence synthesis. *Review of Educational Research, 57*, 293–336.

Slavin, R. E. (1990). Achievement effects of ability grouping in secondary schools: A best-evidence synthesis. *Review of Educational Research, 60*, 471–499.

Slavin, R. E. (1992). When and why does cooperative learning increase achievement? Theoretical and empirical perspectives. In R. Hertz-Lazarowitz & N. Miller (Eds.), *Interaction in cooperative groups: The theoretical anatomy of group learning* (pp. 145–173). Cambridge: Cambridge University Press.

Slavin, R. E. (1995). *Cooperative learning: Theory, research, and practice*. Boston, MA: Allyn & Bacon.

Slavin, R. E., & Lake, C. (2008). Effective programs in elementary mathematics: A best-evidence synthesis. *Review of Educational Research, 78*, 427–515.

Slavin, R. E., Lake, C., & Groff, C. (2007). *Effective programs in middle and high school mathematics: A best-evidence synthesis*. Baltimore, MD: Center for Data-Driven Reform in Education, Johns Hopkins University.

Smith, A., & Schneider, B. H. (2000). The inter-ethnic friendships of adolescent students: A Canadian study. *International Journal of Intercultural Relations, 24*, 247–258.

Stake, J., & Katz, J. (1982). Teacher–pupil relationships in the elementary school classroom: Teacher–gender and pupil–gender differences. *American Educational Research Journal, 19*, 465–471.

Stormshak, E. A., Bierman, K. L., Bruschi, C., Dodge, K. A., Coie, J. D., & the Conduct Problems Prevention Research Group. (1999). The relation between behavior problems and peer preference in different classrooms. *Child Development, 70*, 169–182.

Sukhnandan, L., & Lee, B. (1998). *Streaming, setting and grouping by ability: A review of the literature*. Slough: National Foundation for Educational Research.

Sullivan, A. (2006). *Academic self-concept, gender and single-sex schooling in the 1970 British Cohort Study* (CLS Working Paper). London: Centre for Longitudinal Studies.

Sullivan, H. S. (1953). *The interpersonal theory of psychiatry*. London: Tavistock Publications.

Suls, J., & Wheeler, I. (2000). *Handbook of social comparison: Theory and research*. New York: Kluwer/Plenum.

Swann, J., & Graddol, D. (1988). Gender inequalities in classroom talk. *English in Education, 22*, 48–65.

Tamis-LeMonda, C. S., Way, N., Hughes, D., Yoshikawa, H., Kalman, R. K., & Niwa, E. Y. (2008). Parents' goals for children: The dynamic coexistence of individualism and collectivism in cultures and individuals. *Social Development, 17*, 183–209.

Taylor, A. R., Asher, S. R., & Williams, G. A. (1987). The social adaptation of mainstreamed mildly retarded children. *Child Development, 58*, 1321–1334.

Telfer, K. E., & Howe, C. J. (1994). Verbal, vocal, and visual information in the judgment of interpersonal affect: A methodological limitation of some influential research. *Journal of Language and Social Psychology, 13*, 331–344.

Tenenbaum, H. R., & Ruck, M. D. (2007). Are teachers' expectations different for racial minority than for European American students? A meta-analysis. *Journal of Educational Psychology, 99*, 253–273.

Tennant, G. (2004). Differential classroom interactions by ethnicity: A quantitative approach. *Emotional and Behavioural Difficulties, 9*, 191–204.

Terry, R., & Coie, J. D. (1991). A comparison of methods for defining sociometric status among children. *Developmental Psychology, 27*, 867–880.

Thomas, J. J., & Berndt, T. J. (2004). *Friends' similarity, friendship quality, and academic and psychological adjustment*. Paper presented at the 10th Biennial Meeting of the Society for Research on Adolescence, Purdue University, Baltimore.

Thomson, A. (1993). Communicative competence in 5- to 8-year-olds with mild or moderate learning difficulties and their classroom peers: Referential and negotiation skills. *Social Development, 2*, 260–278.

Tolmie, A., Christie, D., Howe, C., Thurston, A., Topping, K., Donaldson, C., et al. (2007). *Classroom relations and collaborative groupwork in varying social contexts: Lessons from Scotland*. Paper presented at the American Educational Research Association Annual Meeting, Chicago.

Tolmie, A., Howe, C. J., Mackenzie, M., & Greer, K. (1993). Task design as an influence on dialogue and learning: Primary school group work with object flotation. *Social Development, 2*, 183–201.

Tomasello, M. (1999). *The cultural origins of human cognition.* Cambridge, MA: Harvard University Press.

Tomasello, M., Kruger, A. C., & Ratner, H. H. (1993). Cultural learning. *Behavioral and Brain Sciences, 16*, 495–552.

Topping, K. (1992). Cooperative learning and peer tutoring: An overview. *The Psychologist, 5*, 151–157.

Topping, K., & Ehly, S. (1998). *Peer-Assisted Learning.* Mahwah, NJ: Lawrence Erlbaum Associates.

Trickey, S., & Topping, K. (2004). Philosophy for children: A systematic review. *Research Papers in Education, 19*, 365–380.

Tweed, R. G., & Lehman, D. R. (2002). Learning considered within a cultural context: Confucian and Socratic approaches. *American Psychologist, 57*, 89–99.

Underwood, G., Underwood, J., & Turner, M. (1993). Computer thinking during collaborative computer-based problem solving. *Educational Psychology, 13*, 345–357.

Van Avermaet, E. (2001). Social influence in small groups. In M. Hewstone & W. Stroebe (Eds.), *Introduction to social psychology: A European perspective* (3rd ed.) (pp. 403–443). Oxford: Blackwell.

Vandell, D. L. (2000). Parents, peer groups and other socialising influences. *Developmental Psychology, 36*, 699–710.

Vandell, D. L., & Hembree, S. E. (1994). Peer social status and friendship: Independent contributors to children's social and academic adjustment. *Merrill-Palmer Quarterly, 40*, 461–476.

Véronneau, M-H., Vitaro, F., Brendgen, M., & Tremblay, R. E. (2007). *Reciprocal effects of peer experiences and academic adjustment in elementary school: A five-year longitudinal study.* Poster presented at the Biennial Meeting of the Society for Research in Child Development, Boston.

Vygotsky, L. S. (1962). *Thought and language.* Cambridge, MA: MIT Press.

Vygotsky, L. S. (1978). *Mind in society: The development of higher psychological processes.* Cambridge, MA: Harvard University Press.

Warden, D., & Mackinnon, S. (2003). Prosocial children, bullies and victims: An investigation of their sociometric status, empathy and social problem-solving strategies. *British Journal of Developmental Psychology, 21*, 367–385.

Webb, N. M. (1982). Peer interaction and learning in cooperative small groups. *Journal of Educational Psychology, 74*, 642–655.

Webb, N. M. (1984). Sex differences in interaction and achievement in co-operative small groups. *Journal of Educational Psychology, 76*, 33–44.

Webb, N. M. (1987). Peer interaction and learning with computers. *Computers in Human Behavior, 3*, 193–209.

Webb, N. M. (1989). Peer interaction and learning in small groups. *International Journal of Educational Research*, *13*, 21–39.

Webb, N. M. (2009). The teacher's role in promoting collaborative dialogue in the classroom. *British Journal of Educational Psychology*, *79*, 1–28.

Webb, N. M., & Mastergeorge, A. (2003). Promoting effective helping behavior in peer-directed groups. *International Journal of Educational Research*, *39*, 73–97.

Wegerif, R. (2000). Applying a dialogical model of reason in the classroom. In R. Joiner, K. Littleton, D. Faulkner, & D. Miell (Eds.), *Rethinking collaborative learning* (pp. 119–136). London: Free Association Books.

Wegerif, R., & Scrimshaw, P. (1997). *Computers and talk in the primary classroom*. Clevedon: Multilingual Matters.

Wellman, B. (1926). The school child's choice of companions. *Journal of Educational Research*, *14*, 126–132.

Wentzel, K. R., Barry, C. McN., & Caldwell, K. A. (2004). Friendships in middle school: Influences on motivation and school adjustment. *Journal of Educational Psychology*, *96*, 195–203.

Wentzel, K. R., & Caldwell, K. (1997). Friendships, peer acceptance and group membership: Relations to academic achievement in middle school. *Child Development*, *68*, 1198–1209.

Wertsch, J. V. (1979). From social interaction to higher psychological processes: A clarification and application of Vygotsky's theory. *Human Development*, *22*, 1–22.

Whiting, B. B., & Edwards, C. P. (1988). *Children of different worlds: The formation of social behavior*. Cambridge, MA: Harvard University Press.

Whiting, B. B., & Whiting, J. W. M. (1991). Adolescence in the preindustrial world. In R. M. Lerner, A. C. Peterson, & J. Brooks-Gunn (Eds.), *The encyclopedia of adolescence* (pp. 814–829). New York: Garland.

Wiliam, D., & Bartholomew, H. (2004). It's not which school but which set you're in that matters: The influence of ability grouping practices on student progress in mathematics. *British Educational Research Journal*, *30*, 279–293.

Wilson, V. (2003). *All in together? An overview of the literature on composite classes*. Glasgow: The Scottish Council for Research in Education Centre.

Wood, D. (1986). Aspects of teaching and learning. In M. Richards & P. Light (Eds.), *Children of social worlds* (pp. 97–120). Cambridge: Polity Press.

Wood, D. (1998). *How children think and learn* (2nd ed.). Oxford: Blackwell.

Wood, D., & Middleton, D. (1975). A study of assisted problem-solving. *British Journal of Psychology*, *66*, 181–191.

Woodward, L. J., & Fergusson, D. M. (2000). Childhood peer relationship problems and later risks of educational under-achievement and unemployment. *Journal of Child Psychology and Psychiatry*, *41*, 191–201.

Xolo, S. (2008). *Mathematics teachers' beliefs: Post-apartheid South Africa*. Unpublished MPhil thesis, University of Cambridge.

Younger, M., & Warrington, M. (2002). Single-sex teaching in a co-educational comprehensive school in England: An evaluation based upon students' performance and classroom interaction. *British Educational Research Journal, 28*, 353–373.

Youniss, J. (1980). *Parents and peers in social development.* Chicago, IL: University of Chicago Press.

Zajonc, R. B. (1965). Social facilitation. *Science, 149*, 269–274.

Zic, A., & Igri, L. (2001). Self-assessment of relationships with peers in children with intellectual disability. *Journal of Intellectual Disability Research, 45*, 202–211.

Index